KNITTING
IN AMERICA

MELANIE D. FALICK

Photographs by

CHRIS HARTLOVE

ARTISAN • NEW YORK

FOR CHRIS WHIPPLE

My heart is, and always will be, yours.

Production director: Hope Koturo

Library of Congress Cataloging-in-Publication Data

Falick, Melanie

Knitting in America / Melanie D. Falick: photography by Chris Hartlove

ISBN 1-885183-27-5

1. Knitting — United States. 2. Knitting — Patterns.

I. Title.

TT819.U6F34   1996

746.43'2'0973 — dc20   96-21061 CIP

Published in 1996 by Artisan, a division of Workman Publishing Company, Inc.

708 Broadway, New York, NY 10003

Printed in Italy

First printing 1996

10 9 8 7 6 5 4 3 2 1

LOCATION CREDITS

Pages 22, 37, and 58: Audrey's Farmhouse Bed & Breakfast, Wallkill, NY; 914-895-3440

Page 36: Blue Chip Farms, Wallkill, NY; 914-895-3930

Page 47: Red Hook Riding School, Red Hook, NY

Pages 48, 169, and 180: The Grass Harp, Stone Ridge, NY, 914-687-0811

Pages 52, 100, and 198: Gentle Farm, Southern York County, PA (good source of fleeces from Lincoln-Cotswold sheep); 717-235-5631

Page 127: Butterflies with Beads. Linen with glass beads, © 1985 (Courtesy of Goldstein Gallery/University of Minnesota).

CONT...

ENTS

I LEARNED TO KNIT AS A VERY YOUNG child from my mother and my grandmother, then learned to purl from my aunt. I vividly recall the long, thin, pointy metal needles I practiced on, the yellow yarn, and the misshapen fabric I produced. In my mind, I can see myself sitting cross-legged on the floor in my aunt's study while she worked at her desk, carefully counting my stitches—which varied in number almost every row. I have no recollection of creating anything in particular, of even finishing a project during my childhood, though my memories of knitting are happy ones.

As an adult, I had several false starts as a knitter, but once I was knitting consistently, the idea for this book came to me quickly. I worked in publishing so I was, perhaps even more than most knitters, interested in seeing the knitting books available. I searched the shelves at nearly every bookstore and library I visited and noticed that the most beautiful books came from England, and that the subtle message communicated through the lack of lavishly illustrated American publications was that British designers were more talented than their American counterparts—that they were more worthy of this glorious treatment. Even though Kaffe Fassett, one of the most celebrated and talented knitters of all time and the author of the most successful illustrated books about knitting, is American, he has resided in England since the mid-1960s and his early books were published in the United Kingdom prior to becoming available in the United States.

Like most knitters, wherever I traveled I would look not only for bookstores, but also yarn shops or any other fiber-related destinations I could identify, including farms, festivals, and museums. What I found were some of the most fascinating people I had ever met, many of whom worked quietly and with limited recognition in their little corner of the world. I decided to write this book because I wanted to celebrate knitting in this country, its richness and its diversity.

I WORKED ON *KNITTING IN AMERICA* almost exclusively for one-and-a-half years. In the beginning, I met with, talked on the phone with, and corresponded with hundreds of people—including yarn company owners, designers, artisans who create one-of-a-kind garments, gallery owners, farmers, and a profusion of nonprofessional knitters who are impassioned by the medium as well as by fiber in general. Slowly I began compiling the list of people and places I wanted to feature. It was important to me to link together the many different elements that feed into the knitting process—from the breeding of the animals that provide the fiber to the transformation of the fiber into yarn to the actual knit and purl stitches that yield the infinite possibilities that have been fascinating knitters for centuries. I also wanted to illustrate that knitting is not just a method of garment-making but also can be used to make powerful wearable as well as nonwearable visual statements.

I tried to give the designers who created projects for *Knitting in America* a great amount of freedom so that their designs would be representative of who they are rather than who I am. Because I wanted this book to be warm and intimate, a reflection of how knitting fits into real lives, I made the decision to photograph *Knitting in America* without professional models. Whenever possible, I wanted to photograph garments on the designers or on members of their

families or circle of friends, and in settings that represent the places where they live and work. Chris Hartlove, the photographer, wanted to shoot all of the photographs in natural light, which meant that we would be slaves to the weather and, ideally, would shoot only early in the morning and just before sunset, when the light was most beautiful. We traveled around the country together and, in the process of documenting the richness and diversity of knitting, spinning, dyeing, and animal and plant breeding, we documented the changing American landscape.

The making of *Knitting in America* became, for me, an important personal journey. By opening their homes, studios, and farms to me, the people featured in this book not only shared an important part of themselves, they gave me invaluable glimpses of—and confidence in—my own potential in many different aspects of my life. For that, I am truly grateful.

I HAVE SPENT A LOT OF TIME THINKING about why we knit and talking to others about it. I have come to believe that knitting speaks to both an innate pleasure in making, and to a natural instinct to create something that is pleasing to the eye. Even though our world is becoming increasingly reliant on the work of machines rather than human hands—and speed and economic gain often seem to be valued over all else—the instinct to use our hands to create (however time-consuming that process may be) remains with us.

When knitters gather together, whether for a few hours each week or for a week-long retreat, they are making time for an activity they love as well as nurturing social bonds. Many a knitter I spoke to compared her knitting-group meetings to the quilting bees of yesteryear, to support groups, to lifelines. The vast majority of knitters are women. Indeed, knitting is "women's work" and has been for a long time. While it is true that men played an important role in the history of knitting, the practice lost favor among most of them—and, as a result, its prestige—when it ceased to hold potential for significant financial gain. Interestingly, just the fact that knitting is women's work has brought forth a recent wave of feminism within the knitting community. While the trend during much of the late twentieth century was for women to turn away from many of the traditional female roles to which they were once confined, women are now choosing to celebrate—with pride—what they have always done: stitching the stories and emotions of their lives into textiles. And they are celebrating and enjoying one another, sometimes as never before.

The image of knitting within the general, nonknitting public is strangely limited. Somehow the overriding and misguided message is that if knitters had something better to do, they would. After meeting with knitters all over this country, I can attest that they are all ages and come from all walks of life. What they share is a common passion, one that invigorates them in good times and can even help to heal them in bad. What they create runs the gamut—some call their work fashion, others craft, others art, and some simply regard their creations as labors of love. To me, what is most important to understand is that the potential of knitting is limitless. It is my sincere hope that all who turn the pages of this book, knitters and nonknitters alike, will feel inspired in their knitting—and in their lives.

EAST

EAST
PAM ALLEN

CAMDEN, MAINE

PAM ALLEN'S GOAL IS TO DESIGN THE handknit sweaters that transform us, the ones that are so comfortable that we want to reach for them nearly every time we get dressed. She compares the psychological effect of the "right" sweater with how we feel in a favorite T-shirt or faded pair of blue jeans, or with the dress a woman puts on when she wants to feel beautiful. A professional designer since the mid-1980s, Pam claims that she has hit the mark only a couple of times, but that is the perfectionist in her coming out. This is a woman who considers ripping out and reknitting a sweater a luxury. She is intent on getting every detail just right.

Pam lives in the coastal town of Camden, Maine, in a pretty Victorian house with her two children, Caitlin and Ryan. She starts each workday with a mug of tea and thirty minutes of reading, often curled up in a worn and cozy overstuffed chair — the furniture version of that ideal sweater — in front of a roaring wood stove. Writers like Emily Dickinson, E. M. Forster, and Virginia Woolf ease her into a day of designing and knitting for magazines and yarn companies, listening to Irish fiddle music or books on tape; she has already knit through all of Charles Dickens and Jane Austen. Her studio, a newly built addition to her gingerbread-trimmed house, is bright and airy, with enough books, magazines, and yarn spilling onto the white painted wood floor to give it a casual, free and easy feeling — the same feeling that Pam herself puts forward in one of her favorite work outfits: paint-splattered teal overalls, white thermal shirt, and pink silk-flower pin. Above her studio is a loft space that, during my visit, her son was using as a Lego construction site. "When I'm an old lady, I'll turn the studio into an apartment and live there and rent out the rest of the house," Pam explains. "All I'll need when I don't have young children anymore is a studio with a kitchen at one end and a little place for guests to spend the night — and my yarn."

At times, Pam's soft, sweet voice fades into a whisper, which would belie her strength were it not for the power and passion of her words, whether she's speaking about the ills of modern society, the degradation of women in fashion magazines, her latest literary discovery, community support, her love for her children, or even her sweater designs. She is a devoted designer, always seeking to educate herself — in part to make up for the formal art education she feels she is lacking — and improve upon what she has done before.

Above: Pam takes her knitting with her everywhere—to her children's music lessons, to the doctor's office, and in the car to work on while waiting to pick up children when she's responsible for the school car pool. She even takes it with her on her walks. Pam's design goal is to create the sweaters we live in day in and day out, not the ones that make a statement for one season then find their way to the back of the closet.

Left: Pam's daughter, Caitlin, modeled the Girl's Trapezoid Jacket with Mitten Motif on top of Mount Battie in Camden.

Above left: The picot edge, which Pam borrowed from Latvian tradition, lends these mittens a subtle frill. Above right: Pam pins sources of inspiration to the window frame in front of her desk.

She combines color with texture to create sweaters that are at once strong, feminine, and romantic without being frilly or cute.

Born and raised in Chicago, Illinois, the daughter of a minister and a full-time mom, Pam has been knitting for as long as she can remember. She has no recollection of learning the craft, but assumes it was one of her grandmothers who taught her. Unsure of what she wanted to do with her life, she enrolled at the University of Chicago in 1967, then dropped out after a semester and worked as a seamstress in a dress shop. Recognizing her creative talents — and a desire to express her unique ideas in the textile field — she opened Mariposa, her own boutique, in 1970. After two years of fourteen-hour days, she re-enrolled in college at the age of twenty-three and earned a bachelor's degree in French, then a master's degree in linguistics. During an academic year in Paris, she became serious about her knitting again, honing her language skills by reading French knitting patterns and enjoying the yarns and beautiful sweater styles she found in the chic European capital.

Upon earning her master's degree, Pam still didn't foresee a career in knitwear design. She intended to travel around the world teaching English, but ended up in Camden, Maine, working as an editor on a boating magazine. Shortly thereafter, Pam got married and had children. She was selling machine knits and one-of-a-kind children's sweaters at a local gallery in 1985 when she decided to attend The National Needlework Association trade show in New York City. There, she had the good fortune of sharing a cab with an editor from *Family Circle Great Ideas* magazine, who asked her to send in some of her sweater proposals. Subsequently, her initial design submissions to *Vogue Knitting* were rejected, but she received an encouraging note from longtime editor Nancy Thomas, who ultimately became one of Pam's biggest supporters.

Pam remembers Nancy's handwritten words—"Keep up the good work"—and wonders whether she would have had the courage to continue without them.

Sometimes, particularly when the financial difficulties of trying to make a living as a knitwear designer hit her hard, Pam ponders the idea of going back to school to become a nurse, or engaging in a more service-oriented career that assures a dependable income. Whereas some designers boost their earnings by hiring outside knitters, giving themselves more time to generate and sell other ideas, Pam has never found this arrangement truly satisfactory. First, she likes to watch her sweaters evolve on the needles. (Pam usually uses straight wooden needles for colorwork because the wood keeps the yarn from slipping around, and is not particular about the needles she uses for more textural projects.) In addition, she compares giving a project to another knitter to a husband going away to war and coming home several years later: "You know him but you don't know him," she says. When she opens a box containing one of her designs knit by someone else, she hesitates and wonders, "Is this going to be what I thought it was going to be?"

For inspiration, Pam relies on myriad sources, including the natural landscape she sees on her daily walk or bike ride, pages she saves from home and fashion catalogs and magazines, fashion stories that knitting magazines send her to let her know what they're looking for, and books on art. Pam is especially fond of Asian art, all sorts of folk art, and painters that use color abstractly, such as Wassily Kandinsky and Milton Avery. Some ideas go in a file; others are pinned up on the wall or on the frame of the window in front of her desk, but Pam doesn't usually work directly from any of them. She internalizes them and then they find their way into her designs, she believes, by osmosis.

Living in Camden, a moderately progressive, boat- and tourist-oriented New England town, Pam is forced to find her own way. "I don't have fashion parading in front of me," she says. "But somehow, sitting here in the middle of nowhere, I can come up with something that someone will respond to." Interestingly, Pam does not feel that she has yet found her true knitting voice. In order to work professionally, she has been responding primarily to the design needs of magazines and yarn companies rather than to her own aesthetic. The way Pam sees it, the masterpieces—the sweaters we truly want to live in—are yet to come.

THE MITTEN ENSEMBLE

The inspiration for the Girl's Trapezoid Jacket with Mitten Motifs came from two sources: a sweater with teacups on it that Nicky Epstein (page 33) designed for *Vogue Knitting*, and *Latvian Mittens*, a book by Lizbeth Upitis (page 153). Pam was intrigued both by the design of the mittens and by the traditional role they play in Latvian culture, but she was not keen on knitting them. Instead, she used them as inspiration for this jacket, which she made for her daughter, Caitlin, who is the model in the photograph on page 12. Before starting, she swatched the border and the individual mittens many times. She also made a full-size paper cutout of the sweater and laid construction-paper mittens on top of it in order to determine the best placement for the mitten motifs. Even with all of this advance planning, after she had knit the back and the front, she decided to rip back to the border on both. She felt that the mittens were too big and that her use of color was chaotic. To improve the design, she scaled down the mittens, decided to use a color from the border as a background color for each mitten, and added the snowflakes. Rather than tiring of all of this work, she luxuriated in the opportunity to continue working on the project until she got it right. Often when she is working for magazines and yarn companies, her schedule does not allow for the extra time that reknitting requires. The knitting of the full-size mittens and hat that go with the jacket was successful on the first try. Pam chose Classic Elite's three-ply worsted-weight Tapestry yarn (75 percent wool and 25 percent mohair) for this project because she likes the quality of the fiber and the color range. The pattern for this trio of garments begins on page 164.

EAST
THE ART OF KATHARINE COBEY

CUSHING, MAINE

KATHARINE COBEY is wise and powerful, learned and talented. She has much to tell the world and chooses to communicate her message through knitting. She works out of a spacious barn-like studio on the banks of a river in Cushing, Maine, the same town where Andrew Wyeth painted Christina Olson, her brother, and their house. Katharine's art, like Wyeth's famous *Christina's World*, invites the viewer in and encourages contemplation. Often, Katharine's creations are provocative social commentaries—about homelessness, about aging, about marriage, about the environment. They sometimes take the form of clothing—"I knit shapes that are 'about' clothing, and the life that clothing expresses," Katharine wrote in an article in *Spin-Off* magazine—and sometimes they do not.

Katharine's voice roars then whispers, shifting from smooth and satiny to gravelly and staccato depending on the subject of the moment, reminding the listener of her earlier career as a poet and her sensitivity to words and their rhythms. With her windswept white hair, grand body, and dramatic gestures, she looks like a cross between a fairy godmother, a mystic, and a goddess.

To get to Katharine's home and her on-site studio, which her architect husband, David Cobey, custom-built for her, we followed her directions to an unmarked road between two white houses, turned, then drove down a hill and over the river. From the river, she told me, we would see the studio perched on the hill. On the right was her sign: **Katharine Cobey, Fiber Work**. And on the lawn in front of the 1790s house, hanging from an oak tree, was *Knitting Gesture,* a sculpture consisting of three rows (a head row, a body row, and a leg row) of five wire knitting stitches executed in the round, then covered with I-cord knit out of black plastic. "I skinned the plastic on like a snake. It was wonderful," Katharine told me. "It's a piece about knitting, and it's about knitting circles, and it's about circular knitting, and it's about women, and it's about dancing." At such a large scale (about three feet tall) the stitches look as though they are holding hands.

Katharine learned to knit as a child but did not begin to use it as a primary means of creative expression until much later in her life, when she was in her early forties. She grew up in a bookish family, one in which many a morning was whiled away reading poetry aloud and in which Katharine's interest in something as "domestic" and "anti-intellectual" as knitting was regarded as a curiosity. Her father made a living building tennis courts and moved the family up and down the east coast so frequently that

For many years, Katharine Cobey expressed her hopes, dreams, concerns, and fears as a poet, through words. Now she expresses those same emotions through handknitting.

***Portrait of Alzheimers* (right) is a tribute to Clare Raymond Durant, Katharine's mother. After gaining much attention for her plastic works, Katharine wanted to return to traditional fibers (in this case silk and wool), to demonstrate that it isn't any specific material that makes art, but all of the elements of a piece taken together.**

Katharine was actually relieved when her parents enrolled her as a full-time boarder in a strict Catholic high school. She fondly thinks back to the nuns, who let her write and produce her own plays and also helped her to complete her first sweater. "I must have made a terrible mistake on the sleeves because they had to be gathered to be inserted," Katharine recalls. She went on to earn a bachelor of arts degree in language and literature from Bennington College in Vermont in 1959, then married a diplomat and raised four children with him while living in Washington, D.C., Cameroon, Belgium, England, and France.

It was after a divorce, a remarriage, and a life-altering back injury that Katharine turned to knitting as a way to express herself. "I changed from somebody who could dance and climb mountains to somebody who sits down and walks badly," Katharine explains. Desperate to find something to do other than write poetry and read while she convalesced on the back porch of her home in Washington, D.C., she started knitting a coat. Before long she realized that for her there was no point to knitting if she wasn't going to create something important, something with meaning.

When I walked into Katharine's studio, I was immediately faced with one of her most emotionally charged works, *Portrait of Alzheimers*. It is a piece about her own mother, a hanging lace shawl in which stitches come together, then seem to unravel randomly, then partially

Ritual Against Homelessness is a five-part installation (two of the five figures are shown here). After working at a homeless shelter for women in Washington, D.C., Katharine realized that her sensitivity to the women's condition was a result of her own feelings of homelessness as she was growing up—she moved twenty-eight times before she went to boarding school—as well as her lifelong feeling of otherness, a sentiment that extends to her role in the knitting world. The five figures in *Ritual Against Homelessness* are called Against Fear, Against Self-Deception, Against Despair, Against Blame, and For Compassion. Katharine does not reveal the individual identities of the figures to viewers.

Katharine used handspun Churro wool and wood she gathered from the shores of the Potomac River to create this piece. About animal fiber, Katharine says: "I love its wildness, I love that it comes from an animal that lives outdoors in the moonlight and the wind."

come together, and finally pool onto the floor into long cob-web-like shreds. To make the shawl, she first spun silk and wool, fibers that reminded her of her mother. "This is a woman I hated as well as loved," explains Katharine. She finished the piece while traveling on a train from New York to Maine. "I needed to get it done," she remembers. "I was knitting my mother's death in silk and wool. I sat there weeping." The piece, which speaks to both the beauty and fragility of an old woman, of her presence and of her absence, has been exhibited at the Torpedo Factory in Alexandria, Virginia, where Katharine was a juried artist and maintained a studio for eight years, as well as in a special solo exhibition at the Textile Museum in Washington, D.C. Jeremy Adamson, a curator at the Renwick Gallery of the Smithsonian Institution and a juror at the Torpedo Factory when it named Katharine artist of the year, wrote of her work: "I find her creative productions of exceptional quality and intent . . . imbued with a material and spiritual quality that propels them beyond the limits of function and into the realm of meaningful art."

Katharine garnered much attention within Washington art circles (she moved to Cushing full-time in 1992) because of her exploration of nontraditional "fibers," such as plastic garbage bags, forestry tape, six-pack yokes, and wire. For *Loose Ends,* a wedding dress and wreath-like headpiece, she cut tall white Glad bags. She used shiny black garbage bags to knit both *Mime for Gulf War Birds* (a huge floor-length cape with a bird head and a wide border of feathery fringe) and *Slick,* a slinky evening coat. Though Katharine has appreciated the recognition that these nontraditional pieces have earned her, she is

In the gleam of a fading day, in the field between Katharine's studio and her home, we photographed *Loose Ends,* a wedding dress and headpiece knit out of tall white plastic garbage bags.

dismayed when the plastic, and its unusualness, are overly emphasized. "Sometimes the plastic is a distraction," she says. "Sure, it's an added dimension that *Loose Ends* is made of tall white Glad bags. But that's not the major point. It isn't plastic that makes art." Katharine insists that it is neither material nor technique: art can be made just as well with wool or plastic and knitting needles as it can be made with a brush and paints, a stone and a chisel, or a camera and film. Katharine refers me to the work of Magdalena Abakanowicz, an internationally celebrated Polish artist who first gained recognition as a sculptor in fibers. Some know her as a weaver of room-filling environments called Abakans, but she also has created monumental works in such materials as bronze, stone, wood, and iron. Abakanowicz is credited with revolutionizing the once-placid world of weaving. Katharine, who strives to do the same with knitting, remembers the relief she felt when she saw Abakanowicz's work for the first time. "I had been starved to see fiber work of that excellence and scale. I thought, thank goodness that the genre has already produced somebody who I totally revere."

Katharine admits that the courage to take herself seriously—as a woman, an artist, and a knitter—took time to develop. "If I were a man and I were knitting things, I would feel perfectly calm. It would be perfectly ordinary to have a beautiful studio, to say what I do is as important as I can make it," she affirms. But as a woman, how does she do it? "It takes putting both feet firmly on the ground and saying, 'Stand up,' all the way that you can go. Just as big or as little as you are, but as much as you can."

EAST
MICHÈLE ROSE
CAMDEN, MAINE

MICHÈLE ROSE DESIGNS BETWEEN FOUR and five hundred sweaters each year from her studio in Camden, Maine. She rarely knits one herself and rarely even makes a swatch. Instead, most of her designs are knit, thousands of units at a time, in China. She is the design director of Tiara International, a young company that produces hand-knit garments for large American department stores and chain boutiques. She spends much of her workday developing seasonal themes and color stories and designing on her high-powered Macintosh computer. Otherwise, she's on the road—in New York City every few weeks, attending meetings and supervising her assistants, or in Europe or the Far East, where she travels several times each year. She is ever-reliant on her computer and the sophisticated software that she has adapted to serve her own needs—aided by a color printer, a scanner, overnight shipping, jet travel, and a modem. In contrast, there are thousands of women in China knitting Michèle's sweaters in pieces. In one remote village in the south, all the women may be knitting the same front. In another, they will be making the back or the sleeves. Men on bicycles or in ramshackle trucks will pick up the pieces on the assigned day and take them to a factory, where they are embroidered on (if called for by Michèle's pattern), then sewn together and finished. "The fact that completed garments actually get to the stores is amazing to me," says the appreciative design director, who grew up in Florida and has been moving north—farther and farther into sweater territory—since she graduated, with honors, from high school, a very small private academy where she played varsity sports, edited the yearbook, was active in cheerleading, and was homecoming queen.

Gutsy and talented, Michèle prepared for her job by starting at the bottom, as a gofer at a small sportswear firm on Seventh Avenue in New York City, and worked her way up—quickly. Before moving to Manhattan, she was a student at Yale University in New Haven, Connecticut, where she double-majored in fine art and economics. Though Yale is better known for grooming its students to become high-powered lawyers, doctors, academics, and performers rather than globe-trotting knitwear designers, Michèle believes it prepared her well for the fast pace and high pressure she faces today. "It was the overall process of learning how to learn and learning how to work,

Above: Michèle and her husband moved from New York City to Maine in 1990 to improve the quality of their everyday lives. She can design a sweater on her computer, then modem the graph and specs to the office in New York in less than sixty seconds. Michèle worked on the Spice Market Wrap (left) while traveling to and from China on business.

how to handle a heavy workload by stepping back and deciding what can be realistically accomplished in the allotted amount of time that was most valuable," she explains. She also credits the inspirational student body: "Everyone there had an exuberance or amazing intellectual level or something above and beyond that was inspiring." When she departed from New Haven, she realized that not everyone in the outside world tried or worked as hard as many Yale students did, and that her college experience could propel her as far as she wanted to go in whatever career she pursued.

It was also at Yale that Michèle became an avid knitter. During her freshman year, she played on the women's volleyball team, most of whose members, to her surprise, were knitters. On the bus traveling to and from competitions, the athletes would sit with their yarn and needles. Michèle had learned to knit at six years old from her

Above: The beginnings of a knitting project at Michèle's home.

mother — a Dutch woman who had a knack for making things with her hands, for taking something ordinary and making it beautiful — but had never pursued it further than any of the other crafts that she enjoyed. The Rose home was, according to Michèle, Craft Central — the cabinets chock-full of supplies like beads, paint, clay, and fiber. Michèle's father was an architect, and when she set off for college in 1981 she thought she would follow in his footsteps.

"The biggest obstacle for me in becoming an architect would have been three-dimensional thinking," explains Michèle, who concentrates primarily on knitted colorwork, often using a sweater as a canvas for the decorative drawings she creates on her computer. She consciously limits the amount of shaping, or architecture, she designs into her garments, as she says her customers do not ask for it. Michèle is, indeed, best known for her use of color and her impressive ability to combine disparate elements, such as flowers and plaids or textured stitches and Victorian scrolls. She also designs a vast number of pictorial holiday sweaters for her company, interpreting and reinterpreting Santa Claus, snowmen, reindeer, scarecrows, pumpkins, and teddy bears in a variety of different ways each year. That is one part of her job that she accepts but admits to not particularly liking. Michèle's warning to anyone who covets her career: "In mass marketing, it's not just you and your love of knitting and your ideas anymore. You have to make something that is salable and commercial and it might have to be worked into someone else's concepts."

Creatively, Michèle feels she is truest to her own personal aesthetic when she is designing for knitting magazines and yarn companies, a moonlighting job that she started in the late 1980s and squeezes in whenever she can find the time. She is often one step ahead of other designers who work for the same clients—such as *Vogue Knitting*, Tahki, Reynolds, and Classic Elite—because she has access to fashion forecasting reports and because she travels regularly to trend-setting cities like Paris and London to attend trade and fashion shows, and, in garment-industry speak, "shop the stores." "Often I can anticipate what the *Vogue Knitting* themes are going to be," Michèle explains. She is also accustomed to working within other people's design concepts and thus doesn't feel constrained by them.

When faced with a new design challenge, she might flip through books or pictures she has clipped from magazines, which she says she saves like a pack rat and, when she can find the time, look through her files, which cover such subjects as dried flowers, rugs, plaids, and decorative textiles from all over the world. Interestingly, she tends to get more ideas from interior decorating publications than from fashion magazines. Or, she might go directly to the drawing tablet on her computer and start sketching. I watched her create a cabbage rose, her signature flower, in less than a minute, then copy it, move it around, enlarge it, reduce it, then completely change the color scheme and add cables around it. The main flaw of the computer, she says, is that it allows her to overcomplicate her designs—for example, to change colors every stitch. It can also eat instead of save time, as it permits her to explore every option available.

When asked about mentors, Michèle speaks of her mother and father, both of whom have passed away. Her father taught her about the joys and rewards of working hard at something you love. Her mother showed her how to make her environment beautiful. Not unexpectedly, her bright, cheerful house, an early-nineteenth-century white-brick cape that she and her husband, Matt Orne, renovated together, looks as though it could be featured in one of the decorating magazines she regularly scans for sweater ideas. Ethnic rugs share space with florals and plaids, heavy antiques, light rattan, and delicate crystal. "I get a kick out of finding something that needs work at a yard sale or an auction, doing something creative with it, and turning it into something that looks great," she says. Outside, she has started a Giverny-like flower garden. "It's a wild perennial garden," Michèle explains. "My aspirations to tame it go unfulfilled." She compares it to her house and her sweaters, calling them all a hodge-podge: a modest description from a great talent.

SPICE MARKET WRAP

Michèle chose Manos del Uruguay handspun yarn for this project because the spicy, autumn-like palette was especially appealing to her. For inspiration, she looked through books on Indian and Middle Eastern carpets. She began knitting it at her home in Camden, Maine, then ended up taking it on a business trip to China in order to finish by the deadline. Not surprisingly, several people in the airport and on the airplane stopped to ask her about the beautiful ribbon of color growing in her lap. "You're knitting your own blanket," Michèle recalls many of them saying as they admired her work. In fact, it would be easy to turn this shawl into a blanket by making it twice as wide, repeating the patterning twice. Michèle played around with several different hat shapes before she settled on the close-fitting cap shown on page 22. The patterns for both appear on page 169.

EAST

STITCH & SAIL:
PENOBSCOT BAY KNITTING CRUISES

PENOBSCOT BAY, MAINE

WHAT MANY KNITTERS want more than anything—even more than yarn, needles, or the latest pattern book—is more time to devote to their knitting. If they could have one more wish, it might be the chance to sit, knit, and talk shop with others who practice their craft. It is, therefore, not surprising that camps, retreats, conventions, and other knitting-related travel opportunities are generally successful.

The first knitting camp was kicked off by Elizabeth Zimmermann in Shell Lake, Wisconsin, in the summer of 1974, and continues to this day—now in Marshfield, Wisconsin, under the leadership of Elizabeth's daughter, Meg Swansen (page 139). Though admission to Meg's camp is open to all, competition can sometimes be fierce and applicants have been known to send in their deposits by overnight mail to assure their places. Spin-offs of Meg's camp abound, however, and many are directed by former Zimmermann/Swansen camp devotees. One such spin-off is Joan Davis's cruise on Penobscot Bay in Maine. Several times each season, which runs through the summer and fall, a dozen knitters board the mini-cruise vessel *Pauline,* a two-deck, eighty-three-foot boat built in 1948, for up to six days of uninter-

Above: The knitters are aboard and the captain has raised all of the important flags: the flag of Maine, the *Pauline* flag, Joan Davis's flag of a sheep with a body constructed out of stockinette stitches on a needle, and the flag from Blackberry Ridge Woolen Mill in Mount Horeb, Wisconsin. Joan provides Blackberry Ridge yarn for many of the cruise projects. Right: The *Pauline* cruises the bay. The captain lowered the anchor when it was time for a hands-on lesson in chemical dyeing.

rupted stitching and expert instruction.

I joined a fall shawl-knitting cruise on the *Pauline,* one that also included hands-on lessons in chemical dyeing. Joan, our instructor, asked each of us to pick a project, then guided us through it, explaining techniques, picking up dropped stitches, reading complicated instructions aloud so we could watch our hands, untangling knots, and every once in a while (when we were feeling overwhelmed, or, in my case, when I had lost a yarn over one too many times), giving us a gift of a row or two of finished, perfect knitting. Whether it was seven in the morning or eleven at night, Joan seemed always to be around and accessible—in the galley, on the fantail, on the boat deck, in the salon. At least once a day I wished that I could take her home with me to help me finish a few projects there.

But at home I would probably be distracted. And the key to any knitting camp is its location—away from it all—whether on a boat, on a campground, at an inn on the ocean, or at a ski lodge in the mountains. There are even camps in Iceland and the Canadian Arctic. At knitting camp, no one is making demands on our time, and we can indulge ourselves in what we love to do best: knit.

BETH BROWN-REINSEL
EAST

DELTA, PENNSYLVANIA

As a child, Beth Brown-Reinsel dreamed of becoming an archaeologist. Though the grown-up Beth has not gone on a single dig or even once examined fossil relics or pottery shards, she is, in fact, an archaeologist of sorts. Beth studies the history of cultures through knitting. It is with both the knitting women of the past and the modern knitters of today that she feels a connection. She studies historical garments and teaches classes nationwide on their design and construction. The daughter of two educators, Beth thinks often of her father's adherence to the philosophy that students need to have a solid background in the classics in order to go on and be innovative and creative. "I see that in knitting," Beth says. "If you are well grounded in these old and wonderful techniques, then you can do whatever you want."

Beth is best known for her work on ganseys (the British fishermen's sweaters of the nineteenth century). She is the author of the successful book *Knitting Ganseys* and frequently leads classes in their construction. Among the other historic garments for which she has developed workshops are Fair Isles, Arans, the Swedish Ullared, and the Norwegian Fana cardigan. Beth spends about two weekends each month traveling and is booked up to a year in advance to teach at yarn shops, knitting guilds, fiber festivals, and needlework conventions. While at home in Delta, Pennsylvania, with her husband, Bob, and their children, she manages Knitting Traditions, her mail-order company that sells traditional patterns and the supplies needed to make them. She also refines the twenty- to forty-page handouts she has developed and published on her desktop computer for each of her workshops. "I like to put in a lot of information so that the handout becomes a reference for students when they go home," Beth explains, crediting her training as a scientific laboratory technician for her analytic approach and clear technical writing style. Refreshingly joyous about her career, Beth wakes each morning eager to get to work. She has labored hard and devotedly to reach this point, and persevered when many an entrepreneur, teacher, or designer might have lost hope.

In 1980, Beth's house was overflowing with yarn and fleeces, and her exasperated husband urged her to find another place for some of it, to make at least enough room for people to sit on the couch in the living room. She responded by trying to do commercial production spinning and to sell her

As a seven-year-old child, Beth asked all the women at the family church if they could teach her to knit. Finally, a neighbor taught her, and she found a yarn shop she could visit on the walk home from school. During nice weather, the adult Beth enjoys knitting on her front porch.

Our maritime model, Jim Brown (left), fit the part—and the sweater—perfectly. Ganseys are traditionally knit at a fine gauge with strong five-ply wool yarn (which makes them impervious to wind and water) and are close-fitting (with only about two inches of ease). A diamond-shaped gusset at the underarm allows for greater freedom of movement. A neck gusset provides the depth needed to accommodate the round shape of the neck with the traditionally rectangular sweater body.

KNITTING IN AMERICA • 29

The gansey takes on a modern look when it fits more loosely. Teenage model Mara Jonas and her canine friend, Kris, enjoy a morning together at the pier.

handspun yarn as well as handknit sweaters at craft shows, but had very limited success. She could only afford to enter small shows and found that the customers she was reaching did not have the resources to pay her a decent price. In 1981, with two other partners, she opened a spinning and knitting shop. "It limped along for three years," Beth recalls. "It was depressing. But everything I went through helped me to focus more on what I was good at, on what I needed and wanted to do." It was at the shop that Beth began to hone the teaching skills for which she is now renowned and also develop some business acumen. The shop closed in 1985, not long after Beth lost her six-month-old daughter, Chloë, to Sudden Infant Death Syndrome. For two years, as part of the grieving process, Beth knit dresses for Chloë. "I needed to do that," Beth recalls. "I understood that it was healthy."

At the 1987 Knitting Guild of America convention, the first consumer knitting show she had ever attended, Beth entered one of Chloë's dresses in the design contest and won first prize, a win that gave her the confidence to submit a proposal to the guild to teach a workshop on ganseys. She had been studying ganseys for several years, mostly through Michael Pearson's and Gladys Thompson's books on traditional knitting of the British Isles. "The gansey has so much depth to it. It seemed obvious that it had the potential for a workshop," Beth remembers. It was at the suggestion of Mary Rowe, author of *Knitted Tams,* whom she met while teaching at the 1990 convention, that she began to write her gansey book proposal, which was accepted by

Interweave Press two years later. "The contract was signed just in time to save me from having to look for a new job," Beth gratefully recalls. Determined to stay home with her children as much as possible, she had not pursued a full-time profession outside of the house, but had worked part-time in different capacities, including many years as a bookkeeper.

Though Beth's route to success was long and circuitous and continues to be financially challenging, her enthusiasm about knitting has never diminished. Her loyalty to classic, historic garments is probably as much a reaction to her years of toil as it is to their enduring design appeal and cultural significance. While running the yarn shop, she realized how short the life span can be for fashion trends and the yarns that serve them. Through historic templates, she strives to empower her students (mostly women) to knit whatever they want and to inspire them to think about the women who came before them, about their day-to-day reality and the important economic and social roles that knitting played in their lives. At her local community college, Beth teaches a beginning knitting class. "I feel a responsibility to expand the craft, to keep new people coming into it," she says. "Knitting used to be handed down from mother to daughter, but often it isn't anymore. I'm trying to mend that, to continue the sharing—even though they are not truly my daughters."

AT SEA GANSEY

Beth's At Sea Gansey is knit in the traditional manner—in the round and without seams. The pattern begins with the classic Channel Island cast-on and split garter welts, which are knit flat. Once the welts are completed, they are joined circularly and knitting continues through a stockinette stitch area, where initials can be included. It is in this area that lengthening and shortening of the garment can be achieved with ease. Underarm gussets grow out of the cabled side seams. At the midpoint of the gussets, the seam stitches and the gusset stitches are put onto stitch holders while the front and back of the gansey are each knitted flat. The shoulders are then joined, a neck gusset is worked in to allow for depth of the neck, and a rolled collar finishes off the body. The sleeve stitches are picked up around the armhole and knitted down to the cabled cuff; at the same time the stitches of the top half of the underarm gusset are decreased until there are none left. Lengthening or shortening of the sleeve can be easily accomplished in the stockinette stitch area just above the cuff. Beth knit this sweater with a five-ply gansey yarn that she imports from England. The pattern appears on page 171.

NICKY EPSTEIN

NEW YORK, NEW YORK

NICKY EPSTEIN HAD ALREADY WORKED AS an art director in a design firm and a fashion stylist for television commercials when she fell into a career as a handknit designer in 1979. On location in remote Apple Valley, California, where her husband, an advertising executive, was shooting a car commercial, she knit a pictorial unicorn sweater and entered it in a *McCall's Needlework* design contest. She was hoping that she would win second prize, a set of knitting needles in every size. But, to her initial dismay, she won first prize, a cash award of five hundred dollars. Though she never went out and bought herself the full needle set, over the years she has amassed an impressive collection of pairs. "I must have at least a thousand needles," she informed me one afternoon in her cozy New York City apartment. Still, most of the time she knits with mismatched straight steel needles that she pulls from a crystal vase on a shelf in her workroom.

While tapestry-like intarsia colorwork, often whimsical depictions of animals and plants, is Nicky's trademark, she is also known for her versatility and innovation. "There's nothing I haven't knit," she says. In the early days of her design career, no matter what the request — whether it was a sweater, afghan, knitted snails, dogs, or Barbie clothes — "I always said I could do it," she explains. She was one of the first American designers to use more than two or three colors (the unicorn sweater called for about ten), to incorporate embroidery into her handknits, and to add dimensional appliqués to knitted fabrics. Nicky puts great value on being unique; each time she starts to see her work being emulated by others, she sets out to create something new. "I don't want to knit anything ordinary," she says.

Growing up in a protective Italian/Spanish family in a slow-paced mining town in West Virginia, Nicoletta Quinones had a lot of time to indulge her natural affinity for art. From her Italian grandmother, who lived two houses away, she learned the basics of knitting — to cast on and to do garter stitch. Under the tutelage of a seventh-grade home economics teacher, she completed her first sweater: an orange mohair pullover. Then, at age fourteen, her true knitting education began when a woman from Spain arrived in the neighborhood and taught her so many different techniques that, she recalls, "I didn't fear anything anymore." She left home in 1970 to pursue a degree in fashion design at Ohio's Columbus College of Art and Design, but when she realized that the college did

Though Nicky does not often knit on the roof of her building, she does have a beautiful view of the Empire State Building from her bedroom window. For leverage and speed, Nicky knits with her right needle under her arm.

The foliage on Nicky's amazingly comfortable Counterpane Pullover (left) gives it an autumnal feeling — perfect for a hike in the woods.

not have the resources she needed to pursue that degree, she switched to retail advertising and fine art. She helped to pay her tuition by selling her oil paintings of fruits and flowers and, during her spare time, she knit sweaters free of charge for friends who would indulge her by buying the yarn. She never dreamed that she could parlay her love for knitting into a career.

In the years since college, neither Nicky's schoolgirl passion for the medium nor her natural inclination to design have subsided. "I will support anything that promotes knitting," she told me, a friendly whisper of her West Virginia roots still gracing her words. Though she can foresee the day when she will stop designing professionally, she first wants to write a book. Otherwise, she says in earnest, "You're so easily forgotten." That would be hard to imagine in Nicky's case, given the number and scope of the designs she has published (approximately fifty or more per year since the early 1980s) as well as her talent for coming up with fresh interpretations of design concepts that her clients propose to her. After an editor calls with a request, "My head starts to spin," she says. Not designing has, indeed, proven to be a challenge for Nicky as she intentionally slows down her career. She and her husband, Howard, travel frequently in the United States and Europe, and Nicky often finds herself fighting the urge to "think sweater."

Rather than waiting for direction from a publication or yarn company, Nicky usually works out a collection of design proposals independently. "I can pretty much predict who will buy most designs," she admits. Among the best trend indicators, she reveals, is the merchandise in card stores. Once she starts seeing a particular type of flower, animal, or other motif on stationery and wrapping paper, she knows it's time to incorporate it into hand-knits. Nicky gathers up the assorted scraps of paper on which she has scribbled notes as well as piles of resource material — everything from children's coloring books to historic paper doll collections to museum art books — and begins to sketch with the colored pencils that reside permanently on the center of a living room table. Once an idea is accepted by an editor, Nicky will write the instructions and either send it out to be knit, or, more often, knit it herself, sitting in her apartment and watching old movies as she stitches. She generally works from early in the morning until late at night, some days only taking a break for dinner with her husband and a foray to the theater.

The five-room apartment where Nicky works and lives is spacious by New York City standards, the Victorian and art nouveau furniture and light-colored walls accented by a varied collection of needlework. There are Oriental rugs on the floors, afghans and needlepoint pillows on the couch, and a lace doily over the back of a floral-print chair. From her bedroom, where she often knits, Nicky has a direct view of the Empire State Building; surprisingly, she's never incorporated the monolith into one of

COUNTERPANE PULLOVER

Nicky was inspired to design this roomy and comfortable Counterpane Pullover after making an afghan from Mary Walker Phillips's book *Knitted Counterpanes*. Rather than making another bed covering (the traditional use for counterpanes), Nicky envisioned a sweater made up of diamond-shaped counterpanes. She chose Rowan's Fox Tweed DK for the counterpanes and Rowan's DK Light Wool for the foliage.

To create this sweater, you must knit sixty-four triangles (thirty-six of which are stitched together to form nine diamonds) plus an unadorned diamond to be used for the center front. The diamonds and triangles are stitched together to "build" the sweater shape; knitted foliage is appliquéd and embroidered in the center. The sweater can be lengthened by adding an extra row of counterpanes at the bottom edge. The pattern for the Counterpane Pullover appears on page 173.

her designs. She did, however, design a Statue of Liberty pullover for *Vogue Knitting*. From the Oriental carpet in the living room she has derived designs for four sweaters. She has been inspired by her collections of bronze animals and antique cigarette cards, an antique cuff bracelet she picked up in France, and a silver bag given to her by her mother-in-law. Nicky is truly a designer at heart, drawing inspiration from within the walls of her urban nest as well as from the outside world. "I go to the Met [the Metropolitan Museum of Art] and I come home crazy with ideas," she says. About knitting, explains Nicky, "I like the feel, I like the colors. I like to watch my ideas come to life in wool."

Once timid and shy, Nicky has gained confidence from her success and from an awareness of the impact of her own creativity on the industry. She reminisces about the good old days, when more magazines published knitting patterns and when most of the editorial offices were in New York, making it possible for her to walk to *Vogue Knitting* or *McCall's* to share an idea — or lunch — with the editors. But moments after admitting a certain degree of loneliness and dismay with how the industry has evolved, she jumps up excitedly to find a sketch, a photograph, or a sweater that she needs to demonstrate another point. Perhaps the stationery she uses for invoicing tells it all: a drawing of a knitted heart, two needles still at work on the top, a ball of yarn off to the side, and in the center — her name.

NORAH GAUGHAN

HASTINGS-ON-HUDSON, NEW YORK

IN A FRAME ON THE WALL OF NORAH Gaughan's home work space in Hastings-on-Hudson, New York, is a ninth-grade social studies project: a twelve-by-eighteen-inch swatch illustrating ten different stitch patterns and cables that are used in Aran knitting. At the time that she conceived of the project, Norah had no idea that it was to foreshadow her future career. A stellar math and science student, she expected to end up in a traditionally male field — probably biology or physics — rather than a largely female one. When she left her home in rural New York State for Brown University in Providence, Rhode Island, she intended to study biophysics and music. She graduated with an A.B. in biology and art in 1983.

Today, Norah Gaughan is one of America's most well respected designers of handknits, known for her sophisticated silhouettes, innovative use of texture, and fine workmanship. Interestingly, her primary focus has shifted over the years from producing full garments to developing new stitch patterns and selling them (through an agent) in swatch form to design houses on New York's Seventh Avenue. Her sixteen-inch-square swatches, reminiscent of the one that hangs on her wall, are also evocative of shapes and textures found in landscapes and stoneworks as well as what a scientist might see under a microscope.

Norah learned to knit at fourteen years old from a good friend in Princeton, New Jersey, in the midst of a heat wave. It was too hot to go outside so the two girls opted to stay in the air-conditioned house and knit. Norah soon decided to make a fisherman's gansey with wool she bought at the county fair, then became quickly discouraged: at one point, she broke into tears because she couldn't understand the pattern. Her mother, a nonknitter adept at reading instructions, helped her work her way through the project, then found that time-honored solution to her daughter's dilemma: Elizabeth Zimmermann's *Knitting Without Tears*. Norah has been knitting, for the most part tear-free, ever since.

The daughter of two illustrators, Norah initially rejected the idea of a career in design; she thought it would be too hard to make a living. At seventeen, she sold a pattern to *Ladies Home Journal Needle & Craft,* then followed with several others while she was in college. For a period after graduation, while working alternately at a yarn shop, toy store, and sweater

Left: Andrea Danese, a New York City editor, models Norah's Centered Cable and Rib Pullover at Blue Chip Farms in Wallkill, New York, not far from where Norah (above) grew up. With Andrea is Snow Drop, a twenty-year-old standardbred brood mare.

Above left: In this photograph, Norah is knitting with the needles that a former boyfriend carved for her one day when she found herself without needles and itching to knit while at his house. She tries not to carry knitting projects for work around with her, but will take a personal project if she is, in her words, "lucky enough to have one going." The truth is, she rarely has time to knit for herself—at most, one or two sweaters per year.

Above right: The Centered Cable and Rib Pullover in Paloma #313 from Reynolds. The sweater in the photograph on page 36 was knit in color #305.

boutique, she knit samples for the local Providence designer Margery Winter, then gradually started publishing more of her own work—with Margery's support and encouragement as well as the support of another local knitter, Deborah Newton (page 52). Norah remembers fondly how the three of them—all powerfully creative and committed—bounced ideas off of each other during this productive time, when a large number of magazines were still publishing knitting patterns. Despite her reluctance, Norah was making a living as a knitwear designer.

"In the beginning everything was scary—and fun," she says, recalling how she learned to keep track of many cables at the same time, how she perfected different techniques for necklines, how she mastered full-fashioning (a fashion industry term for shaping details designed to be visible and add to the overall appeal of the garment). "Now I have to go for bigger thrills," she says wryly. Innovation is a great source of excitement for Norah, especially when creating swatches. Usually she'll draw a graph for a new idea, then knit the swatch and start exploring the variations: twisting a cable in a different place, letting it go off in another direction, or mirror-imaging it; putting design elements in checkerboards, diamonds, or stripes, making them smaller or larger. From one idea, she can come up with a dozen variations, plus a plethora of new concepts to explore. With the help of a photocopying machine and a few reliable women who knit for her, Norah has been producing, for sale, more than one hundred swatches per year. She compares the creative rush she experiences when creating a new stitch pattern to the way she felt in school when catching on to a new concept or solving a complex math problem. No equation could go unsolved, Norah remembers. She works equally hard to realize her goals in knitting.

Not surprisingly, one of the aspects of knitting that appeals to Norah most is its mathematical neatness. "Each stitch is a discrete unit. It's on the needle, you see it, and you have to know exactly where it goes. There's no guessing," she explains. And on those occasions when Norah is faced with some guesswork, such as when she is figuring out how many stitches and which stitches to pick up for a neckline, she will knit and rip over and over again until the results are just right. Norah admits to a streak of perfectionism that she has to work hard to control. At the same time, the magazine editors and yarn companies she has worked with over the years have come to depend on her for that perfectionism. Because she is able to predict how yarns will behave and which yarns will work best in a particular design, her swatches and sketches always portray accurately what the final garment will look like.

Norah also enjoys keeping up with the fashion trends. Through her work with New York City designers, she has access to fashion forecasting reports as well as the chance to draw on the creative energy generated in the Big Apple. Ideally, she'd like to divide her time between design houses in Manhattan, creating handknits for their collections, and staying at home and working on her own ideas (her swatches as well as sweater designs for handknitting magazines and yarn companies). Norah makes her home in an apartment in a small riverside town thirty-five minutes north of New York City, where she ponders setting up her own company and having her designs manufactured for retail sale. In addition, Norah keeps a box of unsold stitch-pattern swatches that she plans to compile into a book one day. She'd like her volume to appeal both to the manufacturing industry, which, she reports, is always starving for new stitch patterns, as well as to the handknitter. It will, no doubt, take its deserved position on the bookshelf next to classics by Barbara Walker, Mon Tricot, and Harmony.

Norah defines success as being proud of what she is doing, and most days she is. Though, as she was growing up, she thought she was destined for "man's work," she is now glad she has been able to succeed in the professional knitting world, which is dominated by women. "I did have to think about the fact that this is okay," she remembers. "I know that this is absolutely what I do best and that I can put all of the talent and energy that I used to apply to math and science into something else." Norah, like most American women today, is fortunate to have had the freedom to choose.

CENTERED CABLE AND RIB PULLOVER

Norah wanted the Centered Cable and Rib Pullover to have a sinuous feeling, and decided to create it by inventing a cable that required alternately twisting a large number of stitches and a small number of stitches. Because she knew that the physics of the yarn and needles wouldn't allow her to twist as many stitches as she desired, she decreased the number of stitches before the twist and increased the number after it. While working out the cable, she came up with the idea of adding the ribbing. The smooth, lustrous yarn she chose for the project, Paloma from Reynolds, shows off the stitch pattern beautifully. It is made of 50 percent lambswool and 50 percent microfiber, a high-tech synthetic.

Norah says that inventing stitch patterns is a process of constant evolution. Though one swatch is often born of another, she also finds inspiration in abstract forms in nature, such as gullies formed by rain, the texture of a tree trunk, or the flow of a river. The stitch pattern on the Centered Cable and Rib Pullover could easily be compared to any of these. The instructions for this sweater appear on page 174.

THERE ARE PLACES in this world that feel magical. Morehouse Farm is one of them. Peacocks strut through the yard in front of the eighteenth-century house. A cat or two may skitter by. A dog barks, and grazing in the one-hundred-plus acres of pasture are more than five hundred proud and plush Merino sheep, a breed that has been around since the Middle Ages and produces the finest and most valuable wool in the world. During the day, the clatter of animal activity on this beautiful farm is invigorating. As the day moves on and the sun begins to reach down toward the horizon, a cloak of golden light and a peaceful hush settle over the hilly landscape—and over all who live there and come to visit.

Some of the magic at Morehouse Farm can be explained by the efforts of two of the most dedicated, hardworking, and stupendously creative people I have ever met: Margrit Lohrer and Albrecht Pichler, the farm proprietors. Together, Margrit, who came to this country from Switzerland in 1962 to go to high school, and Albrecht, who arrived from Austria in the late 1960s, have reintroduced the Merino breed in the east, transformed a once overgrown plot of land into an energized and immaculate working farm, and designed a line of all-natural yarn that is sold at yarn stores nationwide and in their rustic yet elegant on-site farm shop (actu-

ally a renovated barn with a glass wall separating the merchandise from the animals).

One day, I asked Albrecht his definition of success. He looked over to Margrit, his partner for more than twenty years, and said, "To be able to do things that you like to do, together with the person you love." That streak of romance fuels the magic of the farm in addition to all the hard work. Actually, Margrit and Albrecht bought the house and thirty-five acres of land in Milan (pronounced MY-lin) in 1977 as a weekend getaway, never dreaming that it would become one of the largest pure-bred Merino sheep farms in the country. They were living in Manhattan, two hours away. She was a partner in a graphic design firm. He was—and still is—a partner in an architectural firm. They began by bringing their own menagerie of domestic pets to the farm—five dogs, two parrots, and several tanks full of fish—plus a chicken Margrit had found wandering around a park in New York City. The couple added a few more chickens to keep the first one company, then in 1983 they purchased four Merinos. Other animals took up residence on the farm, including an assortment of peacocks, cats, guinea hens, geese, and ducks, then more Merinos. Gradually, weekends on the farm started to include Friday afternoons and Monday

In their work relationship, Margrit reports that she's the schemer, coming up with all sorts of ideas, some wild and some feasible, about how they can develop the farm and the business. Albrecht, she says, is the stabilizing force. While the dozen or so peacocks that call the farm home, as well as the chickens, ducks, dogs, and cats that live there, do not contribute to what Albrecht calls "a smooth-running operation," they do add to the experience. "They're just really nice to watch, and people wouldn't have nearly as much fun if we didn't have them," he explains.

mornings, then as much time as possible, until finally, in 1992, Margrit moved to Milan full-time and Albrecht followed a year later. Albrecht, however, still works in the city, commuting by train four hours each day. Rather than begrudging the long commute, he describes returning to the farm—and the work that awaits him there—as "having a weekend every day and a vacation every weekend."

Margrit and Albrecht chose to raise Merinos because of the high quality and monetary value of their wool. However, at the time—in the early 1980s—the deluxe breed had a mysteriously bad reputation as greasy, dirty, and hard to shear. Apparently, these white-faced sheep—considered so valuable in Australia that their export has always been strictly controlled—had lost favor in the United States in the 1950s, when the price of wool plummeted and synthetics began to overtake the market. In order to survive, sheep farmers had shifted their focus from wool to meat and, in turn, lost interest in the slower maturing Merinos, who were, indeed, more difficult to shear than other sheep because of their heavy dewlaps and skin folds. By the time Margrit and Albrecht decided to join the business, wool prices were on the upswing but no Americans

had dared to reinvest in the forgotten Merino breed. Calling on her background in marketing (via graphic design), Margrit spearheaded a crusade to call attention to her beautiful animals, including showing up at livestock fairs and festivals with a swanky, custom-made livestock trailer, as though the sheep were the least popular students in the class pulling up to their high-school reunion in a chauffeur-driven Mercedes. She and Albrecht also began a meticulous breeding program that resulted in the bevy of blue ribbons that frame many of the doorways in the house today and captured the attention of breeders out west, who started to pay top dollar for Morehouse breeding stock when the fine wool prices skyrocketed in the mid-1980s. The heavier weight of the Merino fleece combined with the fineness of the fiber were now highly sought. This interest by experienced western breeders in sheep raised by eastern farmers was unprecedented.

None of this would have happened if Margrit had not been an avid and talented knitter. She had learned to knit as part of the grade-school curriculum in Switzerland and chose to raise sheep because she liked the idea of working with their wool. In fact, the original plan was to sell the fleeces to hand-

Below left: The average Merino ram weighs between two hundred and two hundred eighty pounds and will produce a twelve- to eighteen-pound or heavier fleece each year, a much higher yield than most other sheep breeds. The fiber itself is comparable to cashmere in fineness and, because of its crimp, is especially elastic. From the Middle Ages through Napoleon's invasion, the exportation of a Merino sheep from Spain, the only place they were bred, was considered a capital offense. Below right: One of three barns on the Morehouse property.

spinners and the breeding stock to other farmers. The yarn line, the shop, and the public farm events they host each year evolved as a natural outgrowth of everything else she and Albrecht were doing.

Running Morehouse Farm is, for Margrit, a way of life. Her day begins at about seven in the morning, when she goes out to feed the animals, and ends each evening after midnight, when, she says, "I fall asleep over my knitting." Going up to bed before falling asleep somewhere else in the house is, in fact, unthinkable to her. During lambing season, she'll nap on the couch downstairs, then rise every two hours to check on the ewes and newborns. Though she relies on a full-time shepherd from New Zealand as well as on a multitalented office and shop assistant, she is most definitely the boss at Morehouse Farm. It is with her that everyone consults and to her that people come with questions and problems — when to move the animals from one field to another, where to unload the twenty tons of hay that are delivered each month during the winter, how to arrange a display in the shop, which buttons to sew on a sweater, which people from the eleven-thousand-name mailing list should receive a copy of the flyer she has just designed.

The biggest challenge that the farm presents to the ever-energetic and engaged Margrit is learning to leave things undone. "You're never finished. You can work twenty-four hours a day and all you do is uncover more projects," she admits. "It's not a question of setting priorities. They all do matter." Still, the undone projects are rarely visible to outsiders, who are invited to the farm for special events, such as Knitter's Days (weekends of educational programs that Margrit organizes several times a year), as well as to shop in the farm store.

It is only love that could make two people work this hard in a business in which financial rewards are rarely grand. Margrit admits that running a design firm is a cinch compared to managing the farm. About her sheep, she reveals, "I still love them as much as I did the first day. Sometimes I wonder how anyone can get another breed when you have Merinos around." Watching the animals, especially in the evening light, she says, reestablishes her faith in the world. Though Albrecht admits he gets tired more easily than he used to, he says he enjoys working hard physically and suspects that the high emotional pressure of working in the city is more stressful on the whole body than the physical labor of farming.

Around sunset, Margrit and Albrecht will often take a break and go down to the barn with a bottle of wine and two glasses. Around them, the sheep are bleating. A chicken is putting her babies to bed. The ducks have sauntered back to the pond. Two kittens are curled up in a pile of hay. In the high-stress world that so many of us live in, this, for sure, is magic.

MOREHOUSE FAMILY CARDIGAN & PULLOVER

Margrit developed an easy slip-stitch pattern for the classic cardigans the kids are wearing and the pullover worn by the rowboat captain on page 41. She then mixed three natural colors of three-strand Morehouse yarn to achieve a different effect in each one. Margrit did a lot of swatching before she began, as is evident from the photo above. Morehouse yarn undergoes no chemical processing and is so soft that, even when worn next to the skin, it is not scratchy. The pattern for these sweaters appears on page 175.

Margrit absolutely loves the creative and meditative rewards of knitting. She says that when she looks at her yarn, she feels inspired, and when she sees someone wearing a handknit sweater she often feels compelled to ask them about it. During the day, her knitting helps her to make decisions. She believes that when her hands are occupied with her yarn and needles, her mind is free to find solutions.

JULIE HOFF

JULIE HOFF SPENT HER JUNIOR YEAR OF college in Salzburg, Austria, living in a dormitory where all the female students knit for hours each day in the common area. Julie asked a friend to teach her, then set off for a yarn shop to buy yarn of her own. The women there cut the sweater shape and size she wanted out of brown paper, had her make a gauge swatch, then sent her on her way. Julie was knitting a rose- and cream-colored Norwegian-style cardigan in the round. "It didn't occur to me that it was anything difficult," explains Julie, just as it never occured to her to knit as a child growing up in Nebraska even though she saw her grandmother knitting often.

"When I started, I didn't know enough to be afraid to design my own sweater," Julie told me during my visit to her home in Wheeling, West Virginia. There, she lives in a charming 1930s white clapboard cottage-like house with her husband and two small daughters. The only pattern she has ever followed was for a pair of socks that she made when she returned to Colorado College from Salzburg to finish her degree in English literature. Julie and her three housemates would gather in front of the television on Wednesday nights, drink beer, and knit Candide ragg wool socks and fisherman's sweaters to wear with their gauzy Indian skirts and hiking boots. She often had to ask her housemates about American knitting terminology, as she knew the words only in German.

Julie had always liked art and had played around with painting, drawing, and pottery, but as soon as she started knitting, she knew that she had found her medium. Essentially, she wanted to knit all the time. After graduating from college, she worked alternately for an importing company, a stockbroker, and a Laura Ashley boutique before she finally decided to design full-time. In a decision that feels courageous to her only in retrospect, Julie put together her own company at the age of twenty-four, sourcing tweed yarns from mills in England and Ireland, designing sweaters on a machine, hiring women in Ireland to knit them, and then selling them to such American stores as Nordstrom's, Henri Bendel, and Mark Shale, along with boutiques in San Francisco and Aspen. Though she worked successfully for three years, she decided to dissolve the business when she realized that she was spending more time troubleshooting — attempting to get the knitters to ship the sweaters on time, fixing errors when the sweaters arrived, and doing paperwork — than designing,

Above: Julie's daughter Hanna joined Mom for the photo shoot. Hanna doesn't knit (yet), but enjoys playing "spaghetti" with any leftover yarn she can get her hands on.

Julie designed both an adult (left) and child's version (page 47) of her Harvest Fruit Pullover.

which was what she loved. She also realized that she didn't particularly like working on the machine. The three-year pursuit did, however, afford her a plethora of design and business experience and also presented her with the opportunity to meet her German husband, Klaus Weisenberger. The two met and fell in love in London while Julie was in the United Kingdom meeting with suppliers.

Julie is now a frequent designer for Kristin Nicholas (page 59) of Classic Elite Yarns and, when she can find the time to submit proposals, works for other companies and magazines as well. Though she wishes she could be more prolific, she is, first and foremost, committed to her responsibilities as a full-time mom. She is also active in volunteer work with an all-female international group dedicated to improving women's lives.

Julie's handknits, which are always fun to work and often combine color and interesting textural stitches, have a charming Laura Ashley/English-country feeling to them, though Julie says she draws her inspiration from many different sources—an art book, a book on stenciling or Eastern European folk art, one of her great-grandmother's quilts, a gardening catalog, a tablecloth. One of her professional stumbling blocks, she believes, is that she has a hard time designing sweaters that don't fit into her own casual lifestyle. "I want comfortable sweaters I can wear walking the dog, taking the kids to preschool, or running to the supermarket," she explains.

Julie believes that one of the reasons her patterns are fun to work is that she maintains close associations with all types of knitters and sees what they like to create. She has kept in touch over the years with her Wednesday night college knitting friends, and since 1988, when she and Klaus moved to Wheeling, she has been teaching knitting to students of all ages at a local fine arts center. Julie is also a member of a very close yet diverse knitting group that meets once a week. "We're all very different in terms of age, economics, lifestyle, and taste," she says. "We may be knitting various types of things, but we share this interest, this creative energy that links us." Like many knitting groups, this one has become a support system, each member knowing she can depend on the others in times of need as well as celebration.

Julie also credits her knitting group, which she calls "Stitch & Bitch," and a more conservative member simply refers to as "Stitching," with keeping

MOTHER-DAUGHTER HARVEST FRUIT PULLOVERS

Julie's Harvest Fruit Pullovers evoke the feeling of autumnal bounty. Crabapples and ornamental cherries, which Julie sees each October in her backyard in Wheeling, West Virginia, are arranged along with pears and plums within a grid of four different cables and basketweave squares. To achieve a sense of light and shade as well as texture and delicate coloration within the fruit, Julie chose a combination of wool, silk, and cotton chenille yarns from Rowan. For the basket-like background, she opted for Rowan's DK Tweed. The initial inspiration for these pullovers came from a photograph of fruit on the cover of a mail-order catalog. The pattern for these mother-daughter sweaters appears on page 177.

her in line by commenting honestly on her design ideas. For example, one member didn't hesitate to inform Julie that a cluster of small berries she was planning for the Harvest Fruit Pullover she designed for this book looked more like a nondescript blob of color than an appealing pictorial element.

"Julie's designs usually tell a story," says Kristin Nicholas of Classic Elite. "She has an upbeat personality, and looking at her sweaters always makes you feel happy." Kristin also appreciates the clarity of Julie's sketches, her sense of proportion, and the knitability of her designs. While some color-work designers will leave a knitter with a strand of yarn that, in order to be in the correct position for its next use, has to be either cut at the end of a row or carried all the way across the back of a row unused, Julie will make sure this doesn't happen, saving the knitter excess work and interruptions.

Julie Hoff is a knitter's designer and an overall joy to be around. Though she didn't knit with her grandmother, who was a prolific stitcher, she tells me that she was influenced by her greatly. "She had a strong sense of community, which I really admire, and of right and wrong. At the same time, she was able to have a real giggle," recalls Julie. It seems that her creative granddaughter is following in her footsteps.

Our model, Sasha Pearl, jumped at the chance to be photographed at the horse farm where she takes lessons. Her mother, Elena, is the model on page 44.

SELMA MIRIAM

SELMA MIRIAM LOVES TO DESIGN, BE IT a meal, a garden, or a piece of knitting or weaving. "These are the areas that have been open to women," she says. "That's where we use our design capabilities. Men, on the other hand, are told to go build a house." The passion from which all of this stems, according to Selma, is the desire to arrange light, color, or space. "If I had had another life to live and was born a man, I would have been an architect," she speculates.

Selma is actually one of three partners in a feminist vegetarian restaurant and bookstore called Bloodroot in Bridgeport, Connecticut. Five days a week she cooks for four hundred patrons or more. The pace in the restaurant (named after a North American wildflower) is often frantic, and when she has a chance to sit down between rush periods, she either spins or knits — grounding herself and leveling the excess energy generated in the kitchen. On Sunday afternoons, Selma stays around after brunch, available to anyone who would like to learn to spin, knit, or crochet. On a wall in the restaurant reserved for announcements of feminist events and information, Selma has posted a sign that reads:

SPIDERWOMAN'S GRANDDAUGHTERS
SPINNING LESSONS
COME SHARE AND LEARN

"It's such a joy to see someone getting pleasure out of making something with their hands," Selma told me, having called me the morning before our first meeting to remind me to bring my latest projects along to show her. Her recommendations for the beginner's library of resource materials: *Elizabeth Zimmermann's Knitting Workshop*, "because that's the architecture"; Barbara Walker's *A Second Treasury of Knitting Patterns*, "because all of those patterns factor into the architecture"; and Kaffe Fassett's *Glorious Knits*, "to learn about the interaction of color."

Selma grew up in Bridgeport, now the home of her restaurant. Her father was a fabric merchant and her mother sometimes helped him at the store. As a teenager, Selma would sew all her own clothes, including coats and formal dresses, poring over *Women's Wear Daily* and *Vogue* for the latest styles. Often her father would bring home beautiful fabrics — luxurious silks, French cottons, and lengths of complex lace — unable to part with them as he was so enamored with their beauty. In 1952, Selma left home. "I was in search of the

Above: Selma sits outside of Bloodroot, the feminist vegetarian restaurant and bookstore she owns with two other women. Selma and her partners planted the roses in the background over broken cement landfill on the property soon after they opened the restaurant in 1977.

One of the inspirations for Selma's Kousa Dogwood Shawl (left) was Mary Walker Phillips' book *Knitting Counterpanes*.

secret of life," she states with a small laugh, remembering her earnest idealism. She began her quest at Tufts University in Boston, where she earned a bachelor's degree in biology. She then entered a master's-degree program in clinical psychology at New York University, and subsequently studied philosophy at a community college. "Finally, I realized that the secret of life was growing things," she says, fully confident that she found the answer she was seeking. In 1962, with her husband, newborn daughter, and four-year-old son, Selma moved from New York City back to Connecticut — because she absolutely had to have a garden. "I couldn't grow morning glories in the Southeast Bronx," recalls Selma, who now raises orchids in two greenhouses off her kitchen. Flowers and vegetables also flourish in the backyard of her home and on the restaurant property, which sits on an inlet of Long Island Sound.

It was at Tufts that Selma learned to knit. She knit during most of her classes "to keep from becoming overly compulsive in my note-taking," she remembers. It was not until much later — in 1989, at fifty-four years old — that Selma learned to spin. By that time her life had changed completely: she was divorced, had worked and then retired from a career as a landscape designer, and had opened Bloodroot. She purchased handspun yarns for the first time when she couldn't find soft, fine commercial yarns with which to make lace shawls and scarves, then almost immediately decided that she had to learn to spin herself. "I had never knit with yarn that felt so good, alive, and beautiful in my hands," she recalls. Within a year she had not only purchased a wheel and taught herself to use it, but also attended SOAR, the Spin-Off Annual Retreat sponsored by *Spin-Off* magazine. She now makes an annual pilgrimage to this preeminent spinning event.

For Selma, needlework — in addition to cooking and gardening — is a source of spiritual sustenance. The interrelationship between the earth and its riches and what we can do with them inspires Selma's creativity. "This is magic," she says, "whether I take flour and eggs and make something wonderful to eat or spin a fleece and knit a pair of socks, watching the pattern form in front of my eyes." In the introduction to *The Perennial Political Palate,* the third of three Bloodroot cookbooks, Selma wrote, "When people ask about the time needed to produce a handmade object, it means that they

Selma chose a luxurious two-ply fingering-weight qiviut (musk-ox fiber) yarn produced in the western Canadian arctic for the Kousa Dogwood Shawl. She constructed the shawl in several stages: first, she chose a square pattern called Beeton's Flower from Mary Walker Phillips's book *Knitting Counterpanes* and knit three of them. She wove them together to create a V shape (a center diamond with a square on the two top sides) using kitchener stitch. She then added a few rows of eyelet and a curved triangular extension in a simple Madeira lace pattern to the right and left sides, creating an even larger V. Next, she added an eyelet border to the outside edge of the V, followed by a final ruffled sawtooth edge treatment. Finally, the neckline is finished with I-cord and the shawl is washed and blocked. The result is an elegant curved fabric that rests comfortably and gracefully over the shoulders. Selma named her shawl after a Korean Dogwood tree, known as the Kousa Dogwood, because the petals in the center of Beeton's Flower counterpane reminded her of the flowers on that tree. The pattern for the shawl appears on page 179.

do not see that it is the act of making it which provides the 'grounding,' the stitch after stitch that are individual moments of possibility."

Making lace, one of the most time-consuming branches of knitting, is among Selma's strongest passions. She has made shawls and scarves for herself and friends, her handknit lace doilies rest on the backs of chairs in her home, and she is a member of Lacy Knitters, an international organization of lace enthusiasts. "I don't know exactly what I love about it," Selma admits. "It's a kind of architecture; it's about geometry. It's not that I don't like color and texture, but when it comes down to it, what really fascinates me is pattern, the way shapes arrange themselves and can be arranged."

Selma impressed me with her prolificacy and zeal. Each time I visited her or spoke to her on the telephone, she was engrossed in another project. "I'm not tearing around trying to complete things," she explains. "I just become completely absorbed. Sometimes when I finish, I feel a great sense of loss. And then I feel a hunger to get the next project going."

DEBORAH NEWTON

PROVIDENCE, RHODE ISLAND

DEBORAH NEWTON'S APARTMENT USED TO be overflowing with yarn, books, and pictures clipped from magazines for inspiration. Today, her yarn stash amounts to not much more than she is working with at the moment. She has given away many of her books and can fit her clippings into a single manila file folder. Although she has been admired in the handknitting industry for more than a dozen years because of her ability to meet just about anybody's needs — no matter how complicated or demanding — she now reports that she is back to stage one: the stockinette sweater, the work in your hands, the pleasure of knitting. "Now I just like to have a ball of yarn and two needles. To me, that's bliss."

Deborah's knitting career began in 1980, not long after her twenty-eighth birthday. She had earned a degree in English from Rhode Island College and was working for a costume designer in Providence when she sent one of her first handknit sweaters to the editors of *McCall's Needlework & Craft*. Though the editors quickly bought the design — a wine-colored, cabled turtleneck — the model was wearing it backwards in the photograph published in the magazine, and somehow the editors neglected to include the pattern. "An auspicious start," recalls Deborah. "Really, things should have gone downhill from there." But they didn't. Soon after, *Family Circle* bought another of her designs and Deborah was contemplating quitting her costume-design job and embarking on a career as a knitwear designer. Despite some cautionary words from friends, she decided to take the chance. When she recalls the decision years later, she quotes the writer Joseph Campbell: "Follow your bliss." But at the time, she was much less consciously philosophical about it. She was just following an intuition.

Deborah's rise in the handknitting world proceeded quickly. In the early 1980s, handknits were very popular, and a multitude of magazines were publishing patterns. Drawing on her experience in theater and a passionate interest in how clothing is constructed, Deborah became known for her understanding of proportion and fit and her ability to create complex shapes in knitwear — from a wedding dress to a matador's bolero; from a motorcycle jacket to a Chinese robe. At one point, Deborah even designed dog sweaters. Always up for a challenge and believing anything could be done, she would often come up with an idea that she did not know how to execute — and for

Above: Deborah has lived in Providence, Rhode Island, all her life and continues to love it for its small size, village-like ambiance, history, and vibrancy. The photograph above was taken at one of her favorite places, Prospect Terrace, which overlooks the State House and downtown.

Left: Deborah's Unisex Cabled Raglan Pullover.

which she could not find any written instructions. Then, when a magazine editor accepted it, she would be forced to work out the technical details on her own. She learned as she went, and can now usually visualize a finished garment down to the last detail even before she begins to swatch.

From the start, Deborah was more interested in the creative process than in the final knitted product. She owns very few of the hundreds of garments that she has designed over the years and admits that once she sews the pieces of a sweater together and completes all of the other finishing details, the challenge—and the fun—are over. Once she has taken the garment to the point where it couldn't possibly look better, she packs it in a box and sends it off to whatever publication or yarn company hired her to create it—with no remorse. While she is fascinated by fashion—its history and how it continues to evolve and change as well as the psychology of clothing—this fascination does not extend to her own wardrobe. This reveals something about Deborah: for her own daily wear, she favors jeans, T-shirts, and a simple, short hairstyle. Not surprisingly, she says that she doesn't like to draw attention to herself. She sells swatches through an agent to ready-to-wear designers and loves the anonymity of it, never asking which companies have purchased her work.

Deborah believes that among the most important reasons why she has been successful are her earnest desire and ability to meet other people's needs as well as her lack of prejudice against any fiber or design style. Whereas some designers will not work with synthetics, she sees them as a challenge and appreciates the opportunity to reach the great many knitters who use them regularly and sometimes exclusively. "I don't really have a like or don't-like about a sweater," she explains. "There are all different kinds of people: therefore, if you are designing something that isn't particularly suited to you, then it will be suited to somebody else. I've done novelty sweaters that maybe I wouldn't wear. I know that people love them. I've tried to be more spacious. I think it has made me a better designer."

That spaciousness also makes Deborah ever-encouraging and always eager to share her knowledge as well as the credit for her success. She is certain that she never would have reached her present position were it not for the support of her longtime mate, science fiction writer Paul Di Filippo, or the expert knitters—many of whom have become good friends—who have made it possible for her to keep up with her workload over the years. In her design heyday she was, with their assistance, sending out anywhere between two and ten sweaters a month. She also wrote *Designing Knitwear,* a highly regarded guide to design that was published by Taunton Press in 1992. "Knitting brought me a long way," Deborah explains.

CABLED RAGLAN PULLOVER

For this unisex pullover, Deborah experimented with asymmetry and with juxtaposing dissimilar cables. Of the two main cables, one is very soft, round, and textured and the other is angular and confined-looking. Also note the raglan seamlines: one is cabled, the other looks like a textured checkerboard. Deborah chose Reynolds Candide yarn because she likes its rough, rustic look and the heathery color range that is both bright and soft at the same time. The pattern for this sweater appears on page 181.

"I relied on other people and other people relied on me. I knew that I could come through for somebody. It carries over into your life. The knitting is more than just knitting. It is any job well done."

Deborah's only complaint throughout this journey, especially in the beginning, was the lack of technical information available on the intricacies of the handknitting design process. That is why she wrote her book: to share all that she had learned over the years — through trial and error — with her fellow knitters. Deborah saw the book as a way of giving back to the craft that had been "very generous" to her and also as a means of carrying on the legacy that women like Barbara Walker (see page 56) and Elizabeth Zimmermann had passed on to her. In the early days, Deborah would use Barbara Walker's stitch patterns as a jumping-off point for innovation. She would start a cable, then explore what would happen if she made it smaller or larger, took it into another direction, or added another element. Without a graph or any type of notes, she now enjoys knitting swatches that include as many as six cables, all growing in different directions and at varying paces.

Deborah's book brought her to the end of an important stage in her life. These days, she is slowing down, giving herself more time for other activities — a family map-making business, a garden, meditation. Now that she is less pressured to produce, she is returning to the simpler joys of knitting. "I like a string turning into something but I like a string all by itself. I like a ball of yarn even if nothing gets made of it," she explains. She no longer uses a ball winder or an umbrella swift to prepare a skein for knitting. Instead, she puts the skein over her knees and happily winds the balls herself, the way she remembers her mother and grandmother doing it. Sometimes she'll simply cast on and start playing with cables — maybe six, all doing something different, at the same time. Sometimes she'll cast on and simply knit garter stitch.

Gone is all of Deborah's knitting paraphernalia. After all this time, she understands her technique so well that she doesn't have to think about it. Instead, the work flows from within. Deborah remembers a day she and Paul spent at the beach. Without thinking, she picked up a long, skinny piece of seaweed and made knots in it. "It's my automatic nature," she reflects, "to take a long piece of string and do something with it."

BARBARA WALKER'S KNITTING LEGACY

MORRISTOWN, NEW JERSEY

BARBARA WALKER DID for knitting what Webster did for the dictionary and Roget did for the thesaurus. An over-statement? Perhaps, but not a gross one. Barbara Walker's ten published knitting books, in particular *A Treasury of Knitting Patterns, A Second Treasury of Knitting Patterns, Charted Knitting Designs*, and *Mosaic Knitting*, have provided knitters everywhere with a vocabulary so in-depth and extensive that it would take a lifetime to exhaust it.

What compelled her to do it? Necessity first and curiosity second. In 1965, at age thirty-five, Barbara learned to knit from a Bernat yarn company instruction book, started her first sweater, a basic pullover, and quickly felt as though she was going to die of boredom. Uninspired by the repetitive stockinette stitch but not yet ready to give up knitting for good, she tried out a few of the stitch patterns for which she found instructions in magazines. Then she was hooked. But there was a problem. She wanted a compendium of as many stitch patterns as possible so that she could investigate and manipulate them all, but could not find such a compilation. Without realizing that she was embarking on what would become more than a decade-long exploration into the depths of the medium, she started her own collection, hand-copying patterns from magazines, foreign books, yarn company publications, and old pamphlets, then making swatches of all of them. Her first book, *A Treasury of Knitting Patterns*, included instructions and photographs for nearly five hundred fifty stitch patterns. Then came the *Second Treasury*, which chronicled more than seven hundred additional patterns, including many that she had unearthed amid the stacks of the Library of Congress, many that she had devised herself, and many that were mailed to her by fans from the U.S. and abroad.

For nearly thirteen years, Barbara devoted herself to knitting. In addition to writing books, she traveled around the country to promote mosaic knitting, a technique for slip-stitch color knitting for which she created hundreds of patterns and devised a charting system. She also designed sweaters for yarn companies and magazines, until she became disgruntled by the low wage she was paid for her designs. She was also frustrated by the number of her ideas versus the amount of time she had to execute them. Always practical, Barbara started working out her design ideas on a small scale — on her son's GI Joe doll — and stopped selling them altogether. Not a woman inclined to do anything halfway, Barbara designed outfits for close to six hundred dolls, including GI Joe plus Barbie and all of her friends, Dolly Parton, the crew of Star Trek, Scarlett O'Hara, the rock group Kiss, and Elvis Presley — basically, any figure she could find at the toy store. And then Barbara Walker turned her tenacity and devotion to other subjects.

Today, Barbara knits for about thirty minutes each morning. Often, she knits socks

Though she no longer writes knitting books, Barbara displays many of her handknit creations around her house. More than four hundred dolls dressed in hand-knit clothing line three of the walls in her otherwise sparse office, where she writes (longhand) and then types (on an electric typewriter) her manuscripts.

constructed according to her own unique two-needle method (she calls the results "serviceable but not very pretty"). She defines herself as a professional writer and publishes, on the average, one book per year, many of which appear on reading lists in the Women's Studies departments of various universities. Among them are *The Woman's Encyclopedia of Myths and Secrets; The Crone: Women of Age, Wisdom, and Power;* and *Feminist Fairytales.*

She has also written about crystals, symbology, I Ching, and tarot, even designing and painting her own seventy-eight-card tarot deck. The paintings are exhibited in a tarot museum in Connecticut.

She lives in the same pale green stucco ranch in Morristown, New Jersey, that she moved into in 1963 and in which she wrote her knitting oeuvre. Sitting in silence in her living room, with her notes and books spread out on her coffee table, she would knit a row, then write the directions for that row, and continue until the swatch was finished. Soft-spoken and direct, she says that she is not opposed to talking about knitting but does not feel she is on top of the field anymore. "I've been getting a lot more fan letters lately about my feminist books," she explains. "That is rewarding because I am helping these women. They're getting more self-esteem and self-confidence." Advancing the feminist movement has been one of Barbara's lifelong interests. When I tell her I am impressed by her productivity, she answers simply, "This is just what I do."

Born in 1930, Barbara grew up in the suburbs of Philadelphia with a passion for horses (if she had had the money she thinks she would have ended up breeding them in Wyoming) and studied journalism at the University of Pennsylvania. She worked at the now-defunct *Washington Star* in Washington, D.C., until she relocated with her husband, Gordon, a research chemist, to New Jersey. She recalls being prepared to embrace the traditional role of wife and mother when she got married in 1952 and gave birth to a son seven years later, but soon realized that the lifestyle that was expected of her wasn't going to be enough to fulfill her. To enrich her days, she taught modern dance, which she had studied in college, to adults in New Jersey. She calls that her dance period. And, at the same time, she got into the habit of choosing a new topic of study each fall, such as astronomy, geology, and ancient history, and immersing herself in it. She says she didn't get a job outside of the house because she didn't want to give up her research time. Then the long knitting period began. And, according to Barbara, studying knitting patterns led her into symbolism, which led her to study spirituality and comparative religions.

Currently, Barbara is engrossed in an investigation of goddess lore and the goddess movement in America. "To me, the goddess religion is basically nature worship, and nature seems to me very sacred. All of the women's groups celebrate the solstices and the equinoxes and the old Celtic holidays, like Halloween and May Day." Barbara's interest in crystals is also a reflection of her appreciation of nature. She thinks of crystals as the "bones of Mother Earth," but completely rejects New Age beliefs in their healing powers.

Barbara attributes the greater interest in knitting among women than among men to cultural norms and economics. The desire to make things with one's hands is a natural instinct, says Barbara, but most men choose woodcarving or building model ships or airplanes, a different kind of handwork. The first knitting guilds were all male, but when handknitting stopped being a source of profit, the male knitting population declined dramatically. Barbara does, however, report receiving many fan letters from male knitters over the years.

Barbara Walker is an impressive, intelligent woman. It would be a boon for knitters if she would return to the craft with which she launched her writing career. But Barbara Walker's knitting period is, for all intents and purposes, over. Barbara Walker is first and foremost a scholar. And we're all grateful that she turned her genius to knitting for a while.

EAST
KRISTIN NICHOLAS

PEPPERELL, MASSACHUSETTS

KRISTIN NICHOLAS KEEPS EXOTIC CHICKENS in her backyard on a residential street in northern Massachusetts. She likes to have something specific to do in the morning—take care of them—and she also likes to use their manure as fertilizer for her picket-fenced flower and herb garden and the vegetable garden tended by her husband, Mark Duprey. Though Kristin understands the appeal of solid-color stockinette knitting, she says that it bores her a bit. She likes doing something different every row, whether that means colorwork or cabling or both. Kristin also paints, makes pottery, and sews. "I always like to have my hands busy," she explains.

As the creative director of Classic Elite Yarns, one of this country's leading yarn companies, Kristin Nicholas is one of the best-known figures on the American handknitting scene. Her top priorities are developing two collections of handknits each year, designing many herself and contracting out the others, and finding new yarns for her company to sell, choosing colors and textures that she feels reflect the mood of the nation and a wide range of individual tastes. She also organizes photo shoots for Classic Elite patterns and promotional materials in the United States and overseas, designs all of the company advertising and yarn labels on her Macintosh computer, represents her company at trade shows, and constantly comes up with new and interesting ways to invigorate knitters as well as Classic Elite sales. Kristin achieves all of this with hard work, an in-depth understanding of color, fiber, and design, an acute ability to both identify and instigate trends, and great faith in her own unique creative flair. Though knitting has meant serious business for Kristin since 1984, when she started working at Classic Elite, then a lackluster company with a small nondescript knitting division, she approaches each one of her responsibilities with a rare and constant freshness.

Kristin earned a bachelor's and a master's degree in textiles and clothing at the University of Delaware and Colorado State University, respectively, but her handwork and design education began much earlier. Her first teachers were her mother and paternal grandmother, who were accomplished needleworkers. Her mother taught Kristin and her four sisters to appreciate the subtleties of color—an object wasn't blue, it was teal, bright purple, royal blue, or aqua—and the value of fine-quality materials. It was better to have a little of something of high quality than a lot of something of poor quality.

Above: Kristin learned to knit when she was eight years old during a family car trip through Kentucky—she made an orange-and-yellow striped pocketbook—but didn't knit again until her junior year of college. She was about to return east by train after spending a year in Oregon, and a wise professor advised her to buy Elizabeth Zimmermann's *Knitting Without Tears* and a Mon Tricot stitch dictionary and figure out how to knit again on the train. Kristin is now doing her part to perpetuate Zimmermann's philosophy that within every knitter lies a designer, and that knitters need not feel paralyzed by a pattern.

Left: Kristin's Moss Stitch and Cable Cardigan is perfect for afternoons whiled away on a hammock.

Kristin was struck by the rapport between the brown and white eggs laid by her chickens outside and the three yarns she had chosen for her sweaters: Kelso Tweed, Nature's Palette Cotton, and Mackenzie Silk Wool.

The example Kristin's mother used was fabric from the British firm Liberty, whose products have represented the zenith of quality in printed fabrics since the late nineteenth century, when the company was founded as part of the Arts and Crafts movement. It is, in fact, that design movement, which advocated a return to fine craftsmanship and the pursuit of beauty in even the most utilitarian of objects, that best defines Kristin's approach to her knitting and to life.

While Kristin's office at Classic Elite is a seemingly jumbled mix of paper, yarn, and books with no discernible design scheme — she has posted a sign that reads "Creativity Comes out of Chaos" — her house, a pale pink Victorian with high-gloss Mediterranean blue doors, is something altogether different. Inside, it feels like a cross between a Middle Eastern bazaar and a gleefully painted stage set for a fairy-tale performance, a cross that only someone as gifted as Kristin could pull off with such inspired success. The kitchen is sunshine yellow, the cupboards fixed with ceramic doorknobs portraying the faces of her two dogs and two cats, and the counters scattered with her brightly painted pottery. She ragged the dining-room walls (a decorative painting technique) in royal blue with teal, navy, and cobalt accents and added copper stencils of leaves, pottery jugs, and sheep on the ceiling. In the living room, teal stripes with olive green leaves travel up the ragged yellow-tangerine-ocher walls; the floor is kilim-covered, the couch upholstered in a dark, striped brocade. Throughout are fresh flowers and baskets of yarn, both Classic Elite and yarn spun from the fleece of the sheep that Kristin and Mark raise on the Duprey family farm in western Massachusetts. There are also knitting projects in progress, textiles, family antiques, and bric-a-brac that Kristin has collected in her international travels, as well as art, home decorating, and textile books and magazines displayed throughout the home. On the walls hang Kristin's painting. She has knit a coordinating tea cozy for the kitchen and study.

"In America, the school system teaches you to follow rules," says Kristin. "Americans transfer this to all areas of their lives. Following the rules is okay, but you've got to know when to break them, how to change things, to make them better, to make them suit you." At her house, Kristin is pushing this personal philosophy to its outer bounds, at least in terms of color. In her knitting, she seems to have an endless flow of ideas; she remains conservative only by sticking to traditional garment shapes and limiting her designs to those that are generally wearable by the average individual. She is, indeed, designing for the general public and is known for her simultaneously wearable, fashionable, and exciting sweater ideas. "When I put together a collection, I think about my life and Mark's life, the sweaters we would like to wear," she explains. "Then I have to think about people who have different lives than we do."

To nudge knitters to push their own creative boundaries and, perhaps, break some rules along the way, in 1992 Kristin introduced the World Knits Collection, a series of kits for small colorful projects such as socks, gloves, fedoras, moccasins, and tea cozies. With each kit the knitter receives a palette of yarn colors that works well together (Kristin's way of assuring beginning designers successful results), a series of charts for different, often ethnic-inspired motifs, and instructions on how to mix and match these colors and motifs to achieve one-of-a-kind designs. The results have been personally satisfying to Kristin, who meets appreciative knitters at yarn stores and when she teaches a limited number of classes each year. One especially thankful knitter reconnected with her son by making him an ethnic hat from one of her kits to wear on his dreadlocked head. He couldn't believe that his "out-of-touch" mother could produce something so incredibly hip, and the hat became a stepping-off point for improved communication between the two of them.

When Kristin was putting together her ethnic sock kit, she asked the members of a somewhat conservative knitting guild in Amherst, New Hampshire, to make the samples she needed for photography. Initially, many of the members were intimidated by the idea of working with so many colors and motifs, but the group now looks forward to and prides itself on helping Kristin with each and every kit she comes up with. While orchestrating a photo shoot on a country estate in Northumberland, England, Kristin spotted an appealing two-color garter-stitch glove in a basket in the mud room in the house, found out that this type of glove was popular in the region, and within forty-eight hours had a pattern written and a sample pair knit for photography. On the same trip she spontaneously decided to add a knitted stuffed sheep to the collection. She stayed up until 3:00 A.M. designing and knitting it, then had it photographed with one of the bottle-fed lambs on the property the next morning. This kind of quick thinking is typical.

Julie Hoff (page 45), a freelance designer who has been working for Kristin since 1992, marvels at her ability to turn a merely satisfactory idea into a great one. "She brings out the creative in me—and in most people, I would imagine," explains Julie. "She has a great sense of humor and is laid back and trusting, so I can basically do my own thing. She just takes my ideas and makes them better." Kristin accepts this kind of flattery nonchalantly. She is only doing what comes naturally, she says, to someone who has been making things with her hands since childhood. "And because of my art background," Kristin explains, "I am always thinking about how you can change a fabric to make it better." If she breaks a few rules in the process, so be it.

Kristin is inspired to this day by the memory of her paternal grandmother, Frieda Roessler Nicholas (in a photo on the desk below), who, like Kristin, was always making something with her hands.

In a conversaion about her unconventional color sense and home decorating style, Kristin said, "I understand the concept of the white room and sparseness, Scandinavian and modern design . . . but I can't live there!"

HIS & HER SWEATERS

Although Kristin often thinks about what she and her husband, Mark, like to wear when she is designing sweaters, the couple actually own very few of Kristin's creations. So, for this project, I asked her to design sweaters specifically for her and Mark that the two of them would keep for themselves. She found a diamond cable in a Japanese stitch book, started playing around with it, then added the X in the center and the seed stitch (rather than the more typical reverse stockinette) around the sides. To show the different textural possibilities, she chose Classic Elite's two-ply Kelso Tweed (which is 100 percent wool) in Wensleydale Olive for Mark's pullover and Mackenzie Silk Wool (a 70 percent wool and 30 percent silk nubby, textured, single-ply tweed) in St. Croix for her cardigan. Later, to show yet another possibility, she had a second pullover knit in Nature's Palette Cotton (the color made with 50 percent Classic Elite Buffalo Fox Fibre® and 50 percent natural organic cotton). The cotton sweater is modeled on page 75 by Sally Fox. The pattern for these unisex sweaters appears on page 183.

Right: Close-ups of the cables. Far right: Kristin and Mark wearing their sweaters while they watch their sheep in a field on the family farm.

DONNA BRUNTON

TAOS, NEW MEXICO

DONNA BRUNTON HAS NEVER MADE A gauge swatch in all of the years she's been knitting. She doesn't have a needle preference either. Plastic, bamboo, aluminum, straight, circular — it doesn't really matter. Donna likes to cast on and go, though she doesn't often known exactly where she's headed. What Donna responds to is color and texture. She likes to combine yarns and see where they'll take her.

"I taught myself to knit and I don't even know if I do it the right way," she explains. What Donna may lose in technique, she gains in creative freedom. She doesn't know the rules, so she doesn't feel constrained by them. While conservative or technique-minded knitters may frown on her free-for-all sizing or her unique finishing methods, it is the freshness of her ideas that deserves the attention, whether she's translating a poppy field, a piece of stained glass, a cowboy boot, or the fall colors in New Mexico into her impressionistic, sometimes whimsical, and always feminine style of knitting.

There is an air about Donna that is reminiscent of a princess from a fairy tale. It may be the lightness of her step, the gold color of her hair, or the femininity of her dress style. She lives in what looks like an adobe castle that her boyfriend, artist Thom Wheeler, designed. Eventually, she will work out of a Victorian-style studio that he is building for her on top of a barn on their property. She rides a white Arabian horse named Sonny Boy, and after work each day goes on a walk with any number of her four dogs (all saved from the pound) and her Nigerian dwarf goat, whom she calls Nadine.

Donna taught herself to knit at age twenty-one. She had just graduated from the University of New Mexico with a degree in art history and had moved to Tulsa, Oklahoma, to open a craft gallery. Bored and unable to bring her loom into the gallery, she decided to give knitting a try — and was immediately obsessed. Her first project was a salmon-colored vest with a llama on it, which she designed herself. She made the front in solid stockinette stitch, then got bored and added the llama to the back. To this day, she claims to be incapable of following a pattern. She does, however, have a sense of what people want and need, a sense that she cultivated while working at La Lana Wools (page 94) in the 1980s and by selling her work in different galleries and clothing boutiques in New Mexico and Colorado. The gallery experience was, for her, difficult. It was hard to get paid and her pieces weren't always cared for prop-

Above: Donna taught herself to knit at age twenty-one. To this day, she has never followed a pattern.

Left: Donna's Leaf Kimono. When the arms are raised, the sweater takes on a butterfly shape.

erly. Unlike many designers, she likes custom orders and says that the key is listening carefully to what people tell her and also making sure they see the colors of the yarn before she starts knitting. She's learned that everyone sees color differently: what she calls peach may not be what the customer sees as peach.

Although Donna knits in spurts, relying on her job as the manager of a Taos craft gallery and part-time catering as her main sources of income, when she's in the knitting mode she is completely absorbed by it and says she can hardly stop. Often, after she has sewn all the pieces together, she will spend another few days or a week embroidering on them, crocheting a special edge, or adding beads, milagros, or pockets as finishing touches. She absolutely loves clothes. She attended Catholic school and wore a uniform every day for twelve years. "When you get out," she says, "you go overboard."

Donna's garment shapes are always simple and unstructured, which gives them the feel of a wide-open canvas. She uses her yarn as paint, often combining several different fibers, and chooses colors by dumping them all out on a flat surface and picking and choosing with abandon. Donna's sense of color comes naturally, but she also likes to spend time in museums, studying paintings, particularly Impressionist works, and dissecting how the colors are layered for different effects. Her favorite artist — she calls him her hero — is Matisse.

LEAF KIMONO AND PULLOVER

The Leaf Kimono and Pullover were both made with worsted-weight alpaca from On the Inca Trail. The kimono comes to two points at the hip in the front; when you raise your arms, the sweater shape actually looks like a butterfly. The back is straight and waist-length. The pullover fits like an oversized sweatshirt. Both sweaters benefit from the drape of alpaca, which is looser and freer than wool.

Donna says it was easy to decide on colors for the Leaf Kimono, the first of the two sweaters she designed. It was October and she began by picking colors that reminded her of fall in New Mexico, then she added colors she liked to go with them. "It didn't take long," she remembers, "because I picked almost everything on the shade card." When it came time to select the colors for the pullover, the On the Inca Trail owner, Heddy King, who lived in Taos at the time, joined in. Donna was open to everything except deep purple and turquoise, a typical Southwestern color combination that bores her. The pattern for these sweaters appears on page 185.

Rather than graphing out her ideas ahead of time, Donna will usually build shapes with color and texture as she knits along. Though she may forget where she left her wallet fifteen minutes earlier, she says she can pick up an unfinished knitting project after several years and remember exactly what she had intended to do next.

So why didn't Donna Brunton follow in her hero's footsteps and become a painter? She says she's not disciplined enough and could never sit in a studio and paint all day. Cheerful, quirky, and social, Donna often hosts parties along with her boyfriend, and the two of them are regulars on the Taos art-gallery circuit, sometimes attending several openings per week. There is, however, a Matisse-like quality to much of Donna's work. The leaves on the kimono and pullover she designed for this book are reminiscent of the master's cutouts.

Donna Brunton will never be a perfectionist or a technician. She is a colorist who chose knitting as her medium. And if Hans Christian Andersen or the Brothers Grimm had met her, she probably would have inspired them to write a tale about a woman who paints with yarn.

Donna's friend Janine Keller, a construction worker who builds houses out of recycled and other earth-friendly materials, agreed to model the Leaf Pullover with Donna's horse, Sonny Boy.

MOLLY GEISSMAN

ALBUQUERQUE, NEW MEXICO

MOLLY GEISSMAN COMES FROM A LONG LINE of artists. Just knowing that reassures her about her own work and her ability to explore and achieve without a formal art education. Her maternal great-grandfather was a painter and lithographer. His daughter, Molly's grandmother, excelled in an assortment of mediums, including oil and pastels, and lived the life of the bohemian in 1950s Santa Fe. "My mother," Molly relates, "is incredibly creative. As a little kid I came home from school one day, and she had hand-painted primitive early American motifs on the walls of the dining room. Because she felt like doing it. That really inspired me."

Molly is co-owner, along with three other women, of Village Wools, a large yarn shop and fiber arts center in Albuquerque. When she's not taking care of her home and family (a husband and a young son), working at the shop, or knitting samples in order to inspire customers, she is pursuing her own artistic vision in knitting, primarily with wool and silk yarns she dyes herself. Increasingly, she is using her one-of-a-kind handknit garments as canvases on which she can make a personal statement. For example, in a jacket called Inside Looking Out, part of a series that draws on symbolism from Ethiopian magic scrolls (seventeenth-century parchments regarded as good-luck charms), a demonic face peers out of a window framed by bars. X shapes, used by Ethiopians to keep evil away, are interspersed throughout. Molly recalls that at the time she made the jacket she was feeling trapped by bad feelings. The demon, which was worked at a finer gauge with smaller needles and then knitted into the "window," represents those feelings and her attempt to understand them and not let them control her. Always self-reflective, Molly has also done pieces about the night fears she experienced as a child and overcoming fears of the unknown.

Though Molly sells some of her work at the store and through art-to-wear and craft shows, she does not make it a priority. She doesn't wear a lot of her own work either, in part because she is self-conscious about it and in part because after the garment is finished the thrill is over. "The process is enough for me," she says, meaning everything from the designing to the actual knitting. She usually starts with a concept, then figures out the details as she goes. "I have always used knitting as a way of expressing myself, as a type of therapy," she explains.

Above: In addition to knitting, Molly likes to Rollerblade with her son. And she loves watching football. To the dismay of some of the female customers at Village Wools (but to the relief of many male companions), Molly insists that the television at the shop be tuned to the game on weekend afternoons during football season.

Left: The large size of the shawl (ninety-four inches along the top border) gives it a blanket-like coziness.

Molly left the side edges of the hem at the top of the shawl open so that a dowel could be inserted through the openings and the shawl could be displayed on a wall when not being worn.

Being conscious of feelings, her own and other people's, is actually an important part of Molly's job at Village Wools. In addition to keeping the store running efficiently, which includes organizing classes and special events, writing a newsletter, teaching, keeping track of inventory, and producing samples — all of which she does in collaboration with her partners — she is on hand to work with customers at least two days out of every week. "If someone comes in and something has gone wrong in her life that morning, and I say something that really sets her off, I just respond by saying, 'Yes, I understand, I've been there,'" she explains. Sympathy and understanding work wonders, according to Molly. "People hang out here because it's a creative, fun place and because they know they'll be accepted." Many a time a customer has burst into tears or rattled off her whole life story. And even on days when Molly doesn't particularly want to hear it or doesn't have the time, she listens patiently because, she says, "It's an important part of the business." There's always an extra chair around the large work table in the back, and there's always a bowl of M&Ms or other chocolate candy in a bowl in the center.

Molly became a partner in Village Wools in 1986, after ten years as a dental hygienist. She had moved to Albuquerque two years earlier with her husband, John, a professor of geology. She had learned to knit as a child growing up in Michigan but never did any of the finishing on her own projects. She gave them to her mother to sew together. That led her as an adult to sideways knitting (knitting a garment from cuff to cuff), which, like circular knitting, is virtually seamless and requires minimal sewing. It is for this technique and for her color-work that she is best known. "I can look at something done in color and be able to knit it immediately," she explains. She has taken classes and been inspired by Kaffe Fassett and Sue Black as well as by local weaver Gina D'Ambrosio. Complex stitchwork, such as lace knitting, is much more difficult and less enjoyable for her. She'll usually only do it when she is making a sample for the store.

Molly's color palette is generally a combination of southwestern earth tones and intense and vivid contrast colors. "I like colors with a lot of depth," she says, "and colors that have a patina to them." She adds bits of brown to a lot of her dyes to give them a subtle mottled quality; she also regularly dyes many different values of the same color, achieving a subtle progression of colors unavailable in commercial yarns. Molly is drawn to cultures that use color and pattern with abandon, as they do in Egypt and other parts of northern Africa, Mexico, and Guatemala. "The ancient Egyptians would spend their lives constructing something to represent themselves. You walk into one of their tombs and every space is covered," she explains with a mix of enthusiasm and wonder. It was after a trip to Cairo, Luxor, Aswan, and Abu Simbel that she felt compelled to paint her entire house as though it were an Egyptian tomb; she scaled down her plans and settled on the front door. Her idea: to paint geometric banding in oranges, yellows, blues, and black to frame a central section depicting an intense dark blue sky with yellow stars.

When Molly's son, Tom, is grown up, he'll probably tell his friends: "As a little kid I'd come home from school and my mother would have painted the front door to look like an Egyptian tomb. Because she felt like doing it. That really inspired me."

PRE-COLUMBIAN SHAWL

We were enthralled by the interplay of colors when we placed Molly's Pre-Columbian Shawl on an adobe wall in Ranchos de Taos as the sun was setting and a storm was brewing in the distance (see pages 63-64).

To make the shawl, Molly matched a rayon and mohair novelty yarn from Fiesta Yarns in a color called Taos (a melange of gold, copper, rust, and grayish blue) with a two-ply silk yarn called Rapunzel that she purchased from Henry's Attic and dyed herself in a palette of turquoise and purple (using Lanaset dyes) and varying shades of brown (using Cushing's Perfection Acid dyes). The silk yarn has a jewel-like luster that contrasts beautifully with the matte color and the fluffiness of the mohair. The stamp motif is pre-Columbian and was commonly used by Central and South Americans as a fabric motif.

Although Molly's shawl is a one-of-a-kind piece that cannot be recreated exactly, the chart on page 188 can be used as a guide. To create the triangular shape, cast on three stitches, knit one row, then, working in stockinette stitch, increase one stitch at each end of every row until the shawl reaches the desired dimensions. (Without the fringe, Molly's shawl measures ninety-four inches wide and thirty-eight inches deep and requires approximately one-and-a-third pounds of the silk and three eight-ounce skeins of the mohair-rayon yarn.) For a neat finish at the top, knit about seven rows straight, then make a fold line by either knitting on the wrong side or purling on the right side. Next, work about five rows stockinette stitch, cast off, and sew down the edge with a whip stitch. Using a crochet hook, attach the fringe (mixing together strands of all of the different fibers used in the shawl). Be sure to knit the shawl at a medium-loose gauge to assure an attractive drape. Molly worked twelve stitches and fourteen rows to four inches over stockinette stitch, using a size 11 circular needle.

SALLY FOX AND HER
NATURALLY COLORED COTTONS

AGUILA, ARIZONA

FOR THREE WEEKS each spring, the dining-room table in Sally Fox's house in Aguila, Arizona, is totally covered with three-by-five-inch index cards. Typed and printed on these cards is crucial information about some of the 250,000 cotton plants that grow on fifty of the five hundred farmable acres on her western Arizona ranch. On each card, in a scientific shorthand that she has been developing since she came upon her first brown cotton seeds in 1982, is a remarkable chunk of crucial information about a particular plant, including its breeding history, its height, the number of bolls (seedpods around which the lint grows), a description of the bolls, and the quality of the lint. Also attached is a lint sample and a handspun yarn sample; the lint is the cotton fiber (actually 96 percent cellulose). By going through these cards—from the 250,000 plants in the field, about three thousand reach the card stage—Sally is able to select the approximately five hundred to one thousand plants with which she will continue to breed. What she is developing, through careful selection and cross-pollination, is naturally colored cotton that can be organically farmed on a large scale and is long and strong enough to be spun on industrial machines for mass manufacturing. So far, through her company, Natural Cotton Colours, through which she

Sally started out by growing colored cotton in six plastic pots in her mother's backyard. She now maintains a 50-acre certified-organic research nursery on her ranch in Aguila, Arizona. She also grows (for sale to mills) thousands of additional acres of cotton through contracts with independent farmers. At right, Sally is wearing a sweater knit with Classic Elite's Nature's Palette Cotton (made with 50 percent Fox Fibre®). The pattern appears on page 183.

grows, breeds, and markets her product, Sally has introduced a range of both brown and green cottons that have been transformed into yarns and fabrics for such companies as Fieldcrest-Cannon, Levi Strauss, and Esprit. When I visited the ranch, she was focusing on red cotton, trying to produce a shorter plant with a higher number of bolls and longer fiber. It takes about seven to ten years, equivalent to seven to ten plant generations, from the time she starts pursuing a particular color until it is ready to be farmed commercially, then it takes an additional one to two years before it reaches the marketplace.

Sally, a Peace Corps veteran, holds a bachelor's degree in entomology and a master's in integrated pest management (the science of controlling pests without using pesticides). She began this unplanned and now world-renowned enterprise while working as an entomologist in southern California. The twenty-six-year-old was breeding pest- and disease-resistant strains of white cotton when she came upon her first wild brown seeds and lint. Though colored cotton dates back to 4000 B.C., modern growers have always worked hard to keep it out of their fields because they believe it spoils the quality and consistent white color of their crop. But as soon as Sally found the seeds she saw the situation differently. A spinner

from way back (she learned on a drop spindle at twelve years old), she was intrigued by the possibility of hand-spinning the naturally colored cotton that in her mind was comparable to the undyed wool, silk, linen, and dog hair that she had been working with since she was a teenager. In the beginning, the seeds yielded a fiber that was difficult to spin because it was short (about three-quarters of an inch long) and weak, but through a series of cross-pollinations with white cotton, Sally was able to strengthen and lengthen it (to about one inch initially, longer later on) without sacrificing its color. The very best quality, rarest, and most expensive cottons are more than 1.5 inches long. Most of the cotton grown in the United States is between one and 1.1 inches long.

Sally firmly believes that she never would have pursued this experiment, which has brought her international renown, or have been able to succeed at it, were it not for her passions for spinning, knitting, and weaving and the help afforded to her in the low-budget, start-up years by the San Francisco Bay Area and Ann Arbor, Michigan, hand-spinning communities. Because she could not afford expensive laboratory tests, in the beginning she would judge the quality by spinning the fiber herself and, in addition, by sending it to other spinners to test. She also suspects that no professionals before her realized the possibilities inherent in colored cottons because "the cotton breeder is normally a man who works in agriculture and doesn't have any textile connection." Colored cotton is different from white cotton in many ways—for example, it can be more elastic, more lustrous, and bouncier than white cotton—and a breeder who didn't actually work with the fiber would probably, according to Sally, "have seen these improvements as something bad because they are unlike white cotton." Sally tells me all this while we sit on an antique couch upholstered with handwoven FoxFibre® in her business office in Wickenburg, Arizona, about twenty miles east of the home and nursery where she has been doing her research and development since 1993. (FoxFibre® is the trademark Sally established to allow those manufacturers who use her cotton to distinguish it from dyed imitations.) She is casually dressed in clothing made out of her cotton—light brown jeans, a grayish T-shirt (made by combining green and white cotton), and a sand-colored gansey—and it strikes me that her skin tone and her features harmonize perfectly with the dusky, soft colors of the cotton.

Among the small but amazing details of Sally's

story are the fact that her grandfather was a cotton merchant in Greece — she did not find this out until after she had begun to do her own research on colored cottons — and that as a very young child she would amuse herself at clothing shops by feeling all the fabrics with her fingers and identifying them. Sally remembers spinning on her drop spindle on the bus to high school and spinning and knitting throughout classes rather than taking notes. "When my

hands were active, my memory was very good," she recalls, affirming a theory held by many progressive educators. It worked for Sally: she finished high school in three years, earning a scholarship to the California state university of her choice.

Originally, Sally's idea was small: to grow colored cotton on a couple of acres and sell it to other handspinners by mail order. She did, indeed, start a mail-order company called Vreseis (named after her paternal great-grandmother, who raised cotton for spinning in her backyard in Greece), which paid for much of her early work and still exists to this day. But, in 1985, when Sally saw green cotton come out of a cross-pollination of two browns, the only color she had seen up to that point, she realized that she was dealing with something much bigger, more mysterious, and more important than she had previously imagined. Her first big order came from a Japanese mill in 1989 and was followed by a much larger one from Levi Strauss in 1991. In addition to being aesthetically appealing, colored cotton is ecologically friendly because it eliminates the need for dyes and the energy required for dyeing. It also eliminates dyeing costs.

For her impressive work, Sally has received numerous awards, including one from the United Nations. She has traveled throughout the world, and has been written about in scientific, trade, and mass-market publications, including *National Geographic*, *The New York Times*, and *Forbes*. For many years she

Above: Sally compares the patience required for spinning and knitting to that required for scientific experiments. They proceed in small steps and it takes a long time to see the results of one's labor.

has been quite humble about her achievements, something that has come back to haunt her in a certain way. Larger companies are now joining the industry that she virtually created and expecting to quickly surpass her. "What gives anyone the impression that they would know enough about the genetics of these colors to pass me up so rapidly?" she asks rhetorically. "I'm really proud of the science that I have going on. Now I can afford to pay for the tests, to analyze all of the cotton." But, at the same time, she adds, "I do not discount my fingers and my hands. I use the same fingers and hands that spin and knit and weave to feel every cotton plant in the field."

It has been a long journey for Sally. Along with the successes, she has endured her share of difficulties. For example, she was forced to leave her farm in California in 1993 when the local agricultural board began putting so many restrictions on her that it was strangling her business. The underlying issues were the politics of organic farming, which she has always practiced, and independence (farmers there didn't like hers). She has forged her own path, for many years working fourteen or more hours per day. Sally recalls the early years when she was still building confidence, when each meeting, business negotiation, contract, and visit to a mill was a challenge. At the end of my visit, she and I spoke about self-image, children, and confidence, about searching for something we can do with our lives that is so meaningful to us that it becomes, in fact, who we are. "I'm just realizing that I've found it," she told me, clearly pleased with this newfound knowledge. "I want to be able to do this for the rest of my life," she says. "I hope I live a long time." In Aguila, in a rocky desert that would look like the middle of nowhere to many people, Sally Fox has found her oasis, a cotton field, and has put meaning and purpose into her life.

JUDY DERCUM

DILLON, COLORADO

THE HIGH-CEILINGED LIVING ROOM WOULD be stark were it not for the yarn in Judy Dercum's hands or the paintings, the work of her husband, Rolf, on the walls. Like a scene in a Colorado postcard, the snow-covered Rockies rise majestically outside. A perfect match to the white leather couch on which Judy sits, these mountains provide a dramatic backdrop to this couple's creative lives. "My surroundings need to be simple," explains Judy. "I need a blank space so that the object becomes paramount." The object at hand is Judy's latest knitting project. For this one, she has narrowed her choice to about twenty different colors, not very many by Judy's standards. Of course, there's still time for her to add more.

Most days, Judy can be found right there on that bright white couch, surrounded by yarn and the sunshine that beams through the nearly floor-to-ceiling windows. Her husband will most likely be in his painting studio. The pair met on the competitive ski circuit in 1962 — they were both Olympic contenders. Even now, they carry on their outdoor passion every day that there is snow on the ground, cross-country skiing from their doorstep, at an elevation of 10,000 feet, into the wilderness. When they return home, to a contemporary, three-story cedar structure that Rolf designed and built, they devote the rest of their day to their artwork. "I'm aware that I'm incredibly lucky," Judy told me as we drove together to New Mexico, where she and Rolf were helping one of their daughters and her husband build a straw bale house. Neither she nor Rolf needs to work to support their artistic lifestyle, nor do they need to earn money by selling their creations. Judy, however, chooses to sell hers and likes to, for the challenges it provides as well as to pay for the materials and the classes she takes from time to time.

The twenty or so sweaters Judy knits in the course of a year are multicolored studies of geometric motifs, many of which she derives from the Navajo weavings that she and Rolf have been collecting since they began traveling to New Mexico together in the 1960s. It's no wonder that Judy likes simple surroundings, as her tendency is to fill those geometrics with a swarm of colors, subtly transitioning from one to the next, shade by shade. Color is one of Judy's favorite subjects. She likes to speak about it, play with it, and study it. "I like to try to make color bloom," she explains, to achieve the same highlighting effect as Rolf does in his paintings — or the color master Kaffe

Once the snow has melted, Judy and her husband hike rather than ski daily. Judy learned to knit from her mother, who often knit silk bouclé dresses.

Before casting on for the Southwestern Geometric Jacket (left), Judy spent two weeks planning the color progression.

Above left: Judy draws great inspiration from the geometric motifs in Navajo rugs. "My whole life, I have always been struck by geometric figures," she says. "It's just my 'gestalt.' I don't know if I will ever do florals."

Above right: In this copper pot are many of the thirty-six colors of Rowan yarn that Judy used in the Southwestern Jacket she designed for this book. More and more, she is dyeing her own yarns (with natural dyes) to achieve the subtle color grading that characterizes her work.

Fassett does in his knitting. Judy admits to being influenced by Fassett's work but says she wants to develop her own artistic voice, not reproduce what he is doing. Sitting with a color wheel in her lap, she comments on how turning from one combination to another, maybe just a step or two to the right or left, can change her whole mood.

Most of what Judy knows about color and knitting is self-taught. "I'm a true believer that if you're diligent and you read you can learn everything you need to know," she explains. (Amazingly, that theory even extends to building a straw bale house with her children.) Part of this philosophy grew out of necessity, as the area where she lives (between Breckenridge and Montezuma), though an international skiing mecca, does not offer its small nontourist population many educational or cultural diversions. The nearest high-quality bookstore, art museum, theater — or yarn shop — is nearly a two-hour drive away, in Denver. "We've lived a very isolated life," Judy told me; when the throngs of skiers arrive in town, she and Rolf hole up inside. For the few classes she has taken over the years, she has traveled to Denver as well as to Fort Collins, Colorado, and Taos, New Mexico. Though she's been knitting more or less continuously since she started making ski hats with pom-poms as a teenager, for a long time she followed patterns — going through different phases, such as Norwegian ski sweaters, Arans, and Fair Isles — and reserved her design focus for another creative endeavor, ceramics. When not busy raising her three children, for most of the 1970s Judy was creating high-fire stoneware and selling it to private customers and local galleries. All of her pieces were earth-colored — a limitation of the technique she was using — and she gradually became frustrated by that as well as the large amount of gas needed for each firing at such a high altitude. She recalls thinking one day: "I don't want to do anymore dirt-colored things." So she went out and bought yarn in as many shades as she could find and just threw them all together.

Still, those "dirt colors" do tend to show up in Judy's knitting—laughingly, she points to the ochers and browns in one of her pieces. Overall, however, her work is quite bright, a reaction to the brilliant sky and snow that surrounds her most of the year and the large amount of time she spends in New Mexico. Less intense colors would not stand up to the glaring sun and deep shadows of these environments. The appeal of both ceramics and knitting is, for Judy, the same: it is the honesty of the materials, the tactile and meditative nature of the production, and the three-dimensionality of the result. As a potter, she read everything she could get her hands on, including books about Japanese masters and their apprentices. She recalls that in Japan an apprentice is considered of no value until she or he has gone through fourteen years of training, and that within Zen culture you work so that the work flows from you, so that it becomes the essence of you. "That is the goal," she says, referring to her knitting—to get the technique so ingrained into your being that your artistic abilities can come to the surface. "That is Rolf's goal with painting, too," she adds.

These two artists work, like complementary colors, in harmony. While Rolf calls what Judy does art, she is hesitant to define it that way. In her mind, art is more about beauty than function; craft usually has a more practical application, as is the case with most knitting as well as weaving. "At this point, the sweater still has to fit," Judy explains. "It's like a canvas to me. It's someplace that I can put down my visual words." Then she thinks back to the antique Navajo rugs that she so admires. "The Navajos took their weaving to a very high plane. That's what I'm striving for."

SOUTHWESTERN GEOMETRIC JACKET

This sweater pattern combines two of Judy's favorite design tools: color grading and geometric forms. The background grades from black at the bottom through rich purple and red-browns, and finally up into rust shades near the shoulders. The geometric designs are often found in Navajo rugs or in architectural details in the Southwest. The body pieces are knit on the bias. This allows the V pattern, more flattering on most bodies than horizontal patterns, to be easily achieved.

Judy chose Rowan yarns for this project because of the diversity of colors available. She spent two weeks choosing the colors and working out the graph. Though she is willing to make changes while she's knitting, before she starts a new project she likes to work out as many of the details as she can. The pattern for the Southwestern Geometric Jacket appears on page 188. Above is a swatch in an alternate colorway.

PRISCILLA GIBSON-ROBERTS

CEDAREDGE, COLORADO

IT WAS 1961 WHEN THE HEAD OF THE Textile Engineering department at Texas Tech University in Lubbock, Texas, sat twenty-two-year-old Priscilla Gibson down and convinced her that she could not pursue a degree in textile engineering despite the fact that she was the department's most outstanding honor student ever. No one would ever hire a female engineer, he told her.

In many ways, that rejection formed the woman I met nearly forty years later in Cedaredge, Colorado, at the home she designed herself and lives in with her husband, Jack Roberts. Today, she calls herself a "very vocal feminist" and speaks often of her daughters, Sheila and Kimberly, both in their thirties, and how hard she has worked to make sure they have been able to pursue their dreams with as few obstacles as possible. She also speaks passionately of the spinners and knitters of yesteryear with whom she feels a deep connection. Through her work, she tries to honor them. "Women have not been recorded in history. In some small way I'm trying to fix that record — to say that women were and are important," Priscilla explains. "I consider my gift the ability to sit down with old knitting pieces and put myself into the mindset of the knitter, to transport myself into that piece and become that knitter and figure out how she did it."

Priscilla is a highly sought-after teacher and is the author of many magazine articles. Her three books, *Knitting in the Old Way; Salish Indian Sweaters: A Pacific Northwest Tradition;* and *Ethnic Socks & Stockings,* each pay tribute to the artistry and fine craftsmanship of the spinners and knitters who came before her. Her professional accomplishments are as much a result of that early educational rejection at Texas Tech as they are of another reality of our patriarchal culture: moving to accommodate a husband's career. Priscilla married Jack Roberts while they were both in graduate school at Purdue University in Indiana, and when he got a job as a construction geologist with the federal government, the couple started moving from one site to another, living in nine different homes in seven states between 1963 and 1978. At the same time they raised their two daughters and their son, Bret.

In North Dakota in 1969, Priscilla met an elderly Norwegian woman who introduced her to the ethnic knitting techniques that became her specialty and her passion. Ethnic knitting, according to Priscilla, is a common-

Priscilla's first introduction to spinning was watching a Cowichan woman at work in front of her wheel at the Pike Place Market in Seattle. Later, while living in North Dakota, Priscilla decided to learn to spin herself. Because there weren't many spinning teachers at the time, she relied mostly on what she refers to as the Little Blue Bible, a book called *Your Handspinning* by Elsie Davenport. Today, Priscilla does almost all of her spinning on a high-whorl drop spindle.

For the Colorado Cashmere Wimples (at left and on page 85) Priscilla spun the exact amount of fiber she needed. Unlike many knitters, Priscilla does not have a yarn stash. After so many years of moving from place to place and managing all of the packing and unpacking, she likes to keep her surroundings as simple as possible.

Priscilla used Gaywool dyes for the two wimples. Here, she has filled mason jars with the tomato and pumpkin dyes.

sense approach to cultural garment construction, an approach that relies on a thorough understanding of technique and intuitive design skills rather than line-by-line printed patterns. To share this knowledge, Priscilla wrote her first book, *Knitting in the Old Way*, a guide to creating the folk sweaters of the world, including gansey, Aran, Fair Isle, and Bohus designs. In Washington State, Priscilla saw Cowichan sweaters as well as handspinning for the first time. The Cowichans are members of the Salish Indian tribe that live in coastal areas of Washington and British Columbia, and their sweater-making tradition dates back to the nineteenth century. The result for Priscilla was her second book. Though moving around so much was difficult at times, Priscilla also acknowledges how fortunate she has been to meet people of many different ethnic backgrounds in the process. "Luckily for me, we're a multicultural nation," she explains, "and I feel that through my work I am truly American because I am connecting with all of the cultures of the world."

Interestingly, Priscilla was not taken with knitting as a child growing up in South Texas. She was, however, drawn to fiber — at three, she was taking fabric and needles from her mother and pretending to sew. Two of her aunts tried to teach her to knit, but Priscilla describes the results as disastrous. Instead, her passion was horses, and she spent as much time with them as possible. She did sew her own clothes as a teenager, earning money to supplement her college scholarships by stitching Western shirts and other garments for sale. And she did learn how to weave, inspired by a desire to make saddle blankets for the horses. It wasn't until she started graduate school in 1962 and saw a dorm-mate working on a sweater that the knitting bug hit. "I had no need to knit until I went to Indiana and found out what snow was," Priscilla recalls, also remembering her dorm-mate's astonishment when she picked up the skill so quickly and completed her first sweater in two days. Somehow,

COLORADO CASHMERE WIMPLES

Priscilla saw her first wimples in the 1950s. The ones she saw were plain knit tubes and were actually called French hoods or smoke rings. Years later, she decided to elaborate on the concept for a design for *Knitter's Magazine*, and thus her version of the French hood (renamed the wimple by Lizbeth Upitis, see page 152) was born. For this book, Priscilla decided to elaborate even further by designing two new versions, one that is snug around the head and one that fits more loosely and is longer and more shawl-like around the shoulders. Priscilla handspun the cashmere for her wimples, though a commercially spun yarn can be used as well.

Priscilla wanted her contribution to this book to reflect her love for Colorado. She chose the pumpkin color of the loose-fitting lacier wimple because it reminds her of the color of the leaves on the aspen trees just before they drop in the late fall. From where the lace begins around the neck to the bottom edge, the stitches represent the mountains, the Colorado blue spruce, piñon pines, and the wildflowers (repeated around the area that frames the face) that bloom around her home in the spring. She chose the wavy edging to represent the sound of mountain water. The snugger-fitting wimple features a less elaborate design encircling the shoulders. The pattern appears on page 193.

an ancient chord had been struck within her and knitting — and soon hand-spinning — would become her lifelong passions.

When I visited Priscilla at her home in Colorado, she was in the final stages of editing her sock book and was bubbling with excitement about that project. Clad in Birkenstocks and jeans and wearing a silver bracelet with a weaving scene etched on it, an ear cuff, and a spinning-wheel pendant, she told me about her efforts to slow down — to work less and travel less — partly by choice and partly by necessity. She had recently undergone eye surgery and was informed by her doctor that she would have to decide what she wanted to do most with her eyes, as their strength was limited. "A second volume to the sock book," she was quick to tell me. "Then I'll knit for my grandkids, I guess."

When I spoke with Priscilla on the telephone a few months later, she was in the midst of a hectic travel schedule, leading knitting workshops in Virginia, Colorado, and Texas. So much for slowing down, I thought. Before we hung up she did mention that she had suggested to Jack that they go fishing together the next day, a chance for a little relaxation. Although she doesn't fish herself, I could easily see her there, sitting on a rock and spinning on her drop spindle . . . as women have done for centuries.

VALENTINA DEVINE is a portrait of warmth, joy, and creativity. These characteristics come out in the way she dyes her yarn in a kaleidoscope of colors, the way she knits in wildly abstract forms, and the way she sings and plays the guitar. But she has many dimensions, like all of us, and also holds within her a clear understanding and vivid memory of grief and pain.

When Irene Preston Miller, a grand dame of the fiber world and Valentina's mentor, asked Valentina to design a piece for a gallery show, the Berlin Wall had just come down. Valentina had grown up in Germany during World War II, and, in order to finally come to terms with the horror she had endured—as the daughter of a Russian mother and a German father, she was persecuted by the Nazis—she decided to try to knit a torn curtain, a metaphor for what had happened. She recalled in her mind the view from Checkpoint Charlie in West Berlin, which her neighborhood had become part of after the war, across into East Berlin: the bleakness and dismay, the few open windows, the curtains flapping in the wind. She knit irregular pieces with a coarse natural linen and created big holes, or rips, in them. Then one day she turned one of those pieces sideways and saw a screaming face staring back at her and immediately knew what the piece was meant to become. She knit more and more faces, their large, hollow eyes and gaping mouths crying out in anguish over those horrible years of suffering. As in the painting *The Scream* by Edvard Munch, in Valentina's stitches

Above: Valentina sings to Tita Cocq, our model on page 93. Right: *Scream* **is Valentina's knitted statement about the horrors of World War II.**

you can nearly hear the pain.

In another piece, one that is equally personal but in its nature less intense, Valentina has expressed the happiness she has felt in more recent years. In 1990, she moved to Los Alamos, New Mexico, with her second husband. Enamored with the colors she found there—in the landscape, the sky, the adobe buildings, the sunsets, and the costumes worn during the Native American and Hispanic festivals—she knit a celebratory piece: abstract shapes flowing freely from a fiber-covered piñon branch. This vivid work could be considered a metaphor for Valentina's current, more joyful life. She now wakes early each morning and dyes the yarn that she uses for her own knitting projects and also sells from her large home studio and at fiber festivals and craft shows. She knits for hours each day, creating hanging fiber sculptures as well as multicolored and multitextured clothing that is sold in galleries. As she watches one of her pieces flutter in a breeze, she says she is reminded to enjoy her inspirations and to keep on knitting.

Valentina was not always such a daring knitter. Growing up in a strict German home, she recalls being told by her mother, "You will knit for one hour." Often, Valentina felt that her mother also implied, "And you will enjoy it." For many years, while raising two children and living in West Point, New York, with her first husband, an American soldier she met in Berlin, she always followed patterns. Then, in the early 1970s, she met Irene Preston

Miller at her inspirational shop, the Niddy Noddy, in Croton-on-Hudson, New York, and everything began to change. Valentina had never before seen a shop that celebrated color, texture, and creativity so gloriously, nor had she met anyone as supportive of experimental knitting as Irene. Realizing that her new customer was fascinated by what she was doing and technically accomplished, Irene asked her if she would like to knit for her, then told her to choose any yarns that appealed to her in the shop. Valentina spotted a basket of blues and lavenders in different textures and thicknesses that Irene had dyed and dreamily said, "If I could, I would take this whole basket home and do something with it." Irene then handed her the basket. "She has this talent to make people do what they do best, without much coaxing. She gives you that freedom," Valentina recalls about her dear friend. Ultimately, Valentina worked in the shop part-time, when she wasn't at her full-time job as a dietary manager in a hospital. She remembers watching the women who would come into the Niddy Noddy with their husbands, and she imagined, longingly, how wonderful it would be to have the time and financial support to buy all of those beautiful yarns and play with them.

One day in the fall of 1980, Irene called Valentina and asked her to go with her to meet a fiber artist visiting from England. Tired after a long day's work, Valentina refused. But Irene, unwilling to take no for an answer, pressured her fiercely, and very reluctantly Valentina went along with her to meet this stranger, this man whom Irene described as "very important." He had yet to publish a book and was virtually unknown in the United States, but that stranger changed Valentina's life forever in the space of a few hours. His name was Kaffe Fassett. "This was the first time I saw sweaters that were not only beautiful, but also were not neatsy tidy, which I as a neatsy tidy German was taught to do," she recalls. She remembers him speaking passionately about all of the different shades of gray in a stone wall, the rusts in adobe, about using color with abandon. He taught her to see, and the liberation was complete. Together, Irene Preston Miller and Kaffe Fassett had set Valentina Devine's creative juices flowing.

"Be careful of what you wish for," announced Valentina while we were speaking in her color-filled studio in the bright alpine-style house she shares with her husband. "You just might get it." She was in her knitting nest, a window seat strewn with needlepoint pillows, an Oriental rug at her feet. She longed for the chance to devote herself to her knitting and now she has it. Today, Valentina helps to inspire other knitters by teaching throughout the country, including a class she calls Creative Knitting, in which she pushes her students to experiment with abstract shapes as well as interesting textures, to agonize less about color choices, and to mix colors in new and different ways. Sometimes she passes around a paper bag filled with yarn and has each student pick from it, forcing them to find a way to work with whatever colors serendipity delivers. She also advocates an almost stream-of-consciousness knitting technique that calls for no more than switching from knitting to purling whenever the fancy strikes.

This once "neatsy tidy" knitter has come a long way, and when I ask her if she can imagine ever stopping her knitting, her answer is a quick and adamant "No." Her wish for the freedom to play with yarn and color to her heart's content has become a reality and now she is forced to confront the challenges that freedom presents. Undoubtedly, Valentina Devine will continue to push the boundaries of two needles and a ball of yarn — and of herself — for as long as time will allow.

Left: In this hanging fiber sculpture, leaves of color flow from a fiber-covered piñon branch. Above: Valentina uses this shawl, called Windows on the World, as a teaching tool in her workshop.

LOUISE PARSONS

RANCHOS DE TAOS, NEW MEXICO

WATCHING LOUISE PARSONS AT HER spinning wheel is like watching a dance. Her posture is erect, her chin is up, and her left arm fully extends as she draws out the fiber to the beat of the large wheel that she is controlling with her foot. She learned the long-draw spinning method on this Rio Grande Wheel, the Rolls-Royce of spinning wheels, which was designed by Rachel Brown, a Taos resident and renowned weaver. While spinning, an air of peacefulness and relaxation comes over her. "I have tried smaller wheels," Louise says, "but they were too slow and tedious for me." Like so many spinners, Louise enjoys letting her mind wander as she spins. Knitting a challenging project, on the other hand, requires her focus and concentration. "They bring on two different forms of relaxation," says Louise.

Louise knits with an assortment of hand- and machine-spun yarns. She spins on the Rio Grande Wheel that her husband bought for her when she first learned in 1985.

One would never guess by watching this graceful woman at her wheel that finding a place in her life for spinning and knitting has not always been easy. For several years, she put so much pressure on herself to produce sweaters to sell in New Mexico galleries, to be constantly coming up with new and innovative designs, that she burned out and had to stop completely. "I didn't like what I was doing. I was getting in a rut and wasn't enjoying my work anymore," she explains. So she took a year off, but left her imposing Rio Grande Wheel in the center of her studio, which occupies one side of her living room. She left her yarns neatly in place on the shelves; a part of her knew that she would come back to what had once been the source of so much pleasure.

Nearly a year after Louise had stopped knitting, I visited her at her home, a small adobe house in a family-oriented community outside of Taos, and asked if she would be interested in designing something for this book. Before she answered, we talked a while about knitting, and about our dogs and gardens. Then, with a combination of reluctance and enthusiasm, she agreed to design a small child's garment. She said that she thought she was ready to ease her way back into the fiber world, that she had already decided to do some spinning for Luisa Gelenter, the owner of La Lana Wools (page 94). It had been at La Lana that her knitting career had begun.

Louise moved to Taos from northern California with her husband in 1985, with the idea that she would try to make a living as a handknitter. In California, she had studied forestry at a junior college, worked for a map-making company, and served as a housekeeper in a ski resort. Almost immediately upon her arrival in the Southwest, she was overwhelmed and inspired by the creativity she faced. Technically, her work was without flaw, but her designs were cautious; she had never before approached knitting with a sense of adventure or experimentation, characteristics that seemed to typify the garments that were being shown in the Taos and Santa Fe galleries and wearable-art boutiques. "I knit with gray a lot then," she recalls with a smile. La Lana, a fantasy yarn shop and gallery, opened up a whole new world to her. Luisa taught her how to spin and to dye yarn. She learned new techniques from designers who sold their work there, and before too long Louise was among that talented group of creative knitters whose garments lined the walls. In 1987, she started selling her work at the Santa Fe Weaving Gallery, which, along with La Lana, is one of the top galleries for knit and woven clothing in New Mexico.

Through spinning, knitting, and designing, the once-conservative Louise became more alert to the colors, shapes, and textures of the environment around her. Her sweaters became abstract studies of the Southwestern landscape that she loved, photographed, and hiked through so much. She drew inspiration from such images as a rock, its cracks and crevices, and the shadows that fell upon it. Although her designs were selling steadily, she always struggled with perfectionism. She wanted to set up a routine for herself so that she was only knitting when she was in the right state of mind, so that she could comfortably walk away from a problematic project and know that a solution would come to her in time. She was also battling rather than accepting a knitting reality—the time it requires to complete even the simplest of projects. At one point she was trying to churn out a new piece every two weeks, feeling compelled to keep up with the weavers and machine knitters who also sold their work at galleries in the area. Finally, at the end of 1993, she decided to take some time off from knitting garments for sale, to reassess what she wanted and needed to achieve with her knitting.

The child's jacket that Louise designed for this book turned out to be a bridge project, a link between knitting only occasionally for a family member and venturing back into the gallery world. Though it is atypical of her usual style, which has a more abstract, undulating feel, she says it was this project's simplicity and sweetness that appealed to her. Still, there is a landscape-like quality to the way she shaped and connected the patches.

Despite the difficulties she has faced, Louise once again enjoys selling her work. "It's amazing that someone appreciates something from me," she says with typical modesty. Now, she works on a schedule, which frees her from thinking about her designs all the time. As for her goals, she says, "I don't like to get too far ahead of myself. I like to keep things simple." Through her struggles, Louise is learning important lessons about herself—about patience, confidence, acceptance, and fulfillment.

Tita Cocq models the Madeline-inspired Patchwork-Sunflower Jacket. Her mom is the model on page 66.

PATCHWORK AND SUNFLOWERS

Inspiration for this slightly flared jacket came from a picture of the adventurous Madeline, a character in a series of children's books by Ludwig Bemelmans, who wore a blue coat of similar shape. Louise chose seven shades of Dale of Norway Heilo, a four-ply worsted wool yarn, figured out how she would break the jacket into patches, then started swatching and playing with eight different embroidery stitches. The hardest part, she said, was finding stitches that would show up and had dimension. She settled on four stitches for the outlining of the patches—feather, fern, spine chain, and wheat ear—and cross-stitch for the sunflowers. The pattern appears on page 194.

LA LANA WOOLS AND TAOS VALLEY WOOL MILL

TAOS, NEW MEXICO

SITTING IN THE BACK room of La Lana Wools — amid an assortment of unspun fleeces — Luisa Gelenter tells me that she was a free spirit when she came to Taos. She and her husband had been living in Mexico, on the verge of becoming expatriates, when a friend wrote in 1968 and said, "You can come back now. I found the place." Fiber enthusiasts everywhere should be grateful that Luisa took her friend's letter seriously and decided to give the then sleepy Southwestern town of alternative and creative living a try. In Taos, Luisa began to delve into natural dyeing, and it was here, in 1974, that she opened La Lana Wools, a colorist's paradise in the form of a shop and gallery in which she sells spun and unspun fiber, finished garments and other knit and woven objects, as well as natural dyestuffs.

For Luisa, a native of New York City who studied sculpture in high school and originally planned to go to medical school, the fiber trail began in Bolivia. "Everyone was spinning all the time, whether they were scurrying over the Andes or selling potatoes," she remembers. "I was very attracted to it. I bought a spindle and sat down with the ladies at the market." By the time Luisa left South America and moved to Taos, she had a sizable stash of handspun alpaca ready to be dyed, but felt it would be sacrilegious to taint her all-natural yarn with chemical colorants. Recalling the harmonious colors and soft glow of old

Using natural dyes and working with an assistant, Luisa can dye about twenty pounds of fiber in a day. "You do everything you know, you do everything as correctly as possible, and you may or may not get it. This is what keeps me interested." Using chemical dyes, Luisa says she could dye about two hundred pounds of fiber in a day — and get the same color every time. Alas, chemical dyes do not interest her.

Persian, Navajo, and Turkish textiles, Luisa began experimenting with dyes from the plants growing in her driveway, then ventured out into the nearby deserts and mountains. "In the beginning, there were a lot of disasters — blah beiges, weird yellows, disgusting greens. But here and there I would hit on something great like Navajo tea or snakeweed." Luisa now specializes in dyeing with plants native to the Southwest as well as the exotic dyes of antiquity: cochineal, indigo, madder, brazilwood, and logwood. "My feeling is that because the dyes are made out of organic materials you respond to them from your solar plexus, your heart *chakra*."

Today at La Lana Wools, which is housed in the former studio of Burt Phillips, an early Taos artist, Luisa's twenty-plus years of dyeing experience show in the luxurious skeins of yarn that line the adobe walls and fill baskets and display tables. They are also obvious in the handknit garments made with her fiber that are for sale there. Designer Judy Dercum (page 79), who sells her sweaters at La Lana Wools, compares Luisa's yarns to a landscape. "When you look at a landscape, it is never one color. It is a blending of colors, and your eye puts it all together, and that is what makes it beautiful and interesting." Lynne Vogel (page 133), a designer from Cannon Beach, Oregon, remembers discovering the store during a vacation in Taos many years ago. "The

first thing I noticed was the silk basket and those gorgeous colors I had never seen before." Later on, while living in Taos, Lynne would visit La Lana every day "just to look at the yarns."

Most days, Luisa's time is filled with managing the store and dyeing the fiber in her home-based studio as well as helping to run the Taos Valley Wool Mill, which she opened in 1991 with two partners. For hand-spinning, she hires women in New Mexico, Montana, Texas, and California, asking them to use the long-draw method, which requires giving the twist of the fiber a long angle and, according to Luisa, works best with her fibers because it maintains their loft, makes the yarn easier to handle, and helps the yarn to wear better. "The twist is powerful," Luisa says. "Fiber falls apart before it is spun. You put in this tiny little twist and you've got something." Spinning for Luisa does take some training, as her standards are high and at the same time idiosyncratic. She does not want yarn that looks like it was spun by a machine. "I like to keep the life in it," she explains, recalling a star pupil who learned to spin in record time but had to be taught "to lump it up, to let it breathe." She spun too perfectly.

Always the free spirit as well as the philosopher, Luisa credits her lack of formal fiber education with some of her most interesting creations. Consider her Tailspun yarns, rope-like mohair yarn with dangling, silky curls meant to capture the special beauty of fleece as it appears on a goat's back, and Wild Thing, another rope-like yarn, this one with different-colored wool or mohair "flags" shooting out at every imaginable angle. "Because I was never trained, my imagination could do anything," she says. The same goes for her colors. "Working with natural dyes is hard," she explains, "but the colors are so much more beautiful for the same boiling — and unpredictable." Interestingly, the unpredictability that Luisa

values is the same unpredictability that keeps other fiber artists loyal to chemical dyes, with their inherent reproducibility. "If I were getting the same color every time I would have been out of this a long time ago," she admits. There are myriad factors that can affect the natural dyeing process, from the mineral content of the earth and water where the plant grew to the genetics of the particular plant to the weather on dyeing day. Luisa cites brazilwood as an example: depending on the conditions it endured in the rain forest, it can lean toward either pink or orange.

Not surprisingly, Luisa is especially proud of her Forever Random Blends (variegated wool-and-mohair yarns in which the placement of the colors never repeats exactly). These yarns, she says, "talk and move in inexplicable ways." Though she does repeat color combinations — her yarns boast names like Zulu Prince, Faerie Queen, and Tzarina — no two skeins will ever be exactly alike. Luisa explains: "All the colors will be in the blend, but where they appear and how and what they're next to — this is serendipity. That's what makes it so enjoyable to spin and knit."

Luisa admits to having her secrets — where to find a certain plant, a special dyeing formula, exactly how she makes her Forever Random Blends — but she is also eager to share much of her knowledge and enthusiasm and from time to time offers dyeing classes, which she describes as "small and intense." Rather than sitting at a table with eye droppers and formulas, Luisa insists that her students get their hands dirty. "I want them in the pots, sweating, getting things right, getting things wrong, but making their own mistakes and not just watching me dance around." Luisa's advice to a student who wants to spin and dye and start a similar business: Follow your own path, follow what you love.

At the Taos Valley Wool Mill, Luisa and her partners do custom blending, carding, and spinning for customers, small and large, throughout the country.

THE NAVAJO PULLOVER

The Navajo Pullover was designed by Linda Romens, who sells her work at La Lana Wools and has given knitting classes there as well. In order to keep the price down, the black background is made with a machine-spun worsted-weight wool. The color pattern uses three shades of La Lana's Forever Random Blends: Apassionada, Zulu Prince, and Pastorale.

While working out the design, Linda referred to a coloring book of Native American symbols and a book of Navajo rug patterns. For added interest, she decided to add a small cable to the ribbing around the collar, wrists, and bottom band. See the front of the sweater in the photograph on page 99. The pattern appears on page 198.

LINDA ROMENS

CAÑON, NEW MEXICO

LINDA ROMENS BOUNCES FROM ONE ACTIVITY to the next. Not only is she high-energy, she is high-achieving. In addition to knitting, she spins, skis, makes beer and jewelry, and mountain bikes. Most mornings, when I stayed with her at her home in the art- and tourist-oriented town of Taos, she rose out of bed with a smile on her face, made a cup of coffee, then sat down at her spinning wheel. She spoke cheerfully about music, silversmithing, her childhood in Madison, Wisconsin, her full-time job as a medical technologist at the hospital in Taos—whatever was on her mind. Her conversation was always punctuated with bursts of hearty laughter. Often, she would make plans to fix brunch for a friend or meet another so they could fuse glass together, then use the glass to make jewelry. "A Renaissance Woman" is how Luisa Gelenter of La Lana Wools (page 94) describes her. For sale at La Lana are sweater kits that Linda has designed as well as Linda's finished sweaters and jewelry.

The second oldest of six children, seven-year-old Linda learned to knit from her mother using poultry skewers. She made the ubiquitous scarf, then didn't knit again until she was in college in Madison, this time with less pointy needles and older, less tender fingers. She made a fair-isle sweater—she had seen one on the cover of a magazine and was intrigued—but it didn't fit and she did not feel compelled to make another. She had not yet grasped the concept of gauge or learned how to carry more than one color. She recalls that the inside of her sweater was a "horrible mess." The next time she tried knitting was in 1980. She had just finished her college degree and was looking for a job as a medical technologist in Eugene, Oregon, when she passed by a yarn shop. She stepped in, and this time she was hooked, quickly completing several sweaters. Not realizing that there was supposed to be anything difficult about knitting without a pattern, she soon started designing her own garments. She would become intrigued by a yarn, then envision the style of sweater in which it would look best and give it a try.

To this day, Linda continues to let the fiber tell her what it wants to be, in knitting as well as in spinning. After buying a Merino fleece at the Black Sheep Gathering in Oregon, Linda knew it was time to learn to spin; up to that point, she had only a basic understanding of drop spindling. Her aunt loaned her an electric spinning wheel, which she appreciated because it allowed her

Before moving to Taos from Eugene, Oregon, in 1993, Linda did two things: she looked for a good job and a good yarn shop. She found both and moved in.

Left: The wooly sweater and the silky skirt, worn by artist Heather Harrington, form a juxtaposition of textures with the rocky canyon desert around Embudo Station, about twenty-five miles southwest of Cañon, the Taos neighborhood where Linda lives.

David Ashton, the president of a graphic design firm, works on his farm in Linda's rugged outdoor sweater.

to concentrate on the fiber in her hands without having to worry about what her feet were doing. Then, while traveling in New Zealand, she bought her own Ashford spinning wheel; it was time to add the feet. She has learned over the years by first deciding what she wants to spin or knit and then figuring out the necessary techniques, either by trial or error or by finding the information in a book. Often, she relies on pictures instead of explanatory text. One of the best learning tools in her self-education has been her experience writing knitting patterns for Rainbow Mills in Pittsburgh, Pennsylvania, the company that gave Linda her first break in the design world in 1990. Linda was wearing a cotton sweater she had designed with their yarn while browsing in a shop in Oregon when a man approached her and said that if she could write the pattern he could get her money for it. The man turned out to be a sales representative for Rainbow Mills.

For Linda, knitting has always been much more of a creative outlet and something she does for plain old fun rather than a source of income. In fact, most of the time she prefers to be compensated in yarn for her design work because, she says, "If I were paid in money I'd feel like I have to use it to pay the rent." Linda even knows how to manipulate her own leaning toward practicality. It was, in fact, practicality that led the stellar high-school student to pursue a career in the sciences rather than art. She needed to pay for her own education and wanted to know that she would be able to support herself after graduation.

Though Linda seems to have a natural affinity for knitting, she has had her share of upsets over the years. With laughter, she refers to two boxes of not-so-nice sweaters she made before she finally surrendered to the reality that for the type of work she likes to do — lots of color and texture — a gauge swatch is crucial. When a knitter is debating about ripping out a large portion of a garment, she now wisely suggests, "Pretend you're getting more use out of the yarn." Another philosophy: "If you feel you have done your best, that's great." Linda's positive outlook allows her to try many different things — from designing handknits to jewelry-making to sports — and feel successful. While she and I were driving to Abiquiu for a photo shoot, she told me that she thinks most people put up barriers. They say they are not artistic or creative because they are afraid of failing. In the creative community of Taos — Cañon is an old, supposedly haunted neighborhood there — Linda fits right in. Artwork lines the walls of the hospital where she works, and the staff knows her as the knitter and jewelry maker, often stopping her in the halls to find out about her latest project. Everyone knows that it will always be something different. And Linda makes sure it's always something fun.

FAUX CABLE SAGE PULLOVER

Linda says that she is not influenced by colors in nature on a cognitive level, but in an interesting example of inspiration by osmosis, she chose the muted green color for this unisex pullover, then later realized that it matched the sagebrush-swept desert that she saw outside of her front door every day. This rough and tough sweater is made with Brown Sheep Company's Lamb's Pride Superwash Bulky (100 percent wool) in a color Brown Sheep calls Lichen. Though it looks cabled, the texture of the sweater is achieved by manipulating knit, purl, and slip stitches only. The pattern appears on page 197. Linda also designed the Navajo Pullover shown on pages 97 and 99.

WEST

SARAH SWETT

MOSCOW, IDAHO •

SARAH SWETT REMEMBERS LEARNING TO knit from her mother and grandmother as a very young child and making "lots of raggedy magic carpets for my stuffed bears." There is something engaging about this image — a little girl with dark bangs knitting charmed striped squares — and there is something engaging about the adult Sarah as well. She is a spinner, knitter, and tapestry weaver who brings so much intelligence and emotion to what she does that when she speaks of it her gestures become more grand and words begin to tumble from her mouth with increasing speed and animation.

When Sarah's husband, Dan Edwards, a chemistry professor, asked her one day what her favorite aspect of the spinning process was, she couldn't choose one stage over another. She reflected on the fresh aroma of raw, greasy fleece; the fluffiness of a cleaned fleece; the rhythm and meditation of the actual spinning; the sense of accomplishment as she winds each skein. "I can either put the skeins in a pile and just look at them and how beautiful they are," Sarah says, "or I can start knitting swatches." The anticipation and the process are, for this self-motivated artist, almost more enjoyable than the finished product.

Sarah taught herself to spin on a drop spindle that she carved out of apple wood and pine in 1981. She was twenty-one years old, living and working with her first husband as a manager of an old homestead in the Idaho wilderness, without electricity, telephone service, or roads. In a letter to me about the defining six-year experience, Sarah wrote: "In the beginning I brought in mule loads of yarn. Later I hauled in fleece after fleece and even spun and knit with mountain-goat hair." On busy days, she got up before sunrise to squeeze in time for spinning and knitting. She carried her knitting in a fanny pack and knit while she walked and rode her horse. She filled her backpack with knitting projects when on the trail for an extended period. In her isolated existence, the ever-growing number of her fiber creations became Sarah's companions and formed the basis of her identity. "I defined myself not as a mule packer, outfitter, cook, or ranch hand," Sarah recalls, "but as a knitter."

This was not the first time Sarah used knitting to define herself. At Milton Academy, the eminent boarding school in Massachusetts that she attended for three years, she knit. At Harvard University, where she studied for two semesters, it was knitting, she recalls, that made her feel like an interesting

While modeling the handspun, sky-blue-and-red Kestrals Alight Cropped Kimono (left), Sarah spun on her high-whorl drop spindle. At home, she spins on a Schact wheel. The colors of the Kestrals Alight Jacket reflect autumn in Idaho — the expansive blue sky contrasted with the red of the wild currant and gooseberry bushes. Sarah achieved the colors with indigo, cochineal, and madder dyes.

Above: Combed Cormo fleece
ready for spinning. For the yarn
Sarah spun for the sky-blue-and-
red Kestrals Alight Cropped Kimono,
she combined two plies of Cormo
with one ply of Merino.

Below: A Kestrals Alight swatch
featuring a darker background color.

person, that made her feel as though she was effectively rebelling against the city life and intellectualism that Harvard, to her, represented. She left the school in 1979, sure that she didn't belong there. "I wanted to be a hippie farmer, to have milk goats and children and knit and cook great pots of soup and have a huge garden," Sarah explained to me one afternoon while we sat together in her small Moscow, Idaho, home, a one-story poured-concrete structure, nicknamed The Alamo, that looks like a pint-sized cross between a fort and a castle. She worked continuously, adding duplicate stitch to the Kestrals Alight Cropped Kimono that she designed for this book, except when her passion for a topic compelled her to use her hands to express herself, which was often. About adding color to the jacket with the duplicate stitch, she happily announced, "I could do this all day."

Exploring color is a relatively new passion for Sarah. For many years, she knit within a limited palette and tended to rely on safe, traditional color combinations. That began to change when she became a tapestry weaver. She was enrolled at the University of Idaho in Moscow, intending to finish the college degree she began at Harvard and then apply to veterinary medicine programs, when she took her first weaving class and was immediately hooked. "I wanted to spend all of my time on the loom," she recalls. Before she had time to finish her degree, she met and married Dan and gave birth to their son, Henry, then decided that she would devote herself full-time to the fiber arts. "Weaving made me feel freer to play with color," Sarah explains. Her quick and public success — she sold two of her early pieces, and her first submission to the Handweavers Guild of America was accepted for its 1991 Small Expressions exhibition — also built up her confidence and confirmed for her the validity of fiber as an important focus and means of expression in her life.

While the motifs in Kestrals Alight have a natural, tapestry-like feeling to them, the jacket is, in fact, not reminiscent of Sarah's tapestries, which tend to be painterly and surreal and include human figures, usually people she knows. For example, in *Conflict of Interest,* a woman milks a goat while looking out the window of a barn, while the walls of the barn evolve into a mountainside dotted with mountain goats. For Sarah, the large, approximately four-by-five-foot piece represents her own internal conflict between weaving tapestries and being a mom, between domesticity and life in the wilderness.

Typically, Sarah weaves in her studio in her backyard when Henry is in school and on the weekends when Dan is home, then spins and knits in the house whenever she can find the time. She works exclusively with her own handspun yarn, which she dyes using natural coloring agents only. Though Sarah cannot imagine her life without knitting, it is tapestry weaving that brings her the most recognition — her tapestries have been showcased in both one-woman and group shows — as well as the most income, however small. Sarah is acutely aware of the difference in public perception between knitting and weaving. She finds that people can more easily accept weaving as a full-time occupation and are willing to pay a higher price for something they can hang on the wall as opposed to wear on their bodies. During the period between leaving the homestead in the wilderness and returning to school, Sarah made a marginal living as a knitter, selling vests in which she combined handknit fronts with machine-knit backs.

If there were more public recognition for handknits, Sarah says she might devote more time to them, for it is the focus that tapestry exhibitions and commissions call for, Sarah explains, "that pushes me to do better than my best." She does, however, still treasure the time that she spends knitting, for its tactile, rhythmic, and meditative qualities as well as the thrill of watching the fiber glide through her fingers. The knitted fabric, she says, as it grows stitch by stitch, "is almost like a living thing." She compares handknits as well as tapestries to a woman. The Kestrals Alight jacket, she says, "is feminine because it is fiber and because of the way it feels and drapes. Yet you could probably run over it with a truck, then wash it and it would be fine. I think women are like that. All sorts of things happen to them and they still keep people warm and are still strong and there. You don't really ever wear them out."

Sarah models the gray-and-white millspun version of the Kestrals Alight Cropped Kimono amid the sensuous, rolling hills that are typical of the Palouse, the Idaho region where Moscow is located.

KESTRALS ALIGHT CROPPED KIMONO

The Kestrals Alight Cropped Kimono is knit in the round, with steeks at the front and armhole openings. Sarah knit this sweater with her own handspun, naturally dyed, three-ply yarn (two plies from a Cormo fleece and one from a Merino fleece). We then asked another knitter to reproduce the sweater with Classic Elite's millspun ultra-soft Avalon yarn (50 percent baby alpaca, 25 percent angora, and 25 percent lambswool). Sarah graded the colors in the original version, but for the millspun version we decided to omit this step (which would have been much more difficult to achieve with a commercial yarn) and, instead, added duplicate stitch for color interest after the sweater was knit. The name of the sweater speaks to both the birds that were the inspiration for the design and to the birds that "alight" on one's shoulders when wearing the garment. The pattern for the Kestrals Alight Cropped Kimono appears on page 200.

EXTENDING NINETY-six miles from Lost Trail Pass on the Idaho border north to the small town of Florence, the Bitterroot Valley of Montana boasts more temperate weather than the rest of the Treasure State, and awe-inspiring views in nearly every direction—from the Bitterroot Mountains to the west to the Sapphire Mountains to the east. This makes it a popular destination for tourists (hunters and fishermen, in particular) as well as retirees and younger people looking for a slow-paced, country lifestyle. In addition, explains one resident, "It has a small-community feel. Your neighbors are truly there for you all the time. And the kids are much more innocent." The valley does not, however, provide adequate employment opportunities, especially for women—minimum wage is the average salary—and this forces or inspires many residents to make their own way and start their own businesses. Interestingly, an impressive number of Bitterrooters have turned to fiber and fiber-producing animals, including angora, cashgora, and cashmere goats, Shetland and other breeds of sheep, llamas, and musk-oxen, as a means of supplementing their incomes. Following are the stories of three fiber-oriented businesses.

MOUNTAIN COLORS

Leslie Taylor and Diana McKay gave a dyeing demonstration at the first Big Sky Fiber Festival in 1991 and were so gratefully

Above: Bonnie Honohan, a retired sheriff from Los Angeles, maintains what she calls a hobby flock of goats and Churro sheep at her Starfire Farm in Hamilton. Each year she sells goats for packing, as pets (often to retired people), and to landowners who want to use them to control weeds on their property. **Right:** A sampling of handpainted yarns from Mountain Colors are on display along a rocky wall at Castle Crags Ranch, where Diana and Stee Hachenberger raise cashmere goats and a small herd of sheep.

received that they wondered if they might be able to start a business selling their hand-painted yarn. The two friends had met in California and learned to dye as members of the Foothill Fiber Guild of Grass Valley and Nevada City. Each had moved with her husband and children to the Bitterroot Valley in the early 1990s and intended to stay indefinitely. Both women are well educated and boast impressive work experience in California—Leslie has a bachelor's degree in wildlife biology and an associate's degree in computer programming; Diana holds a bachelor's degree in business and marketing—but neither could find a well-paying job in the valley, let alone one that could accommodate the schedules of their young children.

With one pound of undyed mohair each, they founded Mountain Colors in February of 1992. In the spring of that year, they brought a big bag of yarn to Susanna Springer, the spirited proprietor of Joseph's Coat, a yarn shop in Missoula, Montana, and she bought every last skein, providing Leslie and Diana with encouragement as well as additional sales contacts. By 1996, they had moved the business from their homes to a studio in a converted creamery, were dyeing about two hundred pounds of fiber each month, and were selling yarn to about seventy-five shops across the country.

While Leslie and Diana attribute their success to initial support from fiber friends back in California, their own stamina, and their understanding husbands (the business did not draw a profit for several years), when they say this they are underplaying the scope of their talent. Using the mountains, meadows, and woodlands of the Bitterroot Valley as inspiration, the creative pair creates a kaleidoscopic array of handpainted wool, mohair, and alpaca blends in such colors as Bitterroot Rainbow (a rich prism of color that starts at gold and moves through rich and deep oranges, reds, blues, purples, and greens) and Red Tail Hawk (a blend of browns and earthy reds with tinges of gold and mauve).

The most challenging aspect of the business, Leslie and Diana agree, is collecting the money. The most fun, Leslie says, is coming up with new colors. The most satisfying, adds Diana, "is driving to work each day knowing that we put it together ourselves."

THE MUSK OX COMPANY

Nancy and Joel Bender have been raising musk-oxen since 1986, three years after they started researching the feasibility of such a unique venture and trying to find an animal for sale. Nancy, who is five feet, three inches tall and weighs only slightly more than one hundred pounds, is responsible for the day-to-day care of the massive six- to eight-hundred-pound animals, while her strong and tall husband, Joel, who works full-time selling lumber, is responsible for the upkeep of the thirty-acre ranch and is the driving force behind the business. "Joel and the bulls don't get along," says Nancy, who believes it is easier for her to take care of the mighty animals, who as a species have changed little since the Ice Age, on her own. "I don't have a contest with the animals the way guys do. I don't try to overpower them." Instead, Nancy says she respects their power and, as much as possible, sticks to a care system based on our superior intelligence, routine, and reward (mostly grain and scratches in strategic areas that please the animals, such as around their ears and eyes). She also claims that the musk-oxen, reminiscent of yaks in appearance except for horns that swoop down instead of up, have a soft, tender side. She describes Moe, one of her favorites, as a mush and a ham. "He was bottle-raised," she explains, "and in some ways he orients himself more with humans than with other musk-oxen."

When I visited Nancy and Joel, their herd numbered 17; Nancy has determined that she will be able to handle 20 to 25 animals without hiring outside help. Typically, she feeds early in the morning and spends the rest of the day inside — in the timber-frame house that she and Joel designed and built themselves — taking care of production and marketing responsibilities. No matter what she is doing, however, she is constantly checking out the window, counting animals and watching for unusual behavior. The musk-oxen have a tendency to slam into things, and Joel and Nancy are always looking for new and sturdier ways to build fencing. "There's no manual for taking care of musk-oxen," she explains with a chuckle. She and Joel have over the years formed relationships with several different veterinarians and developed a good rapport with zoo curators in the United States and Canada.

It is for the luxurious fiber — most commonly known as qiviut (pronounced KIH-vee-ut) — that Nancy and Joel raise musk-oxen. "They also appealed to us because they're a little bit on the fringe," Nancy admits. Before moving to Montana, the adventurous couple had counted among their non-traditional work sites a fishing camp in Alaska and a hunting camp in the Idaho back country. Finer than cashmere and many times warmer than wool, qiviut (the soft, downy undercoat of the musk-ox) is so highly sought after that Nancy, who has a degree in clothing, textiles, and design from the University of Idaho, has more trouble filling all the orders she receives than getting orders in the first place. Nancy sells raw and dehaired fiber, in addition to commercially spun yarn in the fiber's natural taupe and four handpainted colors, through mail order and trade shows. About her qiviut, Nancy says, "It's the best fiber to wear in the whole world."

Left: It was through handspinning that Nancy Bender was introduced to qiviut. She and her husband, Joel, were working in a fishing lodge in Alaska when a writer from *National Geographic* brought her some raw fiber and said that if she would spin for him he would give her half. Nancy and Joel decided to raise musk-oxen on their Bitterroot Valley ranch as a means of supplementing their family income.

CASTLE CRAGS RANCH

Diana Hachenberger decided to start raising cashmere goats in 1990 in order to bolster the family income and still be available at home for her young children. She knew that her chances of getting a job outside of the house that paid more than she would need to hire a baby-sitter were unlikely. Her flock grew gradually, and before long she faced the American cashmere industry's main bottleneck: dehairing (the removing of the guard hairs from the soft down of a fleece). Diana could have done it by hand, but that process would have required days on end and would have made the final product too expensive to sell. She could have sent her clip to one of the large processors, but it would have been pooled with the fleeces of other breeders and in return she would have received only a small percentage of her own animals' down. The large processors need at least 500 pounds of fiber in order to run their machines, and from an average goat Diana gets only a one-and-a-half pound fleece.

In 1992, Diana's husband, Steve, an electrical contractor, decided to try to build a machine that could dehair small quantities of cashmere. "Someone told him he couldn't do it," Diana recalls, "and he was determined." By 1994, Steve had, indeed, built both a prototype and a 2,000-pound, 15-by-7-foot full-size model, a patented machine still significantly smaller than those used at the large processing plants. Diana and Steve now dehair all of their own fiber, which Diana then spins and sells or uses for knitting. When I visited the Hachenbergers, they had built up a herd of about 150 Australian and Tasmanian cashmere goats plus 30 sheep. They were also preparing to open a shop in Hamilton to sell their fiber products as well as those of other Montana breeders and fiber artisans. Taking care of the animals and spinning, on the average, five hours per day, Diana reports that she is still barely earning minimum wage. She does, however, boost her income by selling some of the animals with which she doesn't want to breed for packing, pets, and as weed eaters. Most importantly, she loves her work, has great hope for the future of the ranch and business — and is enjoying watching her children grow.

KERRY FERGUSON

BAINBRIDGE ISLAND, WASHINGTON

KERRY FERGUSON EXPLAINS HOW SHE became a designer and the owner of a yarn company and a yarn shop by saying, "You grow into these things." Kerry had been working as a fifth- and sixth-grade teacher for nearly sixteen years before going back to school at the University of California at Los Angeles to study design. When she and her husband and business partner, Stuart, moved from Los Angeles to Bainbridge Island, a short ferry ride from Seattle, she took a needlepoint class at the local yarn shop and found out the business was for sale. Kerry and Stuart decided to buy the shop in 1981, selling the family's vintage Porsche to pay for it. "That was a real act of faith," Kerry recalls of her husband's willingness to invest in her vision. In the years that followed, Kerry and Stuart opened two more stores under the name M. L. Mallard, Ltd. — one in Seattle and one in the nearby suburb of Bellevue — then closed or sold all but the Seattle store.

Above: Kerry at Bainbridge Island's Fort Ward, a former military outpost that is now a waterside park.

Left: Jennifer Jewell, a Creative Yarns employee, models Kerry's Snoqualmie Stripes Jacket at the arboretum in Seattle.

One afternoon in 1992, Kerry was working at M. L. Mallard when a man came in and showed her some BioSpun® (chemical-free) yarn from Merino and Perendale sheep raised on an organic farm in New Zealand. She examined it carefully — with her eyes, nose, and fingers — then asked if he had a distributor. "It had a fresh, clean, wonderful feel to it," Kerry recalls. That was the beginning of Creative Yarns International, the eco-conscious company that Kerry and Stuart founded in order to import and sell BioSpun and other yarns from New Zealand. By this time, Kerry had published her own designs in a popular shop newsletter, which had led directors at Cascade, Stacy Charles, and Skacel, all yarn importers and wholesalers, to hire her to put together pattern books for them. With the birth of her own company, Kerry was poised to apply her creativity to her own product.

Kerry had actually started training herself for a career in design as a young child. Her mother, Millie Bliss, who studied apparel design at Art Center in Los Angeles, had taught her daughter how to make paper dolls at six years old, and Kerry has fond memories of drawing and cutting out wardrobes for them. Millie also taught the eager Kerry to sew and to do basic fashion illustration, and one day even predicted that her daughter, who loved shopping at fabric stores, would become a designer. Kerry learned to knit not from her mother, but from her friends in home economics class in junior high. The teacher was trying to orchestrate sewing lessons, and the girls

A field of hand-carved tagua buttons from Ecuador. The colored buttons are naturally dyed in Seattle.

would knit so that she wouldn't see— under the table. Kerry continued to knit, she says, "in spurts through high school, college, courting, and later for my daughter," always preferring to create her own designs rather than follow patterns.

As a professional designer, Kerry brings to her creations years of life experience, even drawing upon her first career in elementary education. While teaching students from many countries, as well as Native Americans, she became intrigued by different cultures. Kerry says she likes to work "in the stream that crosses time and continents," and hopes that knitters who work on her designs feel that they become a part of that stream. It is for its multiculturalism that Kerry loves the United States. For the Snoqualmie Stripes Jacket she contributed to this book, she was influenced by the stripe patterns of traditional African kente cloth, the Tlingit baskets produced by native people of the northwest, and the colors of the Washington landscape. The buttons she chose (which Creative Yarns also distributes) were handcarved in the rain forests of Ecuador from tagua nuts (the ivory-like nut of a certain palm tree). While Kerry pays attention to fashion trends, she works hard to interpret rather than copy them (just as she tries to evoke the feeling of a cultural element without imitating it) and to translate them into garments that are both exciting and wearable by people of varying body types. "I'm not tall or super-slender," Kerry explains. "I've always had to dress with a lot of care in terms of not having volumes around me and paying some attention to proportions of things." Every day, Kerry spends time in her shop, which is within walking distance from the scenic Seattle waterfront and across the street from the Creative Yarns office, and is able to see firsthand what knitters really want — the gauge they prefer, the colors and shapes that appeal to them.

While working out a design, Kerry thinks not only of the look of the finished garment but how to produce it in a manner that is sensible and enjoyable. Taking a cue from the British designer Annabel Fox, who has given two sold-out workshops at M. L. Mallard, Kerry tries to incorporate interesting details into each stage of the knitting process to give the knitters something to look forward to. That might be, for example, a colorwork cardigan in which the bottom band and upper sleeve border are marked by a horizontal cable, or a shawl jacket that combines knit-purl stitch patterning and stranded colorwork, with cuffs worked in a basketweave pattern and finished with a crocheted scalloped edge.

Kerry has also been influenced by Kaffe Fassett, and thinks often of his playful use of color and his suggestion that if twenty-five colors are not working together, add a twenty-sixth. She also recalls a remark he made during a dinner at her home, describing knitting as a very rhythmic activity, whether it is the rhythm of color or of pattern. Kerry, who studied piano and dance throughout her childhood, expands on this concept. "It has a beat to it. The rhythm is something that you say to yourself—K2P1—like a mantra. That's where it becomes meditative and relaxing. It pulls you out of a very staccato kind of life—moving over here, over there, and having to change the pace of things all the time—to being able to sit and be at a regular pace that you choose yourself."

Kerry has the perfect opportunity for knitting built into her daily schedule—the thirty-minute ferry trip across Puget Sound from Bainbridge Island, where she lives in a waterfront home, to Seattle. Often she also spends time on the ferry line before boarding. The great thing about knitting, she says, is that "you need never be bored or impatient while waiting for anything because you're always pleasantly occupied." According to Kerry, knitters can look upon waiting as a gift, an unexpected opportunity to pull out their latest projects.

Between Creative Yarns and M. L. Mallard, Kerry works about sixty hours each week. She admits that managing the two can be difficult. But, overall, she says, "I like how I spend my time." Off-hours, she and Stuart enjoy watching baseball games and taking trips on their boat and in their Triumph TR6. Yes, Kerry and Stuart were able to replace the Porsche they sold in order to finance the first shop with another vintage sports car.

SNOQUALMIE STRIPES JACKET

For the Snoqualmie Stripes Jacket, Kerry drew inspiration from the stripes in traditional African kente cloth and the colors of the northwest. The fabric is composed of rectangles—simple green ones and three different multicolored stripe formations. Kerry chose a woven stitch for the slouched shawl collar and the cuffs, creating a sturdy fabric reminiscent of the baskets of the Tlingit, a native people of the northwest. The proportions are intentionally wide and easy, meant to fit over the layers of clothing Washingtonians generally wear to accommodate the changing weather on any given day. The Snoqualmie Stripes Jacket, made with Creative Yarn's own BioSpun® Merino eight-ply yarn, is named after the Snoqualmie Pass, the Cascade Mountain pass that leads into Seattle from the east. The pattern appears on page 202.

WHEN SHE CAN FIND the time, Jean DePorter, the manager of Northwest Alpacas Country Store, likes to spin amid the animals that provide her with her fiber. She takes her wheel and some alpaca fleece out into one of the many fields on the fifty-acre ranch owned by her employers, Julie and Mike Safley, and before long the curious *machos* (males), *embras* (females), or *crias* (babies), depending on which field she is in, wander by to sniff and peek at what she is doing. Along with the calming whir of her wheel, she is lulled into relaxation by the soft hum of the alpacas, who communicate with each other mostly with hums but also with clicks and whistles.

More than one hundred fifty alpacas live on this spotless ranch, which was founded in 1984, the first year that the South American governments allowed alpacas to be exported. In the same family as the llama (and the camel, guanaco, and vicuña), these gentle, pretty animals have become, ever since that first exportation, popular among livestock investors and breeders like the Safleys who seek to benefit not only from the five- and six-figure prices the animals can fetch but also the luxurious quality of the fiber, which is stronger and warmer than wool and, in many cases, as fine as cashmere.

The yarn Jean spins will be sold in the ranch's two-story shop, actually a converted dairy barn, along with machine-spun yarn, raw and carded fleece, roving, batts, and knit and woven alpaca clothing produced locally and in South America. Julie Safley, who spent more than twenty years working in the fashion industry in New York and Beverly Hills before she opened the store in 1990, also makes the space available to local spinners, knitters, and weavers as well as school and tour groups who come to mingle with the animals, feeding them grain pellets straight out of their hands.

There are two types of alpacas: Suris, whose straight fleece hangs down from their bodies like a floor mop, and the Huacayas, whose fluffy, wavy fiber grows perpendicular to their bodies and is better suited for knitting (the Safleys breed mostly Huacayas). With their long legs, tall, graceful necks, and pointy ears, alpacas appear almost fantastical and whimsical, as though they could have been created by a Disney animator. Some have long, frilly eyelashes, others a flop of bangs hanging in front of their large, flirtatious eyes, which range in color from pale blue to brown. Their facial features are distinct, and there is something knowing in their stare. When alpacas look at human beings they seem to be asking them why they are taking life so seriously. Standing in a field with these peaceful animals, one can't help but wonder.

Right: Jean DePorter, the manager of Northwest Alpacas Country Store in Scholls, Oregon, about twenty miles west of downtown Portland, takes a break from her regular duties. Alpaca is slicker than wool (the scales of its fiber lie flatter) and, therefore, can be harder to spin. To ease into it, Jean recommends carding alpaca with wool at the beginning, then slowly taking the wool away.

NANCY BUSH

SALT LAKE CITY, UTAH

ON THE BULLETIN BOARD IN NANCY Bush's studio in her home in Salt Lake City, Utah, is the following quote: "You can't possibly know where you're going if you don't know where you've been." She wrote down those instructive words after hearing them in a television advertisement for a program about the Civil War. And it is those words, she claims, that guided her through three years of research and design for her first book, *Folk Socks,* published in 1994. Within her sock volume she traces the evolution of footwear from the eighth century B.C. onward and presents new designs based on British and European folk-knitting traditions.

Folk art (which she defines as the art of everyday people) has been Nancy's passion since the early 1970s, when she earned a bachelor's degree in art history from the University of Utah. After college, she went on to study color theory, Japanese and Chinese art principles, and tapestry in San Francisco and then traditional weaving techniques at the Swedish Handcrafts Society in Insjön. It was in Sweden that Nancy became seriously interested in knitting. Under the guidance of her weaving classmates, most of whom were also voracious knitters, she completed two sweaters in the round using yarn spun at a local mill. Though she did not realize the historical significance of knitting at the time (it is now among her principal interests), she was fascinated by the technical process. After leaving the Handcrafts Society, she worked as a nanny in Paris and came to appreciate knitting's portability, especially as it compared to weaving, which she was unable to practice in France because she did not have a loom there.

Nancy's design style is characteristically clean and simple, and she is a devoted circular knitter. She values comfort over fashion and focuses almost exclusively on classic styling and restrained colorways. Her inspiration generally comes from historic garments or textiles and her varied travel experiences. She has designed sweaters based on Hungarian felted horsemen's cloaks, a woven Estonian rug, and the Sissinghurst gardens in England. Her design career began in 1985, when Alexis Xenakis, the publisher of *Knitter's Magazine,* called her at The Wooly West (the yarn shop she opened five years earlier) for photographs of the Shetland Islands. She ended up writing an article about the islands, with which she has had an ongoing love affair for many years, and then began to submit designs to the magazine for publication. Nancy counts longtime *Knitter's*

Above: The degree of passion Nancy holds for knitting is perhaps matched only by her passion for travel. We photographed her — and her socks (left) — in Immigration Canyon, close to her home in Salt Lake City.

editor Elaine Rowley as one of her two most significant mentors. Her weaving teacher in San Francisco, Maja Stampfl, taught her to take her interest in textiles seriously — and Elaine took Nancy seriously. "She had faith in me and gave me a lot of guidance and support," explains Nancy, who penned a column for *Knitter's* for eight years and has also sold many designs to yarn companies such as Dale of Norway, Brown Sheep Company, and Renaissance Yarns.

With the publication of *Folk Socks,* Nancy will be forever associated with foot coverings. Fortunately for her, she has not lost her passion for the subject, which can be traced back to the beginnings of knitting itself, and imagines that she will be designing socks for the rest of her life. The appeal, according to Nancy, is that they're small, portable projects that people can make without committing their lives to them. They can be wonderfully intricate or plain, they are great for trying out new techniques, and they are functional.

Functionality has always been important to Nancy. As an undergraduate pursuing an art history degree, she was especially attracted to the principles of purpose imbued in Japanese folk art. No detail was superfluous, whether creating a tea bowl or a textile. Her attraction to Swedish handwovens stemmed not only from the clean lines of the patterns but also from the tried-and-true traditional techniques and the Swedish custom of creating practicable pieces, such as curtains, rugs, and place mats. Drawn to the Zen concept of orderliness, she displays yarns in her store (located a few blocks from the house she shares with her husband in Salt Lake City) in the order in which they appear

LA PLATA SOCKS

Nancy wanted her design contribution to this book to have its base in the United States and to be derivative of the West, which is where she was born and has lived for most of her life. The pattern motifs in the socks were adapted from a photograph of an Anasazi black-on-white *olla,* or large jug, that was found in the La Plata Valley of northern New Mexico. The colors for the first pair she knit (with the raspberry-colored background) were inspired by the red rock country of southwest Utah and the Four Corners (the spot where Utah, Arizona, New Mexico, and Colorado meet). Subsequently, we asked another knitter to make two more pairs, playing with different color combinations to see how the changes we made would affect the design.

La Plata Socks are knit with Happy Trails yarn, a sportweight yarn made with seventy-five percent wool and twenty-five percent nylon. Nancy describes it as *al dente.* "It's got grip and isn't really slick," she says. The pattern appears on page 204.

on the color wheel. At one point, her desk top was completely clear except for one lone sheet of paper and one pen placed at a right angle to it. While Nancy admits that over time she has lost the discipline required to maintain this degree of order, the ethos that every object has its place remains with her.

Discipline is, indeed, a challenge to maintain when juggling a career as a yarn shop owner, author, designer, and teacher. Nancy spends a fair amount of time on the road, both researching future projects and teaching. A dream, she confides, is to spend one year taking classes instead of teaching them. After meeting June Hemmons Hiatt, author of *The Principles of Handknitting*, Nancy aspired to going through the book, chapter by chapter, in order to refine her own skills. "With knitting, there is so much to learn," Nancy says.

Most of all, Nancy credits "hundreds of folk artists through centuries of time" as having the greatest influence on her knitting career. By studying their creations — whether they are Greek socks, Estonian mittens, or a Norwegian sweater — Nancy feels connected to other cultures. It is by understanding, through travel and reading, the context into which these pieces fit that she gains a sense of history. Nancy's interest in socks was first piqued while learning Scottish country dancing and seeing the hose that the men wore with their kilts. She recalls crawling around on the floor taking photographs of the men's legs. Without a doubt, as Nancy continues to explore the world — from all levels and without inhibition — she will continue to share her findings. For sharing, she says, is the greatest thrill of all.

KATHRYN ALEXANDER

BERKELEY, CALIFORNIA

WE'RE AT A SALVAGE YARD. ALUMINUM, tin, brass, copper, and steel in every conceivable shape surround us in bins, barrels, dumpsters, and crates. Above the roar of the cranes and crashing of inventory, Kathryn Alexander shouts, "I love this place. I think metal is so beautiful." Kathryn is unmistakably recognizable, with her thigh-skimming light auburn hair, suede jacket, straw cowboy hat, and silver jewelry. She and her husband, Mark, come here nearly every Saturday, rummaging through the latest shipments, and pulling out odd metal formations that seem to have been dislodged from the bowels of a faraway building. Together, they carefully select just the right parts to take back to the studio to clean, solder, and form into frames, stands, and sculptural elements to be matched with Kathryn's fiber treasures—her carefully dyed and spun handknit creations.

Kathryn, who moved to Berkeley in 1991 from a farm in Washington State, is best known in knitting circles for her entrelac socks, which appeared on the cover of a 1992 *Spin-Off* magazine and a subsequent sock book. Nine different colors of handspun fiber—in materials like wool, silk, cashmere, and camel down—are used to make interlocking diagonal patches (entrelac), plus stripes and teensy fair-isle patterns, with needles that range in size from 0 to 2. Kathryn favors fine needles for most of her fiber work, as she focuses primarily on small pieces brimming with color and pattern.

Kathryn's voice bubbles and her eyes—one of which is a slightly different shade of green from the other—sparkle as she talks about her evolution as an artist and her growing success. "I am inspired by other people and what they are doing, but my own work drives me," she says. Entrelac has been Kathryn's primary design focus since 1989, when she encountered it for the first time in a dyeing and designer yarn workshop she attended with her mother in Sunlight Basin, Wyoming. Beside her display of yarns, teacher Diane Varney placed a pair of socks she had acquired in a trade with a shepherd in Tibet. The wool was coarse, nearly hairy; the foot was misshapen; and at the top were four rows of orange, rust, and deep blue entrelac. Kathryn remembers the sock as "the coolest thing I'd ever seen," and calls the class and what she learned about color and textured yarns there "an awakening." Kathryn and her mother went home with a challenge: to see who could unravel the mysteries of entrelac. Betty came up with the first pair of entrelac

Like many artists in the area, Kathryn visits the scrap yard at least once every week. At home she cleans, solders, and forms the metal into displays and sculptural elements to be matched with her knitted creations, for example, the piece at left, which she calls a bodikin.

Inspired by an ancient Peruvian cap exhibited in a glass case in a San Francisco museum, Kathryn produced this twelve-stitch-to-the-inch sculptural silk cap on 000 needles, incorporating geometric patterning, I-cord, traditional entrelac, and a three-dimensional entrelac that she originated herself. She then carefully placed the cap on a metal base and matched it with metal forms from the scrap yard to create this surprisingly harmonious hard-soft sculpture.

socks, which were knit flat, then lost interest in the project after she and Kathryn had figured out how to do it in the round. But Kathryn was enthralled and started refining the details, fine-tuning the shape and adding new design elements in the foot and heel tab. Then came the call for socks from *Spin-Off*, and Kathryn sent two pairs to the magazine, hoping that they would at least make it in, never dreaming that they would end up on the cover of the first issue of that publication ever to sell out.

Kathryn became a regular at the scrap yard and began incorporating metal into her work in 1993, when she was looking for an interesting way to showcase her woven scarves. She and her husband, Mark, a Ph.D. candidate at the University of California at Berkeley, salvaged copper pipes and created a sophisticated display area in her studio in a refurbished furniture factory. When a gallery owner told her that she wanted to exhibit her socks in a solo show but wanted them in a frame, Kathryn again turned to copper, bending it to surround the wearable-art foot coverings and sometimes adding a grid of wire within the frame. To display an entrelac-inspired sweater, she and Mark built an avant-garde mannequin out of scrap metal and wire, dressed it in the sweater, then decided that the mannequin was, indeed, a symbiotic element of the piece and that the two elements together—which she named a bodikin—should be sold as a single artwork. Now, she often finds metal formations in the scrap yard first, then designs textiles to go with them. "I am knitting shapes and pieces I never would have thought of before," she explains. Kathryn is also moving courageously beyond the boundaries of garment-making, which is freeing her artistically and allowing her to raise her prices. Her clientele are willing to pay more for a sculpture that includes knitting than they are for a knitted garment alone, however artistic it may be.

As a child growing up on a farm in Wisconsin, Kathryn never imagined that her future would be in the art world. She was a horse-crazy kid and spent most of her time with her animals, only noticing the spinning, knitting, and weaving her mother was doing when she was called into the house to try something on. After graduating from high school in 1971 and spending a year and a half in Madison, she moved to Washington State and got a job planting trees. It was during lunch breaks there that she began to knit, asking a coworker to teach her how to make socks (an interesting foreshadowing of her future). She started to spin many years later, in 1985, after she had gotten married, worked as a horse trainer, and moved to a farm where she raised llamas and rabbits.

Though Kathryn makes goals for herself now, such as getting her work in certain shows or publications, her creative explorations have evolved one at a time. At the point when she took Diane Varney's class, she was already selling handspun yarn and garments, but she had barely worked with color. "Once

I realized I could have a really unique color palette and could have anything I wanted, I think my work took off," Kathryn explains. She usually spends about six days per month dyeing her fiber and can't imagine knitting her bodikins with less than seventy or eighty shades. She never uses machine-spun yarn and feels capable of producing exactly what she needs for any project, a result of years of spinning experience as well as classes with experts like Priscilla Gibson-Roberts (page 83), to whom Kathryn feels deeply indebted. Most days, unless she is teaching a workshop out of town, she can be found in her studio working. "It's not really like work," she says, "because I want to be there. I'm amazed every time I walk in. Everything in there inspires me."

Kathryn's studio is sun-filled and carefully appointed with her fiber work, her loom, her spinning wheel, and an eye-catching display of spinning tools—carders, combs, skeiner, and swift—that metamorphose into *objets d'art* in this elegant environment. "I spend so much time producing each piece and put so much heart and soul into it, I don't want to present it in a shabby way," explains Kathryn, who treats the space, open to the public one day per week, as a personal art gallery.

Kathryn brings an unspoiled spark and spirit to her work. "My designs are the essence of me and everything I do," she told me as she fondled that original sock from Tibet, which Diane Varney unexpectedly and without a note sent to her one Christmas. "Knitting and spinning are really humble mediums," Kathryn adds. "I would like to turn that into something powerful and dramatic. I'd like people to look at my work and not believe what they're seeing."

Kathryn used a blend of wool (from her brother's Columbia sheep) and silk to make this deluxe Christmas stocking.

CHRISTMAS SOCK

As an outgrowth of the entrelac socks, Kathryn started making Christmas stockings to sell during the holidays. This one, made with a sportweight handspun blend of wool and silk, features three-dimensional entrelac peaks, a technique that Kathryn devised herself and uses a lot in her sculptural work. Following a handknit Christmas stocking style initiated by her mother, the foot on each stocking is intentionally misshapen (on this one, the heel is out of proportion to the foot). Any hand- or machine-spun yarn can be used for this pattern, since the size of the finished stocking is not crucial. Kathryn used size 1 needles for the entrelac leg and sizes 2 and 3 for the cuff and foot. The pattern for the Entrelac Christmas Sock appears on page 205.

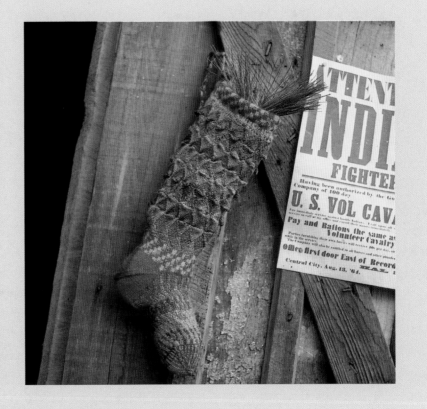

WEST

THE EXPERIMENTAL SPIRIT OF MARY WALKER PHILLIPS

FRESNO, CALIFORNIA

IN THE INTRODUCTION to her seminal book *Creative Knitting: A New Art Form,* first published in 1971, Mary Walker Phillips writes: "The purpose of this book is to establish an awareness of knitting as an independent art style and to describe its many diverse qualities. Most of all, it is to ask the knitter to rethink the long-accepted practice of developing someone else's designs and, by taking a new view, to see knitting as a fresh experience in creative expression."

Rather than simply teaching them how to design a sweater, Mary was challenging her readers to think of fiber and needles as a medium and tools, in the way that a sculptor might think of stone and a chisel or a painter might think of watercolors and brushes. Mary was sharing, through *Creative Knitting,* the knowledge she had gained since the early 1960s, when, as an M.F.A. student in experimental textiles at the world-renowned Cranbrook Academy of Art in Bloomfield Hills, Michigan, she had traded in her loom for two needles and a skein of linen. Thoughout her career, Mary's work—mostly her wall hangings—has been exhibited at more than a hundred museums and galleries in the United States, Australia, New Zealand, Canada, Finland, Norway, and Peru. It is also included in private collections as well as the permanent collections of such prestigious art institutions as the Cranbrook Academy of Art in Bloomfield Hills, Michigan, the Cooper-Hewitt

Museum in New York City, the Art Institute of Chicago, the Smithsonian Institution in Washington, D.C., and the Royal Scottish Museum in Edinburgh, Scotland.

While the fine art and design worlds have accepted Mary, the mainstream knitting world, which focuses mostly on garment construction, has sometimes had a difficult time finding a place for her. "They don't know what to do with me because I don't do anything that fits," Mary acknowledges. She has taught widely, but the few knitters who have followed in her footsteps and pushed the boundaries of knitting even farther have not been as broadly recognized for their talents and achievements. Still, there is much for all knitters to learn from Mary's work, from her spirit of experimentation as well as her technical approach to the medium.

Mary adamantly opposes any discussion of the right or wrong way to knit a stitch or hold the needles. She advocates many different ways—through the front, through the back, yarn thrown under, yarn thrown over—and avers that it is only after carefully studying the possibilities and how each different maneuver affects the stitches on the needle, both visually and mechanically, that a knitter can begin to knit seriously. In her classes, she gives students instructions for several different stitch patterns, plus variations on each one. Her hope is that in the process of exploring the variations students will begin to understand

Early each morning in Fresno, Mary takes a brisk dash around the neighborhood on her yellow Schwinn bicycle. In 1978, the American Craft Council made her a fellow for "turning knitting into an art." In 1984, she received a Visual Arts Fellowship Grant from the National Endowment for the Arts to help her finish her work on *Knitting Counterpanes.*

the mechanics and will be inspired to explore further. But she never shares with her students everything she knows. "I think they should have to do their own homework," she insists, but does recommend to them that they buy copies of *Mary Thomas's Knitting Book* and *Mary Thomas's Book of Knitting Patterns*, which she believes contain just about all of the technical information anyone could need. Mary is trying to push her students to be independent and disciplined, to find their own new questions and their own new answers. Her frame of reference is her fondly recalled experiences at Cranbrook (she earned a B.F.A. in 1947 and her M.F.A. in 1963), where self-motivation, experimentation, and innovation were the norm; her contemporaries and teachers included such accomplished fiber artists as Marianne Strengell, Jack Lenor Larsen, and Ed Rossbach.

I visited Mary at her mother's house in Fresno, California, where for many years she spent part of her summers. For over thirty years she maintained an apartment in Greenwich Village in New York, and she now lives in her own home in Fresno. Distinguished and sophisticated, with a clear appreciation of fine things, she welcomed me with tea served in pretty china cups and an assortment of delicate cookies arranged neatly on a plate. We talked about her career, which she says was completely unplanned. She was an accomplished San Francisco-based weaver with no particular inclination to change mediums when she went back to Cranbrook in 1960. It was Jack Lenor Larsen who challenged her to get off the loom and try something new. She experimented with both knitting and macramé. After finishing her degree, she moved to New York, and the art as well as publishing worlds opened up to her because, she says, "no one was doing the knitting I was doing. For the most part, I had freedom to do whatever I wanted." At the time, even

In her elegant knitted wall hangings, Mary celebrates the purity of the stitches — their shapes and their effect on positive and negative space — rather than how they can be used to make something else. She also pioneered the use of non-traditional fibers in knitting, such as paper, linen, real silver and gold, and wire.

Mary's choice to knit with linen, traditionally a weaver's fiber, was seen as groundbreaking.

Mary recalls fondly the publication of each of her books and the rewarding responses. In addition to *Creative Knitting*, Mary wrote *Step-by-Step Knitting* (1967), *Step-by-Step Macramé* (1970), *Knitting* (1977), and *Knitting Counterpanes* (1989). The counterpane book came about as a result of both her interest in the history of knitting and inquiries from readers of *Step-by-Step Knitting* about a photograph of an antique counterpane (a knitted white cotton bed covering) shown in that book. To keep an important body of design from being overlooked, over a nearly twenty-year period Mary scoured nineteenth-century needlework books and visited museums, historical societies, and private collectors in the United States and abroad. When she could not find a printed pattern for a counterpane, even for the most complicated example, she sat down with her needles and figured it out herself. (For two examples of how designers have been inspired by Mary's counterpane book, see Nicky Epstein's Autumn Counterpane Pullover on page 32 and Selma Miriam's Kousa Dogwood Shawl on page 48.)

Throughout our afternoon together, Mary jumped up from her chair regularly to go find a treasure of some sort to show me: a nineteenth-century knitting book that she had recently acquired, a piece of complex lace that she had yet to decipher, a counterpane, one of the large number of pot holders she has knit as gifts over the years. She was eager to share her knowledge and her stories. "I am disappointed that more people are not being more experimental with their knitting," she lamented. "Just knit for the fun of it. Don't think about the end result." In a way, Mary is only wishing for others the same successes and joys that she has experienced for herself — a wish of marked generosity.

KATY BLANCHARD

LIKE SO MANY PEOPLE, KATY BLANCHARD spent her youth and much of her adult life searching for her path, for what she was really meant to do. Married and the mother of an adult son, she has over the years studied music, designed jewelry, worked as a secretary, and in 1980 opened a graphic design studio in San Diego, California, which she runs to this day. But in 1993, Katy found truth in the old adage that what you're looking for may be right in your own backyard. A thirty-year knitting veteran who had never before attempted to make even a simple garter-stitch pullover without a pattern, Katy decided to try to design her own vest, incorporating into it Native American symbols that were meaningful to her. Never before had she knit with such passion and intense purpose, and that first effort, made with yarn unraveled from a garment knit in New York City in the late 1960s (during her hippie period), resulted in a commission for a cardigan. Katy now sells her handknits on a steady basis under the label Urban Eagle Designs and dreams of the day when she can close her graphics business and devote herself to knitting full-time.

Rather than tracking fashion or any other kind of trend, Katy follows her own inner path, focusing on the power of Native American symbology and how it can be incorporated into a garment and then transferred to the wearer. On a hang tag attached to each sweater, she writes, "This is a one-of-a-kind sweater. It has been carefully and thoughtfully designed to bring a sense of well-being to the wearer and to honor the Native American spirit and tradition." Each sweater is also sold or given with a legend card that explains the meaning of the symbols within the garment — Katy uses colorwork and bas-relief stitchwork to create the symbols — as well as a blessing pouch. A triangular muslin sachet filled with pine needles, sage, and tobacco, the pouch is designed to be stored with the sweater in a drawer or chest. The pine needles come from Katy's Christmas tree; sage and tobacco are both sacred herbs among some Native American tribes. The pouches create a connection with the earth as well as another link between Katy and the wearers, whom she hopes will enjoy her sweaters for a lifetime.

"Knitting, for me, is about adding positive energy into someone's life, passing on good energy," she explains. She placed the thunderbird, the sacred bearer of happiness, across the shoulders of one of her vests and wrote on the legend card: "We carry so much responsibility across our shoulders all the

Though Katy's use of symbols in her knitting is relatively new, her interest in symbology goes way back and has included, over the years, a study of the work of Carl Jung as well as of tarot cards and the I Ching.

Left: Katy's father-daughter sweaters feature — in colorwork and bas-relief stitchwork — such Native American symbols as crow, snake, morning star, corn, and clouds.

buffalo in bas-relief (representing fulfilled prophecy and prosperity); an eagle (for lessons well learned and spiritual awareness); and Spirit Man and Earth Woman holding hands. Those who admire and buy Katy's sweaters are, of course, receptive to her philosophies.

Though Katy is a very fast knitter, she recognizes the equal importance of process and product and tries never to rush through a garment or push an idea. She rarely knows exactly how she is going to design an entire sweater before she casts on and feels that she is at her best—in knitting and in life—when she is following her gut rather than when examining each and every move. She rarely places symbols symmetrically on a garment, though always manages to achieve a sense of balance, a skill honed through her work as a graphic artist. She does, however, graph the symbols on her computer rather than trying to knit them free-hand or remember from one sweater to the next how to execute them. Sometimes the symbols or colors she incorporates into a design come to her in a dream. Other times, she looks for inspiration in her Medicine Cards, a deck of cards that depict Native American symbols.

When it comes time to sew the pieces of a sweater together or do other important finishing work, Katy checks herself to make sure that she is completely focused, as this is the only part of the process that she doesn't innately enjoy. Unless she is making a piece on commission, she doesn't worry about sizing at all. In her view, the sweater will fit the person who is meant to have it. Her craftsmanship is superior, which means her garments hang beautifully on many bodies. Since childhood, Katy has always been able to do whatever she has desired with her hands, from playing the piano and flute well enough to consider pursuing a career as a concert musician to carrying out complex knitting techniques learned from a book on the first try.

Although she has no proof of it, Katy feels that there might be some Cherokee in her blood. "I feel an almost cellular connection to the Native American belief system," she explains. When not working or knitting, Katy spends much of her time at home (in a compact house in the amusingly named Normal Heights section of San Diego) reading books about Native American culture. She is constantly building her vocabulary of Native American symbols and trying to understand their meanings more thoroughly so she can incorporate them into her designs and also use them to gain insight into her own life and the human experience in general. When I visited her—after enduring a series of travel mishaps—then had difficulty getting my tape recorder to work, she reminded me of the power of coyote, the trick-

CROW-BEAR CARDIGAN & SOUTHWEST MOTIF JUMPER-VEST

Katy designed these father-daughter sweaters for a lawyer and urban planner in Berkeley, California, and his one-year-old daughter, both of whom can be seen modeling on page 129. Katy felt that it was very important that the child's jumper-vest be expandable so that it could be worn over the course of more than a few months. To achieve this effect, she worked adjustable ties into the shoulder seam, thus allowing the garment to grow with the child. She chose Brown Sheep's Top of the Lamb worsted-weight wool for the adult cardigan and Brown Sheep's Cotton Fleece (80 percent pima cotton, 20 percent merino wool) for the child's garment. The patterns for these sweaters begin on page 206. Also included there are Katy's interpretations of the meanings of the symbols in each one.

ster who pops in every once in a while to remind us not to take life or ourselves too seriously.

Not surprisingly, Katy sticks to natural fibers, often seeking out small companies that raise their own sheep and only minimally process the wool. Her color palette is notably earthy, though in each design there is usually at least one surprising blast of color, such as a golden yellow or pale blue in the midst of grays, browns, and russets. While many fiber workers believe that the wool of Churro sheep, the sheep brought to the New World by Columbus and the first sheep of the Navajo, is too coarse for knitting, Katy is enamored with it for its heartiness and soul.

Indeed, it is through Native American teachings as well as knitting that Katy Blanchard comes to terms with the complexities of the universe. And it is with warmth, enthusiasm, and knitted beauty that she seeks to share that understanding with all who are open to receive it. Among Native Americans, there are two schools of thought regarding the white person's use of their symbols. One school resents it, the other sees sharing as the only means by which our troubled society can be healed. In borrowing these symbols, Katy seeks to show both honor and respect.

LYNNE VOGEL

CANNON BEACH, OREGON

AT SEVEN YEARS OLD, LYNNE VOGEL would walk to Landis Department Store in the Larchmont neighborhood of Los Angeles and buy Coats & Clark wool yarn. She would take it home and make little square purses with stripes and give them away to family members who would, Lynne remembers, almost immediately put them in the back of a drawer. She slowly proceeded to scarves, then vests, and at fifteen years old she managed to finish a whole sweater. Today, Lynne sells her sweaters for two thousand dollars or more to private customers but those first purses — the early Vogels — are lost forever. Lynne thinks it may be for the best.

I visited Lynne at her home on the Oregon coast in the spring and was almost as impressed with her ability to predict changes in the weather as I was with her knitting. We would be trying to take a photograph and she'd look out to the sea and say, "You have about ten minutes." Then, nearly ten minutes later, she would say, "You have forty-five seconds, thirty seconds . . ." We'd go running for shelter . . . and the rain would start, almost as though she had been controlling it. It is this same sensitivity to nature, to color and light as well as texture, that Lynne uses to create her very special handknits.

Lynne learned to knit (and sew) from her mother, who studied fashion design in college. For her understanding of color, she credits her father, a professional animator who worked at one time for Disney. Father and daughter would sit together in the evening and study art books. He'd open Johannes Itten's *The Art of Color* and lecture her on color theory. They would discuss complementary colors and simultaneous contrast and color mixing. He would explain what made a particular Matisse painting work.

Lynne knit and painted throughout her youth (and continues both to this day), but did not pursue a formal art education. In 1975, she earned a degree in English from the University of the South in Sewanee, Tennessee. And for a long time the closest she came to turning her love of color and fiber into a paying profession was selling handpainted needlepoint canvases. The first milestone in Lynne's knitting career came when she moved to Taos, New Mexico, in 1984. Within her first week in the Southwest she discovered La Lana Wools (page 94) and the naturally dyed, handspun yarns sold there, and she quickly realized that her days of solid-color knitting were about to come to

Lynne (above left) and her good friend, spinner Sandy Sitzman (above right) have been collaborating and inspiring each other since 1988. Left: Lynne's friend Dede Coyne, a former ballet dancer, modeled the Tree of Life Mosaic Jacket at a beach near Lynne's house.

The Tree of Life Mosaic Jacket is transformed completely when it is knit with four colors of machine-spun wool and silk yarn (above) versus many colors of handspun wool, silk, and angora (right).

a close. She started making her first multicolored, multipaneled garments and soon began selling them at the Santa Fe Weaving Gallery, considered one of the top galleries for knit and woven clothing in New Mexico. Enjoying the work but not making a living at it, she enrolled in massage school. She was interested in therapeutic body work and thought professional pursuit of it would still leave her time to knit.

Lynne was particularly enamored with the variegated yarns for sale at La Lana and the way they created waves of color that wandered through her knitting at different intervals. To take advantage of this yarn, and because she didn't like circular knitting or sewing pieces together, Lynne started perfecting her panel knitting techniques, creating flat knit pieces that she can build on horizontally and vertically, ultimately creating a garment that requires minimal finishing. She uses an invisible cast on so that she can pick up the stitches and knit in the opposite direction when necessary; rather than cast off when she finishes a panel, she leaves it on waste yarn, then builds on it when she is ready. She favors slip-stitch patterns (such as the mosaic knitting patterns originated by Barbara Walker/see page 56) because they offer an intricate effect but only require working with one color at a time; in addition, because of the higher number of rows per inch, they tend not to draw in as much as traditional stockinette knitting when stitches are picked up along the side edge of the rows.

As Lynne learned more and more skills, she also evolved into a perfectionist, intent on controlling the quality of her work down to the most minute details. Luisa Gelenter of La Lana Wools recalls watching Lynne spend hours sprawled on the floor of the shop, examining each and every skein of yarn before buying one in order to make sure she was getting exactly what she wanted. To this day, Lynne values the control she has achieved in her knitting in terms of both technique and color, especially as it compares to painting. "In painting," she says, "something always changes when it dries. Oil paints get darker, watercolors get lighter. You never know what you're really going to end up with. With yarn you do."

Surprisingly, Lynne has never learned to spin, which would, of course, give her more of that coveted control. When she moved to Cannon Beach, Oregon, from New Mexico, she finally did learn to dye her own yarn—from good friend and spinner Sandy Sitzman, who was co-owner of a local yarn shop at the time. But even this was only after some strong persuasion on Sandy's part. Lynne confesses to not liking change very much and to having resisted strongly. "I had a bad idea of dyeing. I thought it was very difficult," she recalls. "Sandy took me in her kitchen and showed me how really easy it was." The results: a gorgeous space-dyed skein of mohair with deep cobalt blue, violet, and turquoise, and a new dye enthusiast. Lynne soon began to combine handspun yarn she had dyed herself with Sandy's yarn and yarn from La Lana. Sandy and Lynne's collaboration has proven fruitful for both of them. About Sandy's spinning, Lynne says, "She pulls this cloud and it just floats into the wheel." From Lynne, Sandy has learned to see colors in nature and appreciate how they work together. She describes Lynne as "the best knitter I've ever met," and loves to see her yarns knit up into one of Lynne's sweaters.

Although Lynne's pieces are expensive compared to the work of some other handknitters, she is refreshingly confident that they are worth the asking price — if not more. After calculating the cost of the materials and time she puts into each piece, she knows that she is still knitting for love of the medium and not for money. Ideally, she'd like to limit her commercial output to only specially commissioned pieces — in the past she has sold much of her work through galleries — and keep the rest of her knitting personal and without pressure. Although this might disappoint some of the many people who like to collect Lynne's work, it is clearly an artist's dream. She would spend more time walking on the beach. She would spend more time watching the rain clouds come in. And she would be even more intent on communicating what she sees and what she feels, stitch by stitch, within a sweater.

TREE OF LIFE MOSAIC JACKET

For this project, Lynne decided to make a simple version of her Tree of Life Mosaic Jacket using Tahki's Tweedy Lamb and Chelsea Silk. She did, however, want to include in this book an example of her more complex work — thus the multicolored, handspun version also shown here. The jacket is constructed by knitting basic body panels of mosaic knitting and then picking up selvage stitches to knit perpendicular panels. This style of construction allows for the use of complex shapes within the design with a minimum of sewing afterward. Much of the finishing work is done in the knitting itself.

The multicolored Tree of Life Mosaic Jacket can never be repeated exactly, as it was made with an assortment of mostly handspun wool, mohair, silk, and angora, some of which Lynne dyed herself, some of which she purchased from other sources, including Sandy Sitzman and La Lana Wools. Since the multicolored version was made in basically the same way as the black-and-white version created for this book (see left), advanced knitters who do not want to add color by simply choosing additional shades of the Tahki yarn called for in the pattern can use the pattern on page 211 as a basic guide, making their own personal and creative fiber choices.

EST

MEG SWANSEN

PITTSVILLE, WISCONSIN

TRAVELING TO CENTRAL WISCONSIN TO SEE Schoolhouse Press and to meet Meg Swansen felt like a pilgrimage to a sacred place: simultaneously exciting, intimidating, and a long way away. But once within the cozy confines of the rambling former schoolhouse that is also the Swansen residence on Cary Bluff in Pittsville (population: 610), I was immediately at ease. A warm and welcoming Meg had fixed a pot of tea, which she was keeping hot under a beautiful felted wool tea cozy. She quickly leaned back into her chair and lifted her stockinged feet onto a cedar chest that also serves as a coffee table.

I had entered the labyrinthine compound through a side door and wound my way through a crowded office into a hallway lined with shelves of wool, then meandered into a large, bookshelf-lined computer workroom that melded into an open and sunny living area. The living space (actually the original circa-1940 schoolhouse onto which Meg's husband, Chris, built additions) was packed with bookshelves, paintings, and eclectic curios—huge pine cones and beaded necklaces, a piñata, and ornate trim salvaged from an old Victorian home scheduled for demolition. In a pretty silver frame on a shelf I caught a glimpse of Elizabeth Zimmermann, arguably the most famous knitter of the twentieth century—and also Meg's mother.

Meg willingly spent a portion of her adult life in the shadow of the woman she refers to frequently as Elizabeth and every once in a while as "my Ma." Within the context of the knitting world, Elizabeth Zimmermann, retired since 1988, is a legend in her own time. She revealed through her writings, videos, and Knitting Camp not only the commonsensical, empowering approach to hand-knitting and design for which she is renowned but also her personal family history, spirited wit, and life philosophies. But now it is Meg's turn, and she has moved into the limelight gradually and with grace—and with a dedication to and love for knitting that is as deep and unbounded as her mother's.

"I feel absolutely passionate about knitting," Meg says. "The soothing repetition, the same motion over and over again, the songs that are hidden within color patterns." Like Elizabeth, Meg knits almost exclusively in the round and focuses on texture work and stranded color knitting as opposed to intarsia. "Knitting is rhythm," Meg explains. "With intarsia, the rhythm is interrupted." Meg firmly believes that there is no right or wrong way to knit. "If you are getting the results you want, then you're doing it right," she says. She is

Meg doodled on her computer to come up with the pattern motifs for her Schoolhouse Shetland Pullover (left). Interestingly, when the sweater is worn in a nautical setting, the yoke pattern looks strikingly similar to the helm of a boat.

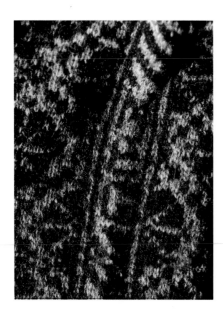

Meg knit her name and the year of construction into one of the side panels of her Schoolhouse Shetland Pullover. The side panels also permit the knitter to adjust the body circumference of the sweater in small increments without worrying about full pattern repeats.

also a stickler for technical details, thrilled and invigorated when she invents (or unvents) new ones (unventing being a word Elizabeth coined for unearthing methods that, though undocumented, have probably been employed by at least one other knitter in the long history of the medium). Techniques Meg has unvented include decreasing stitches within color patterns down the top of a sleeve as opposed to the underarm; a method to achieve a split-stitch increase when working with unspun two-ply Icelandic wool; a way to apply double and triple I-cord borders to stockinette stitch; and the "purl-when-you-can border" used in the Schoolhouse Shetland Pullover she designed for this book, a border that is neither hemmed nor ribbed but still doesn't curl.

Throughout my research for this book, I repeatedly heard gratitude expressed toward Meg. Beth Brown-Reinsel, author of *Knitted Ganseys*, recalls sending Meg a very rough draft of her book proposal: "Meg called me right away and said she thought the proposal was wonderful. That gave me the confidence to go ahead and submit it to Interweave." Therese Inverso, the New Jersey-based knitter and felter who made Meg's tea cozy (from a felted Aran sweater), says, "She's like a gift to people who find knitting." She has never forgotten what Meg told her the first time she called Schoolhouse Press as a beginning knitter: "You are on the threshold of knitting. There are so many wonderful things ahead of you. I wish I could be you, to experience all of that again."

Knitters everywhere have watched as Elizabeth's knitting fame has been transformed by Meg into a family legacy. Schoolhouse Press has progressively grown as a knitting book and video publisher and mail-order company. Meg also continues to host three sold-out sessions of Knitting Camp each year (campers gather in Wisconsin for three-and-a-half days of uninterrupted instruction and camaraderie); produce and publish *Wool Gathering*, a biannual publication with original patterns first published in 1969; teach workshops around the country; and write articles and design garments for several knitting

SCHOOLHOUSE SHETLAND PULLOVER

Meg's Schoolhouse Shetland Pullover, full of interesting technical detail, is worked in the round, with steeks at the armholes and the neck. The sleeves are shaped on the top side, which causes them to slope down from the shoulder in a more anatomically correct manner than a straight dropped shoulder, which is typically shaped under the arm. The neckline is finished and the shoulders united with I-cord. Instructions are given for continuing the I-cord from the shoulder down the sleeve or ending it at the armhole. Instructions for decreasing to create a bloused sleeve (as in Meg's prototype) as well as instructions for a standard tapered sleeve are also provided.

Interestingly, the lower border is neither ribbed nor hemmed but is prevented from curling by a technique Meg calls "purl when you can." Anytime the pattern graph calls for the background color to be used above a stitch of the same color, the stitch is purled. The resulting texture is close enough to garter stitch or seed stitch to obviate curling and still not have any "purl bloops" showing ("bloops" will show if you purl over a stitch of a different color). Meg chose Jamieson & Smith's Shetland fingering-weight wool in Loch Maree, a very dark green, and Slate Blue for this sweater. The pattern for the Schoolhouse Shetland Pullover appears on page 213.

magazines. In fact, when knitting editors and publishers are preparing to make an important decision, they will often call Meg to get her advice and her opinion.

Meg and her husband, Chris, who passed away during the writing of this book, created out of the one-room schoolhouse that Elizabeth bought at auction in the early 1970s a world both exceedingly private and exceedingly public. With offices, a warehouse, and a video production studio on the premises, there is barely a need to leave the bluff. Together, Chris and Meg, along with their son and daughter and extended family, created their own intimate vocabulary, including a "cat language," seasoning their conversation with a charming eccentricity. At the same time, through Schoolhouse Press, to which Meg gladly devotes seven days a week, Meg, or Swand, as she was known to Chris, has shared the very essence of who she is. When I asked her to differentiate among Schoolhouse Press, her identity as a knitter, and her identity as a human being, she said that all of those areas overlap, that they are inextricably entwined.

Chris Swansen, Meg's husband, constructed the "holster" shown above to hold Meg's supplies while she knits on the couch.

In the swatch below, Meg shows four different colorways for her Schoolhouse Shetland Pullover: Persimmon and Dusty Rose, Blue Lovat and White, Bressay Blue and Tartan Blue, Ghillie Green and Honey Beige (note that these are the names that Schoolhouse Press has assigned to Jamieson & Smith yarn colors; Jamieson & Smith assigns the yarns numbers only).

Meg learned to knit from her mother when she was about five years old, but for a long time gave it only minimal attention. In high school, she knit for boyfriends, and several times traded her sweaters for paintings by local Milwaukee artists. Meg recalls that she and her family were "out of spec" for 1950s Wisconsin. "I was unconventional. I used to wear black stockings and high heels, and my hair was past my waist. People thought I was a witch," she giddily recalls. After high school, Meg traded the chance to go to college for the chance to travel. She worked as a telephone operator and in a dress shop in California, worked at ski lodges for two seasons with her sister, crisscrossed the U.S. by car, and studied art in Munich for two semesters.

It wasn't until Meg married Chris Swansen, a composer, in 1964, and moved to New York City with him that she began to knit bountifully, producing sweaters on commission for such jazz greats as Stan Getz and Gary Burton. Since then Meg has built what she calls "an arsenal of technique and knowledge," essential, she believes, for any designer. "They are the base from which you can free yourself to do anything you want, to go in any direction that you like," she elucidates, comparing her philosophy to a triangle — technique and knowledge at the bottom, and design at the top. "Your sweater should be an expression of you. It's a self-empowerment deal," Meg explains, "and it spills over into the rest of your life." In her patterns and videos, Meg (like her mother) tries to educate the knitter rather than promote blind following of instructions. "I feel an obligation to let people know all of the possibilities so they can decide what's best for their particular situation," explains Meg, who in some ways is still "out of spec" with the general public. She lives and works in her own private hamlet. She devotes herself wholeheartedly to knitting. "What will happen when you retire from Schoolhouse Press?" I asked her. "I have no idea," she answered.

TEACHING LITTLE FINGERS TO KNIT
AT THE WALDORF SCHOOL

DETROIT, MICHIGAN

THERE ARE FEW SIGHTS MORE affirming to an adult knitter than a classroom full of six- and seven-year-olds, boys and girls, sitting quietly and knitting. This is a common scene at Waldorf Schools around the world. At these private learning institutions, propelled by the teaching philosophies of the Austrian educator and social philosopher Rudolf Steiner, students learn to knit even before they start to read or write. Through knitting, they are believed to be refining an assortment of skills, including eye-hand coordination, fine motor control, concentration, and counting, and developing a sense of self-esteem. Imagine the pride they feel when they finish a project. Recent neurological research and Waldorf educators also support the theory that when the hands are occupied, the ability to think and concentrate is strengthened.

These photographs were taken at the Waldorf School in Detroit, Michigan, where the first and second graders knit (using two needles) finger puppets, striped recorder cases, pencil cases with simple fair-isle patterning, and shaped animals, such as horses and cats. The fifth graders make socks and hats on four needles (during the third and fourth grades, students crochet, embroider, and do cross-stitch). As is the custom at all Waldorf Schools—there are about six hundred around the world—the craft teacher in the Detroit school uses a rhyme to help the students remember the order of movements required to make a knit stitch: in through the front door (right-hand needle inserted in stitch on left needle); run around the back (wrap the yarn over the right needle); out through the window (tip of right needle through the original stitch on the left needle); and off jumps Jack (lift original stitch off the left needle).

FUN, FUNKY, AND FUNCTIONAL—THOSE are Sue Flanders' adjectives for the types of handknit designs she is interested in creating. An industrial hygienist for the state of Minnesota, Sue finds time to knit during her breaks, her evenings, and her weekends—that is, when her husband, Chuck, and her young daughter, Alice (the inspiration for many of her designs), do not need her attention. Sue designs kits, mostly for children's clothes, for the Three Kittens Yarn Shoppe in St. Paul, Minnesota, (not far from her home) as well as patterns for such publications as *Knitter's Magazine* and *Better Homes and Gardens Country Crafts*. Among her fun, funky, and functional creations are fish-shaped mittens, whimsical themed hats with tassel-like three-dimensional hanging figures (such as penguins, clowns, cats, maple leaves, and polar bears), and the Sand Castle and Starfish Tunic she designed for this book. Norwegian-style stranded color knitting and the simple shapes of Norwegian sweaters remain, however, her steadfast favorite. Sue learned to knit as a child but didn't become serious about it until after graduate school (she earned a degree in environmental health from the University of Minnesota in 1984), when she took a class on how to make a Norwegian sweater. "I found myself staying up half the night to work on projects," she recalls.

Sue compares the role of knitting in her life to a vitamin: she's got to have a little bit every day. Because of her busy work and family schedule, she purposely limits the number of design proposals she submits to publications. "I want to keep knitting fun and without pressure," she says. Impressively efficient, Sue carefully assigns each proposal a file folder and photographs her swatch and sketch before sending them off to an editor. After the proposal has been accepted, she knits the garment, takes a photograph of it, and places the photograph in a card file; the garment, of course, is sent to the publication. Finally, once the pattern has been published, she catalogs the clippings in a three-ring binder.

Sue's first success in the design world—not counting handfuls of state-fair ribbons—came in 1990, when she won first prize at The Knitting Guild of America convention for a multicolored Kaffe Fassett-type cardigan. "I think everyone who knits a sweater like that should get a medal," Sue states, recalling the hard work that went into the garment and the scraps of yarn she gathered from members of her long-standing knitting group (called the Elegant Needle

Left: Sue's daughter, Alice, enjoyed a morning of water play on Lake Calhoun while we photographed her modeling her mother's designs.

Group, or ENG) because she didn't have enough colors in her own modest stash. The following year she won again for a Double-Knit Petroglyph Shawl; the third year she earned third prize for her fish mittens. That's when Sue started thinking about submitting ideas to *Knitter's Magazine* and when Karen Weiberg, the owner of Three Kittens Yarn Shoppe and a member of ENG, asked her to design kits that she could sell at the shop and to other yarn stores.

When *Knitter's* accepted Sue's first two proposals for double-knit coasters and a hat with polar bear tassels, she, understandably, thought designing for publication was going to be a cinch. Then she endured a year's worth of rejections before she sold another design. "Working with editors, trying to figure out what they want, has helped me to learn to deal better with criticism and rejection in all aspects of my life," Sue reveals. Still, success and acceptance are more often the operative words for Sue, whose ideas are endorsed much more regularly these days and who holds celebrity status at Three Kittens, where much of her work is on display. "Sue tries to downplay her accomplishments," says Karen Weiberg of her down-to-earth and modest friend. "Her designs appeal to people with a sense of humor. They are cute and fanciful but they're still practical."

"I get embarrassed when people ooh and ahh over something," Sue told me one afternoon in her small, comfortable home—a 1927 Craftsman-style house in Robbinsdale, a Twin Cities suburb. She credits some of her success to her sewing background; at five feet, ten inches tall, she has trouble buying clothes to fit her. She also recalls Sister Dennis, a college pottery teacher who taught her to look at her work critically. The nun would break the students' work in half so they could see the structural imperfections. "We would see how uneven the walls of our pots were and how thick or thin the bottoms were. It was eye-opening," Sue recalls. "Now I think of her when I rip out my knitting."

Sue continues to hone her technical skills by taking classes locally and at trade shows, such as Stitches and The Knitting Guild of America conventions, where she often helps to run the Three Kittens booth. Interestingly, many of her designs feature water themes, which she attributes to the environment in which she grew up—first in New Jersey, then on a lake in Minnesota. Always a lover of the outdoors, to this day Sue enjoys swimming, canoeing, fishing, and tubing in the summer and ice skating and ice fishing in the winter. Though many of her designs include three-dimensional elements, she keeps the overall effect simple and often playful.

As Alice, her daughter and muse, grows, Sue expects for her design style to evolve as well. "I like to knit for Alice," Sue explains. "But I'm sure once she gets older she won't want me to. She'll say, 'Oh, Mom, do I have to wear that?'" By that time, Sue's fantasy may have come true—a house on a lake and a full-time and profitable career as a handknit designer.

We chose colors with a sandy and sun-bleached feel for the beach-tunic ensemble, then Sue knit four additional tams in bright and playful shades of blue, green, orange, and red. They are shown here with the starfish purse, perfect for a tube of lip balm or another small treasure.

SAND CASTLES AND STARFISH

For Alice's beach tunic (page 144), Sue first created a stitch pattern that looks like fishnet (adapting a lace stitch pattern she found in a Mon Tricot stitch guide), then graphed a sand castle scene on her computer. Finally, she added the starfish appliqué. The matching accessories (see right)—a starfish hat and purse—are especially fun for young children. The entire ensemble is made with Reynolds Saucy, a mercerized cotton. The pattern appears on page 214.

THE DAY I ARRIVED at Mount Bruce Station, proprietor Yvonne Uhlianuk threw a Mad Hatter's Tea Party in my honor, inviting knitters and spinners who work for her and local women who raise sheep. About a dozen of us gathered in the circa-1930s dye house on her fifty-acre farm for tea (served in mugs with sheep painted on them) and delicious sweets, including a towering Lady Baltimore cake that Yvonne's husband, Peter, had baked the night before. A huge Mad Hatter's top hat was passed from head to head, making each one of us feel suitably silly but also eliciting enough laughter to put us all at ease. We talked knits and purls and increases and decreases, and we all tried on and critiqued sweaters that Yvonne and an assistant were designing for Sheep Stuff, the farm-based shop.

Bringing people together and spreading enthusiasm are, perhaps, Yvonne Uhlianuk's greatest strengths — if you're not counting her natural affinity for animals, her vast knowledge about raising sheep and yarn production, and her gourmet cooking. "When I am really interested in things, I go ahead and do them and I usually achieve," explains Yvonne, who credits her can-do attitude to her upbringing in New Zealand. "The pioneering spirit is indigenous to New Zealanders," she says. And, like many of her compatriots, she chose to leave her homeland for greater opportunities. When she left, however — in 1964, at the age of twenty-one — she couldn't have imagined that she would end up sheep farming in Michigan. It was, indeed, unlikely, given that she was abandoning a land populated by nearly twenty times more sheep than people. And though she knew how to knit, she didn't find the activity particularly intriguing.

The route to Mount Bruce Station, which she and her husband bought and restored in 1992, was, in fact, a long one. In the intervening years, she trained as a chef in Europe, ran several highly acclaimed restaurants and specialty food shops in the Detroit area, and launched a line of gourmet food products for a supermarket chain — and did come to love to knit. But it wasn't until she married Peter, a chemist for DuPont and an after-hours farmer, and moved to his farm in southeastern Michigan that the sheep idea even occurred to her. By then, she had acquired the marketing savvy to turn a small sheep farm into a profitable, creative venture; she was also tired of the high pressure of the restaurant business. Though she typically works on the farm from 5:00 A.M. until 10:00 P.M. (hours unmistakably similar to those of a chef), she has no complaints. "We're having a really good time. The whole operation is done for pleasure and satisfaction."

The operation to which Yvonne refers includes managing a flock of forty to sixty Corriedale, Romney, and Jacob sheep as well as a retail shop; designing hand- and machine-

Yvonne picks flowers for dyeing with Lindsay Mott, her young neighbor who comes by regularly to help out (page 136). Right: Jars of natural dye left to "brew"; a bouquet of zinnias from the dye garden; and freshly dyed yarn hangs to dry. The napping Irish Setter is Lucy, one of five dogs who call Mount Bruce Station home.

spun yarns using the fleece of her own sheep as well as of the sheep, goats, and alpacas that are raised on farms nearby; designing garments that she then contracts outside knitters to produce; and putting on a yearly fiber festival that attracts nearly three thousand people over the course of one weekend. Understandably, Mount Bruce Station is always abuzz with activity, with Yvonne comfortably in place at the helm.

As I watched Yvonne whiz around the farm, on foot and in a golf cart, often with one of her five dogs or twenty (or so) cats in tow, I began to wonder if there is anything she can't do. When I asked her if it's hard to manage a two-hundred-pound ram, she insisted it is not. "You have to be in command of the situation," she told me as she used her hip to push Mortimer, a four-year-old silver Romney ram, out of her way. Yvonne gives all of her sheep names (as opposed to numbers, which is common in the sheep industry). "They all look different," she says. The sheep named Julia Child and Marcella Hazan were born during the year that Yvonne named all her sheep after chefs; Delphinium, Sweet Pea, and Johnny-jump-up were born in the year of the flowers. Yvonne is clearly very close with her animals. On our way to bottle-feed a newborn lamb whose mother had rejected her, we passed by

Eliza, a colored Corriedale whom Yvonne bought for the black color and density of her fleece. "I'm going to sell you to the gypsies," she said to Eliza with a chuckle, explaining that Eliza's lambs were all white this year. Later, I saw Banjo, a speckled Corriedale that was a bottle-fed baby and later became a pet, riding with Yvonne on the golf cart. In the shop, Yvonne pointed to some roving and said, "Here's some from Peggy Sue and Mortimer."

When I asked Yvonne if she has to write down a schedule or goals in order to stay organized, she said she doesn't. "It's a seasonal cycle that goes by itself. If you breed the ewes, then you have to handle the lambing. When the ground thaws, you move the dye plants from the greenhouse. It's the same as making jam when the raspberries are ripe." She emphasizes that it's a team effort and that she relies greatly on several part-time employees, her husband (he is in charge of the greenhouse and does a lot of the renovations and repairs on the house and farm buildings), and a local support system on which she can call at busy times of year, such as in the fall at festival time. "I don't believe that any one person can do everything from A to Z successfully. You'll get much more of a charge out of it when people are working together according to their strengths."

Below left: Lindsay holds a Corriedale lamb. Yvonne chose to raise Corriedales because she was familiar with them from her childhood in New Zealand. Below right: The Mount Bruce Station farmhouse. Mount Bruce is the name of a mountain in New Zealand; station is the term used for a sheep farm there. Opposite page: A lineup of curious baby lambs.

Yvonne does admit to one weakness — overambition. "I try to do ten things when I can only do four."

Yvonne was never formally trained at sheep farming, but she did begin this venture with a vast amount of fiber know-how, having grown up on a farm with one hundred sheep (Corriedales) and one hundred fifty cows in New Zealand. Her father sheared sheep, her brother-in-law was a wool grader and skirter. "I didn't know I was learning," recalls Yvonne, "but micron count and Bradford count [American and English systems for grading wool], twist, ply, all of that is second nature to me." For now, Yvonne says she does not want her flock to grow much bigger. Instead, she is focusing on maintaining the high quality of her fiber and educating and increasing her customer base.

For each of the three rooms that make up Sheep Stuff, the farm's carriage house-turned-retail shop, Yvonne has designed one or more teaching displays. For example, in one display, sample skeins of yarn are labeled by sheep breed to show the different characteristics of each breed's fiber and how those characteristics are affected by the age and diet of the sheep. The Dorset skein is rough and coarse; this type of sheep is raised mainly for meat. The Lincoln yields a very strong fiber (which Yvonne likes to use for the heels of socks). A healthy Romney sheep yields a lustrous fiber ideal for outerwear. The soft Corriedale, Merino, and Rambouillet yarns are well suited for finer garments worn close to the skin. Yvonne also tries to teach her customers to be dis-criminating both when they buy sweaters and when they choose yarn. She explains, "People think they should pay more for handspun, but there are all different kinds of handspun." She then shows me a skein of overtwisted Corriedale yarn that would certainly cause a distortion in shape in any knitted fabric. To maintain the quality of her own handspun fiber, Yvonne works closely with about eight women who live in the area. The rest of her yarn is sent to small spinneries. For the three hundred to four hundred handknits that she sells in the shop each year (some made as custom orders and some sold off the rack), she relies on a crew of about seventy knitters ranging in age from thirty to eighty. It can take up to twelve months to get a knitter to the point where she can knit an entire sweater to Yvonne's specifications. During the training process, she has knitters work on part of a garment or small pieces, or sometimes asks them to come into the shop so she or one of her employees can check on their progress or show them a new technique.

To those who became acquainted with Yvonne during her restaurant days, her attention to detail comes as no surprise. She was known locally as the chef who found farmers to raise vegetables to her specifications and, in fact, met her husband when she placed a special order with him for sixty herb plants to keep in the restaurant. Impressed by her ambitiousness (he called the size of her order "staggering"), he decided to ask her out on a date. Yvonne understands better than anyone that it is attention to detail that will set her apart and help her to reach her goals.

LIZBETH UPITIS

MINNEAPOLIS, MINNESOTA

UPON FIRST MEETING, LIZBETH UPITIS seems reasonably conservative and controlled. Her voice is soft and serene, her movements graceful, her clothing tasteful, simple, and comfortable. In terms of knitting, she is best known for her Latvian mittens, the intricately patterned folk mittens from the Baltic country of Latvia. She is completely uninterested in so-called fashion knitting, anything that hints even mildly of trendiness in terms of color, texture, or shape. She prefers the beauty and design endurance of traditional ethnic garments, which she likes to work out on small needles with fine yarns.

As Lizbeth shares her stories, a free spirit begins to surface. She studied literature at Miami University in Ohio, where she grew up, then moved to Manhattan in 1967 to get a master's degree in library science at Columbia University. Unable to resist the wealth of adventures the city had to offer, including more modern dance classes than she had ever before encountered, she dropped out after only half a semester. Next she got a job writing instruction manuals for IBM, but one evening, a light turned on in her head: weaving — not dancing (which she was studying at the Martha Graham School) — was her calling. This was a surprise even to her, as she had never yet warped a loom. In August of 1969, just after attending Woodstock, Lizbeth quit her job. But before beginning her fiber education, she made a year of pit stops, including a tour of the United States and a trip to Singapore to visit her brother, which she ended up extending to include a few months backpacking in India and several more months in Germany, where she worked at odd jobs. By the time she returned home to Ohio, ready to enroll at Utah State for a graduate degree in fine arts, she looked, by her mother's account, "like a hippie."

In Utah she met her husband, a photography student of Latvian ancestry. When he was offered a job in Minneapolis, they moved, even though Lizbeth was one quarter short of a degree that remains to this day unfinished. "We were thinking of each other as nomads," recalls Lizbeth. "We thought Minneapolis would be fine for four or five years." Lizbeth and her husband, Alvis, have been in the Twin Cities ever since, bringing up a daughter and a son there, though in 1989 they bought property in Hawaii on which they are building a home.

Growing up Lizbeth had never been an avid knitter. She had learned to knit in high school, but much preferred sewing. In college, she knit a few

Using the same motifs as those featured in the Trio of Mittens (left), but connecting them at different angles, Lizbeth designed the sweater that she is wearing above, which she calls Transitions. The name of the sweater derives from the transition of color from one sleeve across the sweater body to the other sleeve, as well as the transition in Lizbeth's life from the knitting she has done in the past (primarily Latvian mittens) to the knitting she will do in her future home in Hawaii — projects that will reflect many different cultural influences.

sweaters but didn't feel inspired by the patterns she found. She recalls, "If it wasn't totally engaging mentally and physically, I didn't take to it," a statement that holds true to this day. During an ethnic textiles class at University of Minnesota in 1978, she made a presentation about Latvian needlework, exhibiting handwovens and knitted mittens, and caught the attention of Sue Baizerman, a fellow student who was starting up a fiber-oriented publishing company. Sue and her partner, Karen Searle (page 156), asked Lizbeth to write a book on the Latvian mittens for the company, Dos Tejedoras (now part of Interweave Press in Colorado), and Lizbeth was off on a mammoth research project that involved, for starters, learning the Latvian language.

Lizbeth never questioned her commitment to the project from the moment she spontaneously agreed to it, though she had never made a single mitten, and in the process of doing it—the research, writing, and knitting took more than two years—she developed a love for knitting as well as for the small Baltic country from whence the mittens came. Lizbeth still recalls the

Lizbeth has knit nearly seventy pairs of Latvian mittens. Here, they tumble from a basket on the shore of a lagoon between Cedar Lake and Lake of the Isles in Minneapolis.

first time she saw a pair of the intricate Latvian hand coverings at her mother-in-law's house. Her reaction: "I could never knit a pair like that." Now she has written the book, made about seventy pairs, and lovingly devoted more than 100 hours to several particularly complicated models.

Mittens are an integral part of the Latvian culture. They once formed a major portion of a girl's dowry; they are the subject of many traditional folk songs; and the symbols within the mittens are believed to reflect the traditional mythology of the original Baltic tribesmen as well as the personal experience of the knitter. For Lizbeth, the main appeal is the discipline of working within the boundaries of tradition, of exploring the creative possibilities within time-honored parameters. She likes knowing which colors and motifs can be combined, which techniques can be used, and, in emulating the oldest of mittens, keeping the motifs symmetrical. "If I knit only mittens for the rest of my life, I still couldn't exhaust the design possibilities," Lizbeth told me, also explaining that this kind of in-depth study extends to other areas of her life. When she became interested in Mozart, in addition to listening to his music, she read three biographies and all of his letters. When she started to study taiji quan (a soft martial art also know as tai chi), she quickly committed to three to four classes a week and has traveled to several international conferences. "You find a genre and you totally explore it," she says, and I began to understand her early interest in studying library science. She has approached Latvian mittens with the tenacity of the most dedicated librarian and has become the world's leading authority on the subject.

While working on the book, knitting overtook weaving in Lizbeth's heart. If the mittens hadn't been enough to convince her that knitting was her true calling, meeting Elizabeth Zimmermann was. She took a one-week course with the knitting matriarch and quickly became one of her loyal followers, one of a core group of women that at the Zimmermann Knitting Camp (now run by daughter Meg Swansen; see page 138) came to be known as "oft-timers." "She instilled in us the knowledge that we could do anything we wanted, that there were no boundaries," Lizbeth warmly and gratefully recalls, also noting that she immediately latched onto Zimmermann's focus on circular knitting. "Intuitively, flat patterns didn't make sense to me," she explains. "As the body is three-dimensional, the sweater should be built around it."

Soon Lizbeth would become one of the founding contributors to *Knitter's Magazine,* an intense and gratifying experience that led to her becoming an editor for the publication and obsessed her for four years. It was only when she realized that she was hardly available to her family anymore that she decided to resign. "I was here but I wasn't approachable," she recalls. Still, the experience enriched her, and the process of editing and proofing other designers' work helped her to develop her own knitting philosophy.

"Knitterly" is an adjective that comes up often in Lizbeth's conversation. "Knitterly is so important to me," she says. It is about flow, about the work going 'round and 'round. It is not mosaic knitting or intarsia, because there is too much stop-and-go in those techniques. "One reason I love knitting," she says, "is that you sit with a ball of yarn and you never have to stop." Then she relates part of a favorite Latvian tale. A prodigal son goes home to see his father, who is dying, and wants to make peace with him. The father says, "Would that life were like a mitten. You could rip it out and start again." Lizbeth giddily continues: "Knitting can do that; it flows and flows; but you can see a mistake and just take it back out."

This man's lined mitten, knit at an extremely fine gauge, is impervious to wind and water.

A TRIO OF LATVIAN MITTENS

The three pairs of Latvian mittens shown on page 152 are all based on a traditional mitten pattern from the Alsunga township in the Kurzeme district of Latvia. The large man's mittens (center) are knit at a very fine gauge (thirteen stitches to the inch) and include a liner. Thus, they are extraordinarily warm; Lizbeth made them for her photographer husband, who had challenged her to make mittens that would keep his hands toasty in Minnesota during a winter sunrise photo shoot. The woman's mittens, with the slightly flared cuff, have a slightly looser gauge (10.5 stitches to the inch). Both versions are made with a fine but strong two-ply wool yarn from the Vuorelma Oy company in Finland. The child's mittens, at seven stitches to the inch, are a much simplified version of the adult models and are made with Peer Gynt four-ply wool. All three pairs draw upon the same traditional Latvian motifs, starting from the cuff: Austra's Tree (from which the sun leaps each morning); Jumis (symbolized by crossed stalks of grain that are bent and heavy with seed; this symbol represents fertility and well-being); and, on the palm, Sun within Morning Star surrounded by Four Moons. Lizbeth's advice to the beginning Latvian mitten knitter: it's still one stitch at a time; just pay more attention to each stitch. The patterns appear on page 216.

KAREN SEARLE: CELEBRATING KNITTING'S PAST, PRESENT, AND FUTURE

ST. PAUL, MINNESOTA

KAREN SEARLE ENJOYS acting as a bridge between cultures. She has been filling this role for a long time—as a translator of Spanish and Portuguese; a publisher and writer of books on fiber traditions of foreign cultures; a popular Twin Cities weaving and knitting teacher; a leader of textile tours of Guatemala and Belize; and the mother of two adopted children—a daughter from Korea and a son from Vietnam. She is also a fiber artist, using varied forms (including knitting, weaving, crochet, and papermaking) and an advanced technical facility to express many of her own emotional and spiritual struggles and convictions as well as her novel sense of humor.

Karen is best known as the cofounder of Dos Tejedoras, the publisher of such seminal books as *Salish Indian Sweaters, Andean Folk Knitting*, and *Latvian Mittens*, as well as many other important knitting and weaving works, including two weaving books that she wrote with Sue Baizerman, her publishing partner for the first eleven years. "I am very proud of the fact that we brought information to light that hadn't been written down before, and that we brought an awareness of different cultural traditions to the English-speaking world," Karen told me not long after selling Dos Tejedoras to Interweave Press. The knitting books Karen published are not typical pattern collections. They are intellectual texts, supplying techniques, charts where necessary, and historical and social background so that readers can understand the technical methods as well as cultural significance of particular knitting genres. When step-by-step patterns are provided, they are intended only as a jumping-off point for more independent work.

With the everyday pressures of running a publishing house behind her, Karen devotes most of her time to her own writing and artwork, much of which combines imagery, techniques, and traditions of foreign cultures with her own sense of sculpture, experimentation, and play. For example, Karen became interested in knitting dolls, a long-standing tradition in Peru and Bolivia, after publishing *Andean Folk Knitting*. She has knit primitive-looking, shamanistic figures out of raffia, crocheted a series of faceless, androgynous free-standing figures meant to represent varying aspects of communication and withholding, and knit the lizards that adorn the tubular card-woven snake shown in the photograph at right. "I've learned that every doll I make is in some way a reflection of myself," Karen explains, noting that she has also hand-sewn and woven many dolls. "Each one is a piece of a great ongoing self-portrait." The snake-and-lizard necklace is symbolic of Karen's exploration of feminism and ancient feminist symbols. The snake is a symbol of the life cycle (birth to death to renewal), and both snakes and lizards are symbolic of protection.

Karen learned to knit as a child, but it never held significant interest for her until her first year in college, when her roommate reintroduced

Karen is a highly skilled knitter, weaver, crocheter, spinner, and papermaker. When she embarks on a new project, she instinctively chooses the techniques and fibers that will best suit her needs.

her to it and she became, in her words, "one of those people who knit in classes and in the dark." Intending to pursue a career as a translator, Karen earned a degree in Spanish and Portuguese from the University of Wisconsin in 1965, and moved to Washington, D.C., but after three years met and married a homesick Minnesotan and moved with him to St. Paul. Unable to find translation work, the twenty-five-year-old Karen embarked on an intensive weaving and general textiles education in the Twin Cities and, before long, started teaching classes herself.

Dos Tejedoras (which means "two weavers" in Spanish) was born in 1976, when Karen and fellow weaving guild member Sue Baizerman wrote *Latin American Brocades* to supplement a class they were teaching at Convergence, the bi-annual convention of the Handweavers Guild of America. They followed their writing debut with *Finishes in the Ethnic Tradition,* and slowly began publishing the work of other writers. By 1984, Dos Tejedoras had become a full-time enterprise, requiring office space (other than the dining-room table on which the business had started) and a small staff. It also required that Karen give up the handknitting and production weaving business that she had begun in 1978.

Karen's experiences in the fiber world—technical, scholarly, professional, and artistic—have been multifaceted. She now sees them as tools that she can draw upon for expression. As important to her as that expression is the support of other artists—she is a mentor in an emerging artists program of the Women's Art Registry of Minnesota and a member of her local chapter of the Women's Caucus for Art—as well as her ongoing work to preserve cultural traditions and crafts. Karen believes that increased experimentation is the only means by which knitting is going to grow, change, or attain the dynamism it needs to become an accepted form within the fine art world. Karen is, indeed, a bridge. Through her dedication, she spans the past, present, and future of the boundless world of knitting.

Below right: In this playful necklace, three hand-knit lizards travel around a tubular card-woven snake. Karen chose a combination of fine cotton, rayon, and metallic thread for this reptilian work because she wanted it to glisten and sparkle—in the same way that real-life snakes and lizards do. She constructed the lizards on size 0000 lace needles and stuffed them with polyester batting. Below left: For this piece, which will ultimately be mounted, Karen embedded a stockinette-stitch metallic fabric between two sheets of sheer paper made out of a long-fibered Japanese vine called *kozo*. She uses this same technique to create three-dimensional vessels and is working out a way to make doll figures with it as well.

MIDWEST
LISA PARKS

LISA PARKS LEARNED TO KNIT IN ORDER
to spend one-on-one time with her mother. In order to be
with her father, she went to the symphony and the ballet
and watched sports on television. "Wasn't that smart?" she
asks rhetorically. "It was a ploy on my end." Zoning in on her
parents' interests was Lisa's way of getting attention in a family
of seven children, a family in which she held the notorious
middle position, in her case between two sets of twins, who
were in turn sandwiched between an oldest and a youngest
sibling. While most beginning knitters make scarves, seven-
year-old Lisa Parks was busy with an Icelandic sweater, a royal
blue one with white snowflakes and white and red reindeer.
"My mother would take me to the knit shop," Lisa recalls.
"She'd say, 'Knit three with blue, pick up your white, knit one, drop your
white,' and so on. We'd sit side by side. She'd say, 'Look at this [pointing at
the pattern]: this is what you're doing.'" And so another knitter was born.

Lisa Parks is today the enigmatic owner of Lisa Parks Knits, the
retail shop/design studio in elegant Birmingham, Michigan (a suburb of
Detroit), in which she sells her one-of-a-kind handknit sweaters. Whereas
many other handknit designers have struggled with this kind of retail
arrangement—bemoaning the long hours and the lack of adequate compen-
sation—Lisa's business has been around since 1982 and continues to do
well. Why is Lisa Parks successful where others are not? For starters, Lisa
Parks is not really like other people.

This forty-something designer/business person/mother of two has what
seems like infinite energy, drive, curiosity, and style. She has figured out how
to get what she needs from her customers and her employees in much the
same way she once figured out how to get what she needed from her parents:
by zoning in on their desires and making them her own. Customers at Lisa
Parks Knits visit the store as much for the sweater designs as they do for
a taste of the passion with which Lisa seasons her every move: the way she
sets up the store (which has the feeling of an old-fashioned salon that is
simultaneously warm, cozy, and on the cutting edge); the titles she gives her
sweater designs (Morning Edition, Light Years Ahead, Every Little Thing);
the music she plays; the books she reads; her philosophies on fitness,
Zen, and fly-fishing. Buying her sweaters may, in fact, reflect a desire on the

Lisa gives all of her sweaters names.
Liu Had a Dream (the cardigan
and vest set that she is modeling
here) is part of her Dreams Series.
Additional sweaters in the series
include Let the Dreams Begin
and Georgia on My Mind (based
on a dream Lisa had about being
inside a Georgia O'Keeffe painting).
"You can feel a little bit of old
knitting in what I do," says Lisa,
"but the look is always modern."

This photograph was taken
on the Huron River, near Ann Arbor,
Michigan. Lisa goes fly-fishing there
a couple of times a month.

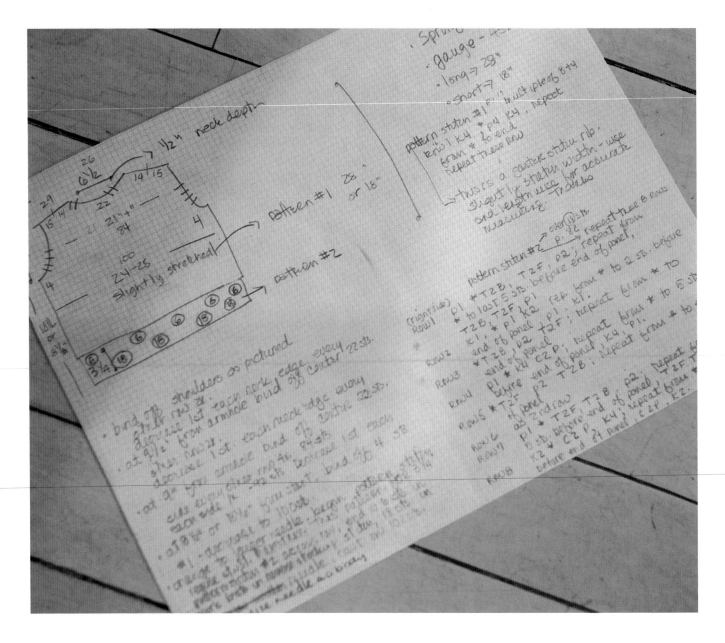

Lisa writes her patterns from the bottom of the page to the top, so that they correspond to the way her sweaters are knit—from the bottom band to the neck. Most of her knitters deliver individual pieces; then she and several finishers sew the sweaters together and add the ribbing for the button band, neckband, and armholes. Lisa believes that pattern writing comes easily to her because she learned it from her mother at a very young age.

part of her customers to take Lisa home. It's no wonder that whatever the designer/proprietor wears herself tends to sell best.

All of this attention works well for Lisa, who designs garments that meld tradition with progressive fashion. She'll start with a straightforward cardigan and a traditional stitch pattern and mix it all up by making the back longer than the front, combining several different fibers, adding ribbing where it's not expected and taking it away where it is, and mismatching the buttons. Each sweater is part of an intimate family of garments, which might include a short and long cardigan, a vest, and a short and long pullover, that are also part of a themed collection, such as Dreams, Goddesses, or Modern Retro. Customers may buy only one piece from a family, or layer several pieces together. Around the shop, which is decorated with an eclectic mix of antiques and contemporary folk art, are cones and bins of the yarns used in the sweaters, plus a select sampling of shirts, pants, skirts, and accessories. Lisa finds that the less merchandise she buys for the shop the better off she is and the more regularly her customers stop in. "If a customer comes in and we don't have her size, we say, 'We're sold out.' We don't reorder," explains Lisa. "What you see today is not what you're going to get tomorrow. It goes along with our sweaters being one-of-a-kind." For her own wardrobe, Lisa chooses to combine two or more layers of handknits with pants by such fashion-forward designers as Comme des Garçons or Yohji Yamamoto, but doesn't stock their merchandise in the shop because it's too expensive and competes with her sweaters, which generally sell for between $200 and $700.

To keep up with — and often ahead of — the trends, Lisa travels to New York City six times a year for trade shows as well as street research. She walks in different neighborhoods, studying what the people are wearing, the stores they are shopping in, the buildings, the archways, the windows, and the window coverings. She also reads incessantly — newspapers, magazines, and books (during one of our meetings she encouraged me to read *Into the Lighthouse* and *Mrs. Dalloway* by Virginia Woolf, *Time and Again* by Jack Finney, and all of the "Zen of" books, in particular *Zen and the Art of Climbing Mountains*, which is her favorite). She reads the *New York Times*, the *Wall Street Journal*, two local newspapers, *Women's Wear Daily*, and *Crain's Detroit Business* regularly, and subscribes to more than twenty other publications, which she reads all together, in a gargantuan binge, about four times a year. On the long list are the major European and American fashion publications (both consumer and trade) as well as sports, fitness, and classical and jazz music magazines.

When it comes time to design, however, Lisa puts all of these outside influences aside, sits down with her sketchbook, and turns the music up high. She doesn't want to be affected, at least consciously, by what other people are doing. The sixty or so sweaters Lisa designs annually are executed in different colorways by about thirty-five freelance knitters, some of whom she has worked with since the beginning of her career. Lisa believes that she can continue to be prolific after so many years because she is constantly changing as a person. Her knitters know that just because Lisa did something one way on one sweater does not mean she will do it the same way on another.

Lisa knits every day, but does mainly finishing work and repairs. The last time she made a sweater from start to finish was in 1985, a striped pullover for one of her sons. I asked her if she longs for the day when she can cast on and cast off. "Yes and no," she said. "Because I live and breathe my knitters' lives, I can imagine where they are when they cast on and I can look at their work and know if their tension is different. I do it vicariously." Then she recalled the start-up years, when she did almost all of the work herself. "I loved what I did then," she told me. "I love what I do now, and I'll do something else later. I'll do it all. And then I'll cook . . . and I'll have a neat house . . . and I'll live on a river."

LIU HAD A DREAM

Lisa designed the Liu Had a Dream cardigan and sleeveless vest while listening to the opera *Turandot* by Puccini, in which a maid named Liu dreams of marrying a prince. In a Parks-like reversal of the expected, Lisa chose a lattice stitch for the bottom band and a ribbing stitch for the body; the lattice is repeated in panels on the sleeves. The yarns, imported from Germany, are both from Muench. The raspberry yarn is called Wuhan and is 65 percent wool and 35 percent silk. The multicolored (purple, blue, mustard, and teal) accent yarn, called Sprint, is 75 percent cotton and 25 percent polyamide. The buttons on the cardigan and vest are all different, a Parks trademark. Knowing she was going to model the sweater while fly-fishing, Lisa included a wooden button with a fish painted on it. The pattern for this cardigan-vest set appears on page 219.

PATTER

SIZES
To fit Girl's size 8 (10-12, 14) or 27 (29-31, 35)" chest. Directions are for smallest size with larger sizes in parentheses. If there is only one figure it applies to all sizes. Shown on page 12 in size 10-12. Hat and mittens are one size fits all.

FINISHED MEASUREMENTS
Chest at underarm: 35½ (38, 42½)"
Length: 24½ (25½, 26½)"
Sleeve width at upper arm: 14½ (15¼, 16)"

MATERIALS
JACKET:
13 (14, 15) 1¾ oz/50g skeins (each approx 95yd/85m) of Classic
        Elite Tapestry in #2226 Persian Purple (MC)
4 skeins in #2258 Rug Red (A)
2 skeins each in #2260 Kani Teal (B) and #2280 Ibex (C)
1 skein each in #2252 Merchant's Eggplant (D),
        #2251 Tibetan Gold (E), #2235 Frond Green (F),
        #2257 Empress Blue (G), #2272 Goblin Green (H),
        and #2284 Sacred Saffron (I).
One pair each size 5 and 6 needles *or size needed to obtain gauge*
Size H crochet hook
Tapestry needle
4 small plastic rings for buttons
HAT AND MITTENS:
2 1¾ oz/50g skeins (each approx 95yd/85m) of Classic Elite
        Tapestry in #2258 Rug Red (A)
1 skein each in #2226 Persian Purple (MC), #2260 Kani Teal (B),
        #2280 Ibex (C), #2252 Merchant's Eggplant (D), and #2272
        Goblin Green (H).
Size 6 circular needle 16" long
One set (5) size 6 double-pointed needles
Size H crochet hook
Tapestry needle

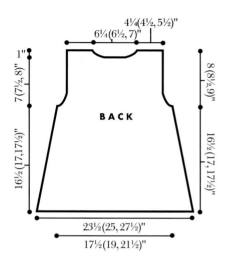

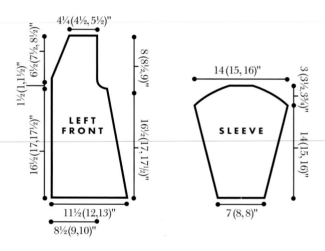

GAUGE
20 sts and 26 rows to 4" over St st using larger needles. *To save time and to ensure accurate sizing, check gauge.*

Note 1: When changing colors twist yarns on WS to prevent holes. **Note 2:** For border pattern, carry each color twisting yarns every 3 to 4 sts on WS across row. **Note 3:** Use a separate bobbin of yarn for each large motif. **Note 4:** Read RS rows on chart from right to left and WS rows from left to right.

BACK
With larger needles and MC, cast on 117 (125, 137) sts. Work chart in St st through Row 6. **Dec row (RS):** K 1, SSK, work across to last 3 sts, k2tog, k 1. Cont to foll chart, work dec every 6th row 14 times more — 87 (95, 107) sts. Cont chart through Row 106 (110, 114), ending with a WS row. ARMHOLE SHAPING Bind off 3 (4, 4) sts at beg of next 2 rows, 2 sts at beg of next 2 rows. Dec 1 st each side on next row, then every other row 1 (1, 2) times more — 73 (79, 89) sts. Cont to foll chart through Row 152 (158, 166). NECK SHAPING **Next row (RS):** Work 29 (31, 35) sts, join 2nd ball of yarn and bind off center 15 (17, 19) sts for neck, work to end. Working both sides at once, bind off from each neck edge 4 sts twice. Bind off rem 21 (23, 27) sts each side for shoulders.

LEFT FRONT
With larger needles and MC, cast on 57 (60, 66) sts. Work chart in St st through Row 6. **Dec row (RS):** K 1, SSK, work across. Cont to foll chart, dec every 6th row 14 times more — 42 (45, 51) sts. Cont chart through Row 106 (110, 114). ARMHOLE SHAPING Work shaping at side edge

only (beg of RS rows) as for back, AT THE SAME TIME, work as foll: NECK SHAPING **Row 117 (RS):** Work to last 2 sts, k2tog. Cont to dec 1 st at neck edge every other row 9 times, every 4th row twice, every 6th row 2 (2, 3) times. Work even until all chart rows have been worked. Bind off rem 21 (23, 27) sts for shoulder.

RIGHT FRONT
Cast on and foll chart for right front.

LEFT SLEEVE
With larger needles and B, cast on 35 (39, 39) sts. **Row 1(RS):** Purl. **Row 2:** With MC, purl. **Rows 3 and 4:** With MC, purl. Foll chart for left sleeve through Row 6. **Inc row:** K 2, M1, work chart to last 2 sts, M1, k 2. Cont to foll chart through Row 90 (96, 104), inc 1 st each side every 4th and 6th row alternately (working incs sts into chart pat) until there are 69 (75, 79) sts. CAP SHAPING Bind off 3 (4, 4) sts at beg of next 2 rows, 3 sts at beg of next 2 rows, 2 sts at beg of next 10 (12, 14) rows, 3 sts at beg of next 2 rows, 4 sts at beg of next 4 rows. Bind off rem 15 sts.

RIGHT SLEEVE
Work same as left sleeve, substituting mittens as drawn for right sleeve.

FINISHING
Weave in ends. Block pieces to measurements. Work embroidery on mitten motifs as shown on charts. Sew shoulder seams. BUTTONBAND AND COLLAR With RS facing, using smaller needles and MC, beg at center back neck, pick up and k 17 (19, 21) sts along back neck edge, 41 (43, 45) sts

along left front neck edge, then 86 (88, 90) sts to lower edge of left front — 144 (150, 156) sts. **Row 1 (WS):** *K 1, p 1, rep from * to end. **Row 2:** Sl 1, *k 1, p 1; rep from *, end k 1. **Rows 3, 5 and 7:** Rep Row 1. **Rows 4 and 6:** Rep Row 2. SHAPE COLLAR **Rows 8 and 9:** Beg at center back, sl 1, work 60 (62,64) sts in pat, wrap next st (with yarn in back, sl next st onto right hand needle, bring yarn to front, slip st back to left hand needle). Turn, work across in pat. **Rows 10 and 11:** Sl 1, work 57 (59, 61) sts, wrap next st. Turn, work across. **Rows 12 and 13:** Sl 1, work 54 (56, 58) sts, wrap next st. Turn, work across. **Rows 14 and 15:** Sl 1, work 51 (53, 55) sts, wrap next st. Turn, work across. **Rows 16 and 17:** Sl 1, work 48 (50, 52) sts, wrap next st. Turn, work across. **Rows 18 and 19:** Sl 1, work 45 (47, 49) sts, wrap next st. Turn, work across. **Rows 20 and 21:** Sl 1, work 42 (44, 47) sts. Turn, work across. Place 144 (150, 156) sts on strand of yarn for holder. Place markers for 4 buttons, the first ½" below beg of neck shaping, the last one 5 ½" above cast-on edge and the other 2 spaced evenly between. BUTTONHOLE BAND With RS facing, using smaller needles and MC, beg at right front lower edge, pick up and k 86 (88, 90) sts along right front edge to neck shaping, 41 (43, 45) sts along right front neck edge and 17 (19, 21) sts along back, ending at center back st — 144 (150, 156) sts. **Row 1 (WS):** Sl 1, *k 1, p 1; rep from *, end k 1. **Row 2:** *K 1, p 1; rep from * across. **Row 3 (buttonholes):** Work in est seed st to first marker, *bind off 2 sts, work to next marker, rep from * 2 times more, bind off 2 sts, seed st to end. **Row 4:** Work in seed st, casting on 2 sts over each set of bound-off sts. **Rows 5 and 7:** Rep Row 1. **Row 6:** Rep Row 2. Cut yarn. COLLAR **Rows 8 and 9:** Using smaller needles and MC, join yarn at center back, work 60 (62, 64) seed sts, wrap next st. Turn, work to center back. **Rows 10 and 11:** Sl 1, work 57 (59, 61) seed sts, wrap next st. Turn, work across. **Rows 12 and 13:** Sl 1, work 54 (56, 58) seed sts, wrap next st. Turn, work across. **Rows 14 and 15:** Sl 1, work 51 (53, 55) seed sts, wrap next st. Turn, work across. **Rows 16 and 17:** Sl 1, work 48 (50, 52) seed sts, wrap next st. Turn, work across. **Rows 18 and 19:** Sl 1, work 45 (47, 49) seed sts, wrap next st. Turn, work across. **Rows 20 and 21:** Sl 1, work 42 (44, 47) seed sts, wrap next st. Turn, work to center back. Sl sts to same holder as button band and Collar. BAND AND COLLAR EDGING **Next row:** With WS facing and B, beg at cast-on edge of left front, p 86 (88, 90) sts, p 116 (124, 132) sts across collar (work wrapped sts by working tog st with loop wrapped at base of st), p 86 (88, 90) sts. Bind off all sts purlwise. BOTTOM EDGING With RS facing and MC, pick up and k 229 (241, 261) sts around bottom edge. **Row 1 (WS):** Knit. **Row 2:** With B, knit. **Row 3:** Knit. **Row 4:** With C, knit. **Row 5 (picot):** *K2tog, yo; rep from *, end k 1. Bind off. Turn bound-off edge of picot to inside and tack down. Crochet desired color yarns around plastic rings for buttons. Sew on buttons opposite buttonholes.

HAT

With dpn and A, cast on 4 sts. Work I-cord as foll: with 2nd dpn, k 4; sl sts back to beg of needle and k4. Cont in this way until cord measures 22". Cut yarn and without twisting cord, sew or weave ends tog to make a loop. With circular needle and MC, pick up and k 108 sts evenly around cord loop. Join and beg Rnd 1 of border chart for Hat. Work chart through Rnd 19. SHAPE CROWN **Note:** Change to dpns when crown becomes too small to work on circular needle. **Rnd 1:** With MC, knit. **Rnd 2** (dec): With MC k 7, *k2tog, k 1, SSK, k 13; rep from * around, end last rep k 6 — 96 sts. **Rnds 3 and 4:** Foll chart for next 2 rnds. **Rnd 5** (dec): K 6, *k2tog, k 1, SSK, k 11; rep from * around, ending last rep k 5 — 84 sts. Cont to foll chart through Rnd 22, working decs as est every 3rd rnd having 2 sts less in each rep on each dec rnd — 24 sts. **Next rnd:** *Sl 1, k2tog, psso, k 1, rep from * around — 12 sts. Work 2 rnds even. **Next rnd:** K2tog around — 6 sts. Work 1 rnd even. **Next rnd:** [K 1, k2tog] twice — 4 sts. Place all sts on one dpn with yarn at left. Work I-cord for 3". Cut yarn leaving a 3" end. Draw end through rem sts, pulling tog tightly. Bring end to inside. Tie cord to make a knot.

FINISHING

With C, cast on 3 sts. Work I-cord as for beg of Hat until it measures 22". Sew or weave ends tog. Stitch cord to Hat at foldline (purl row and last row of Hat border). With C, work overcast st around bottom edge cord and with B around cord at foldline. **To Work Overcast st:** With tapestry needle, bring yarn from WS to right side at top edge of cord. Bring needle under to WS and out again 3 sts to the right. Cont around bottom edge, then work back in opposite direction. At fold edge, work in one direction only. With crochet hook and B, starting at beg of crown, work slip st along 6 lines of sts between decs as foll: Insert hook from front to

back into st, draw B through, *insert hook in next st one row above, draw B through to front and through lp on hook; rep from *. With tapestry needle and A, work overcast st along slip st line.

MITTENS

RIGHT MITTEN

Note: Chart (p. 168) shows back of mitten only, worked on 2 of 4 dpns. Cont pat for palm side by working est reps. With dpn and A, cast on 42 sts, divide sts evenly on 4 dpns. Join, being careful not to twist sts. **Rnd 1:** *K2tog, yo; rep from * to end — 42 sts. **Rnd 2:** Knit. P 2 rnds B, 2 rnds C. Cont in St st (k every rnd) and work chart as foll: Work chart through Rnd 14. **Rnd 15** (dec): Foll chart, work 20 sts, k2tog, work to last 2 sts, k2tog — 40 sts. **Rnds 16-27:** Foll chart. THUMB OPENING **Rnd 28:** Foll chart, work 21 sts, with scrap yarn k 8, sl 8 sts just worked back to LH needle and work them again from chart, work to end of rnd. **Rnds 29-47:** Foll chart (Note: after working through chart rnd 38, cont to rep rnds 29-38). **Top shaping; Next rnd** (dec): With A, SSK, foll chart to last 3 sts of 2nd needle, with A k2tog, k 1; at beg of 3rd needle work SSK, work chart to last 3 sts of 4th needle, with A k2tog, k 1 — 36 sts. Cont in this way to dec 4 sts every other rnd twice, then every rnd 5 times — 8 sts. Transfer 4 sts of mitten back to one needle, 4 sts of palm side to one needle. **Rnd 57:** With A, sl 1, k2tog, psso, k 1 on first then on second needle. Cut yarn, leaving a 4" end. Draw end through rem 4 sts, pulling tog tightly. Bring end to inside and fasten off. THUMB Pull out scrap yarn and sl 8 bottom loops to 2 needles. Pick up necessary loops from top of opening and sl them on 2 more needles. **Rnd 1:** With A, k across bottom loops, pick up loop from left side of opening, work across top loops (k2tog as necessary to make 8 sts), pick up loop from right side of opening — 18 sts. **Rnd 2:** [K 7, k2tog] twice — 16 sts. With A, knit thumb in rnds for 2". **Dec rnd:** *SSK, k 3, k2tog, k 1; rep from * once —12 sts. **Dec rnd:** *SSK, k 1, k2tog, k 1; rep from * once — 8 sts. **Next rnd:** *Sl 1, k2tog, psso, k 1; rep from * once — 4 sts. Cut yarn, leaving a 4" end. Draw end through rem 4 sts, pull tog tightly. Bring end to inside and fasten off.

LEFT MITTEN

Work as for Right Mitten through Rnd 27. THUMB OPENING Foll chart, work 21 sts. With scrap yarn, k 8, sl 8 sts just worked back to LH needle and finish rnd. Cont working as for Right Mitten.

MITTENS FOR RIGHT SLEEVE

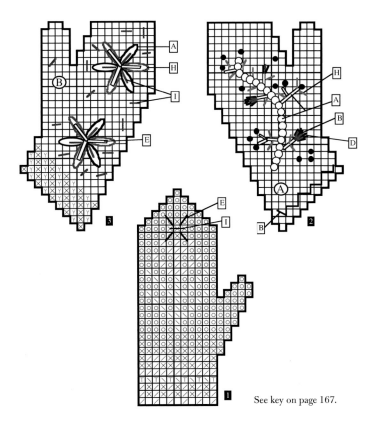

See key on page 167.

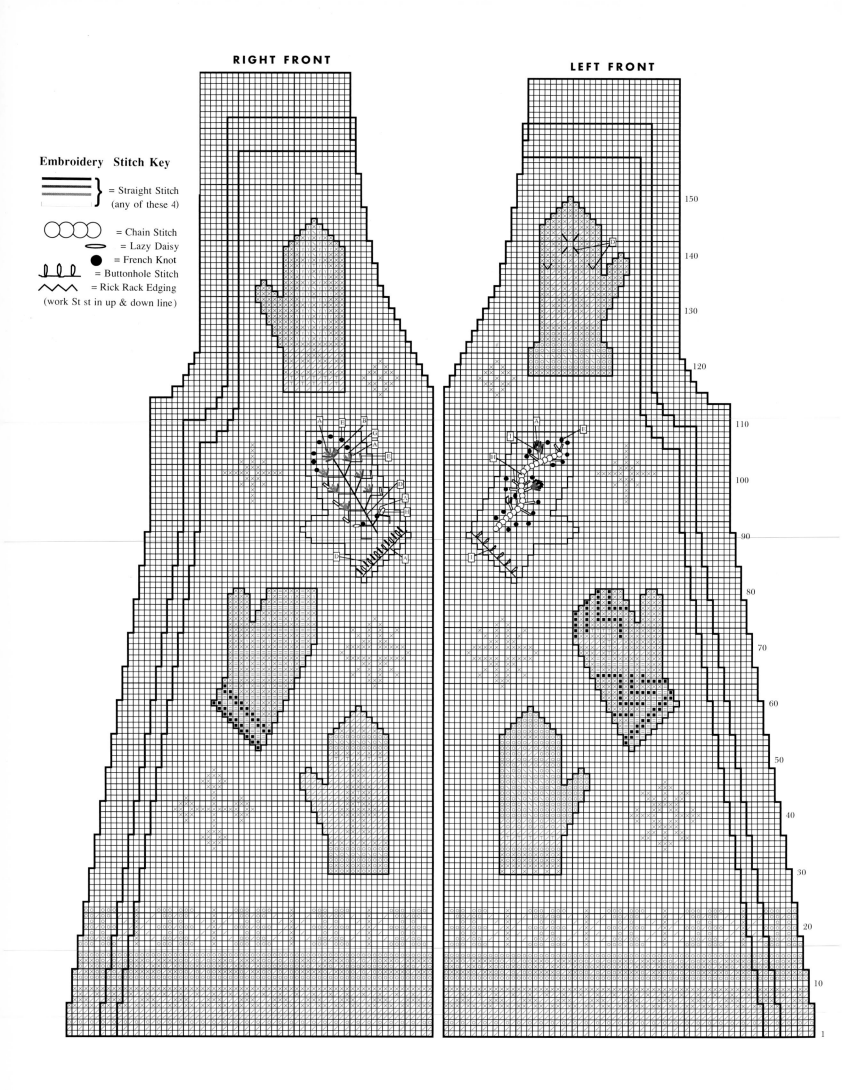

RIGHT FRONT

LEFT FRONT

Embroidery Stitch Key

= Straight Stitch
(any of these 4)

= Chain Stitch
= Lazy Daisy
= French Knot
= Buttonhole Stitch
= Rick Rack Edging
(work St st in up & down line)

150

140

130

120

110

100

90

80

70

60

50

40

30

20

10

1

BACK

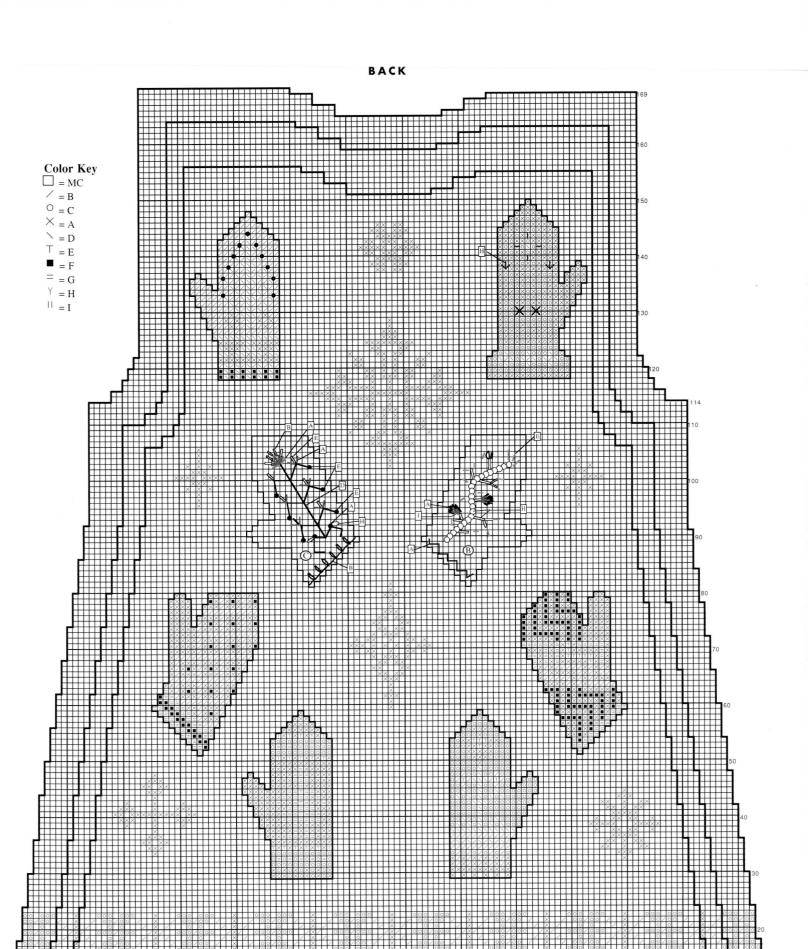

Color Key
☐ = MC
╱ = B
O = C
✕ = A
╲ = D
⊤ = E
■ = F
═ = G
Y = H
‖ = I

LEFT SLEEVE

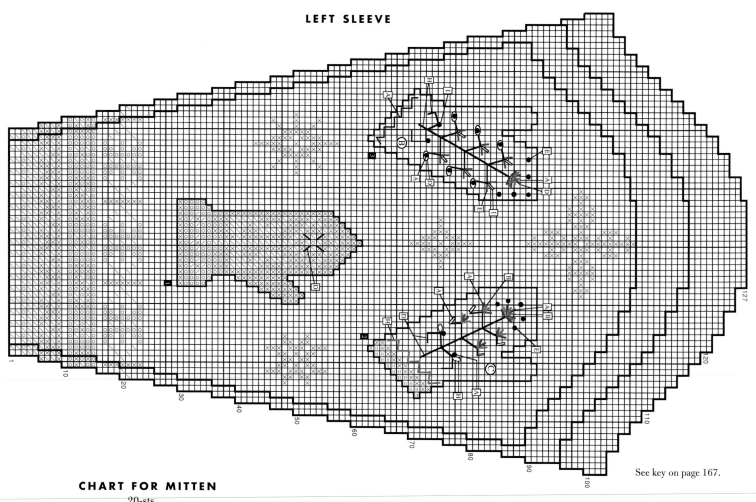

See key on page 167.

CHART FOR MITTEN

20-sts

HAT BORDER

CROWN

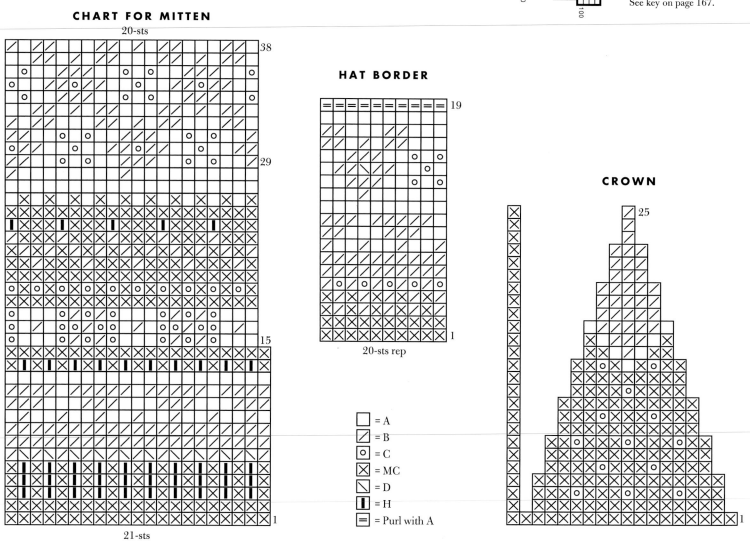

20-sts rep

21-sts

☐ = A
◪ = B
◉ = C
☒ = MC
◩ = D
▮ = H
▤ = Purl with A

SPICE MARKET WRAP AND HAT

INTERMEDIATE

SIZE
One size fits all. Shown below and on page 22.

KNITTED MEASUREMENTS
Wrap: approx 20½" x 66"
Hat circumference: 21"

MATERIALS (for wrap and hat)
1 3½ oz/100g hank (each approx 138yd/124m) of Manos del
    Uruguay in #54 Wine (A), #08 Black (B), #28 Clay (C),
    "K" Bisque (D), "M" Bordeaux (E), #51 Jade (F),
    #48 Berry (G), #49 Coral (H), #61 Peony (I), #52 Flesh (J),
    "W" Yellow (K), "E" Bottle Green (L), #37 Brown (M),
    #55 Olive Green (N), "G" Mossy Brown (O), and
    #35 Thistle Green (P)
One pair size 9 needles *or size needed to obtain gauge*
One set (5) size 9 dpn for Hat
Stitch marker for Hat
Size H crochet hook for Wrap

GAUGE
16 sts and 20 rows to 4" over St st and chart pat using size 9 needles.
To save time and to ensure accurate sizing, check gauge.

STITCH GLOSSARY
Double Dec: Sl 2 sts tog knitwise, k1, pass 2 slipped sts over k st.

WRAP

With size 9 needles and A, cast on 81 sts. Work rows 1-166 of chart; rep rows 127-166 once. Work row 166 again, keeping all sts in St st. Work rows 125-1 of chart. Bind off. *Note:* When working chart backwards from row 125-1, it will be necessary to reverse the garter ridges and some of the texture areas; use first half as a guide. General rule - don't work rev St st unless previous row was St st using same color (Rows 125 and 124 are a garter ridge. Row 125 shows rev St st but work as St st; row 124 shows St st but work as rev St st).

FINISHING
With RS facing, crochet hook and A, work 1 rnd sc and 1 rnd backwards sc (from left to right) around outside edge of wrap.

HAT

With size 9 dpn and A, cast on 84 sts. Divide sts evenly over 4 needles (21 sts on each needle). Join and place marker for beg of rnd. With A, k 1 rnd, p 1 rnd, with O, k 1 rnd, p 1 rnd, k 1 rnd J, k 1 rnd D. Work rnds 10 – 21 of chart as foll: Work sts 2 – 80 once, then sts 9 – 13 once. K 2 rnds I. Work rnds 80 – 82 of chart. With L, k 1 rnd, p 1 rnd. Work rnds 94 – 97 of chart. **Next rnd:** With I, k10, k2tog, with P, k10, k2tog, with I, k10, k2tog, with N, k10, k2tog, with G, k10, k2tog, with K, k10, k2tog, with A, k12. *Turn work* and beg to work back and forth, matching colors as foll: p 1 row on WS. **Next row (RS):** [K4, double dec, k4] 7 times, k1 — 64 sts. P 1 row. **Row 34:** [K3, double dec, k3] 7 times, k1 — 50 sts. P 1 row. **Row 36:** [K2, double dec, k2] 7 times, k1 — 36 sts. P 1 row. **Row 38:** [K1, double dec, k1] 7 times, k1 — 22 sts. P 1 row. **Row 40:** [Double dec] 7 times, k1 — 8 sts. P 1 row. **Row 42:** K8 tog. Fasten off last st. Sew back seam.

COLOR KEY

▢ St st with A		▯ St st with I	
▣ Rev St st with A		‖ Rev St st with I	
✳ St st with B		⊞ St st with J	
✴ Rev St st with B		✳ Rev St st with J	
◿ St st with C		✕ St st with K	
◢ Rev St st with C		▢ St st with L	
⊞ St st with D		◹ St st with M	
✚ Rev St st with D		╱ Rev St st with M	
◇ St st with E		◺ St st with N	
◆ Rev St st with E		◥ Rev St st with N	
▪ St st with F		◲ St st with O	
○ St st with G		◣ Rev St st with O	
● Rev St st with G		▽ St st with P	
⊞ St st with H		▼ Rev St st with P	
⊟ Rev St st with H			

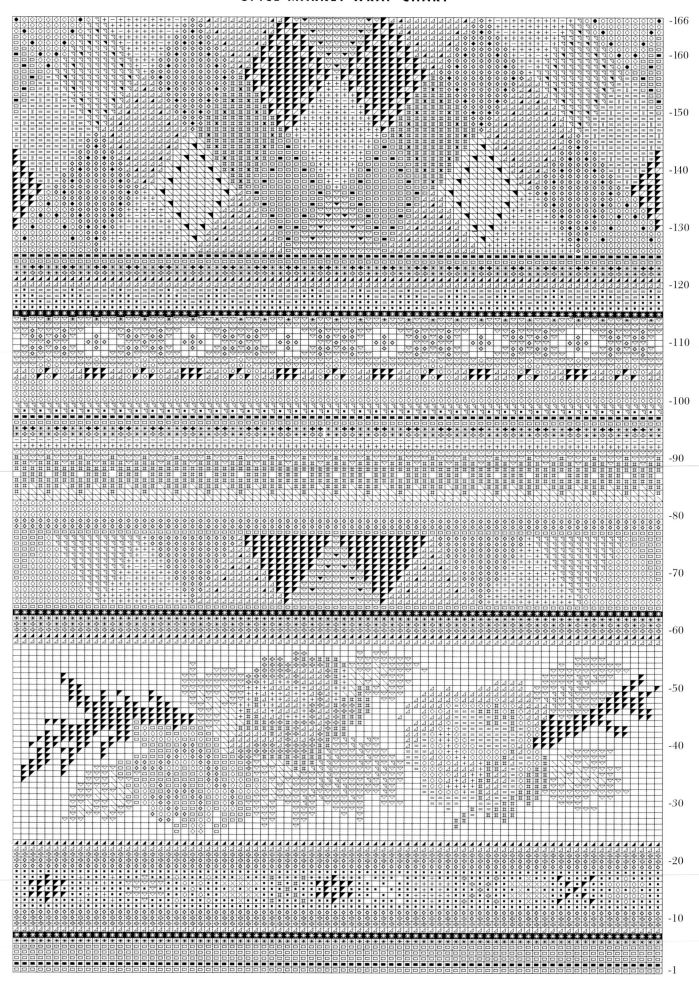

- -166
- -160
- -150
- -140
- -130
- -120
- -110
- -100
- -90
- -80
- -70
- -60
- -50
- -40
- -30
- -20
- -10
- -1

See key on page 169.

AT SEA GANSEY

EXPERIENCED

GAUGE
28 sts and 40 rnds to 4" over St st using size 1 needle. *To save time and to ensure accurate sizing, check gauge.*

STITCH GLOSSARY
2-st Cable: K2tog but do not drop sts from LH needle, k into first st again, drop both sts from LH needle.
8-st Back Cable (BC): Sl 4 sts to cn and hold to *back* of work, k4, k4 from cn.
8-st Front Cable (FC): Sl 4 sts to cn and hold to *front* of work, k4, k4 from cn.
Right Leaning Raised Inc (M1R): With LH needle, pick up horizontal bar between 2 sts from back to front. K into front lp.
Left Leaning Raised Inc (M1L): With LH needle, pick up horizontal bar between 2 sts from front to back. K into back lp.

ST ST K every rnd.

GARTER ST: *K 1 rnd, p 1 rnd; rep from * for garter st.

GARTER RIB (multiple of 3 sts)
Rnd 1: *K2, p1; rep from * to end. **Rnd 2:** Knit. Rep rnds 1 and 2 for garter rib.

DOUBLE SEED ST (multiple of 4 sts)
Rnd 1: *K2, p2; rep from * to end. **Rnd 2:** *P2, k2; rep from * to end. Rep rnds 1 and 2 for double seed st.

7-ST CABLE SEAM
Rnds 1 (RS) and 2: [P1, k2] twice, p1. **Rnd 3:** [P1, 2-st cable over 2 sts] twice, p1. **Rnd 4:** Rep rnd 1. Rep rnds 1-4 for 7-st cable seam.

8-ST CABLE
Rnd 1 (RS): 8-st FC. **Rnds 2-10:** K8. **Rnd 11:** 8-st BC. **Rnds 12-20:** K8. Rep rnds 1-20 for 8-st cable.

WELTS
With 3 ends of yarn and 32" circular needle, cast on 140 (160, 180) sts, not including the slip knot, using the Channel Island Cast-on as foll: This cast-on method makes two sts at a time. *1.* Using three ends of yarn, make a slip knot. (This slip knot should not be included in your stitch count, and should be removed after casting on is completed). *2.* *Hold the single yarn over your left forefinger and wrap the double yarns twice around your left thumb in a counter-clockwise direction. Your needle is in your right hand. *3.* Bring the needle over, behind, and under the single yarn, just like a yarn over. (This forms the first of the two sts made). *4.* Then insert your needle up into the two loops on the thumb (this forms the bead), pick up the single yarn again as in step *3* (this is the second st) and pull it through the thumb loops, drop loops from thumb; rep from *. Even tensioning is tricky and comes with practice. *Do not join.* Remove slip knot and work back and forth in garter st (k every row) for 15 rows. Set aside, breaking the yarn. Make another welt in same way. **Row 16:** Knit across second welt, inc 7 sts evenly spaced, then knit across first welt, inc 7 sts evenly spaced, to last 4 sts. Place marker (pm) for beg of rnd (at this point, the welts are joined at one side, but not into a circle) — 294 (334, 374) sts.

LOWER BODY
Rnd 1: P1, k2, p1, (join welts without twisting), k2, p1, pm, k140 (160, 180) for front, pm, p1, k2, p1, k2, p1, pm, k140 (160, 180) for back. From this point on, the cabled seam sts will be worked between the markers until the gusset is begun. **Next rnd:** *Work 7-st cable seam, k140 (160, 180); rep from * once. Rep last rnd 7 times more. **Next rnd:** Beg initial in purl sts and tree motif from chart B, rnds 6-23, if desired, at left front, about 5 sts in from the cable seam. Cont cable seams and St st until piece measures 5 (7, 9)" from beg. Work 35 rnds of chart A, cont cable seam sts.

MAIN BODY
Next (Inc) Rnd: *7-st cable seam, k9 (15, 21), k35 inc 4 sts evenly over these sts to 39 sts, k10 (14, 18), inc 1 st in next st, work 30 sts chart C, inc 1 st in next st, k10 (14, 18), k35 inc 4 sts evenly over these sts to 39 sts, k9 (15, 21); rep from * once. **Establish Pat - Next Rnd:** [Work 7-st cable seam, 9 (15, 21) sts garter rib, *work sts 18 and 19 of chart B, 8-st cable, 19 sts chart B, 8-st cable, sts 1 and 2 of chart B*, 12 (16, 20) sts in double seed st, cont 30 sts chart C, 12 (16, 20) sts double seed st; rep between *'s (39 sts) once, work 9 (15, 21) sts garter rib (beg p1)] twice. Work even in pats as established until piece measures 13 (14, 15)" from beg. Work underarm gusset between the 2 cables in the side seams as foll: **UNDERARM GUSSETS** *Work cable seam pat on next 3 sts, M1R, k1 (gusset st), M1L, 3 sts in cable seam pat*, work front in established pat; rep between *'s once, work back in established pat. Work 4 rnds even, keep 3 sts each side of gusset in cable seam pat, work gusset p1, k1, p1. **Next (Inc) Rnd:** *Work 3 sts cable seam pat, p1, M1R, k1, M1L, p1, 3 sts cable seam pat*, work front; rep between *'s, work back. Cont to inc 1 st at each side of gusset (working inc sts into St st) every 5th rnd until there are 23 sts between seam markers each side — 346 (386, 426) sts.

UPPER BODY
FRONT On a RS row for cables, put the gusset and seam sts onto a stitch holder (23 sts), work across front 150 (170, 190) sts in pat, turn work. Put rem gusset and seam sts on another stitch holder, and back sts onto a piece of yarn. Work back and forth for 9 (9¾, 10½)". On the last (WS) row, dec 2 sts in each 8-st cable to allow for a smoother transition into the shoulder seam. Place rem 142 (162, 182) sts on a holder.

BACK
Work as for front.

SHOULDERS AND INVERTED TRIANGULAR NECK GUSSET
Slip 43 (51, 59) sts of left front onto a needle and 43 (51, 59) sts of left back shoulder onto another needle. Beg at armhole, with wrong sides facing, using a third needle, work bind off as foll: K tog first st from each needle, then *k tog next st from each needle, pass first st over second st; rep from * until 7 sts rem on each needle, and 1 st rem on third needle. Working back and forth, beg neck gusset: Turn garment to RS. Cont to use third needle to knit. **Row 1 (RS):** K1 (from LH needle), turn work. **Row 2:** Sl 1 purlwise wyif, p2, turn work. **Row 3:** Sl 1 knitwise wyib, k3,

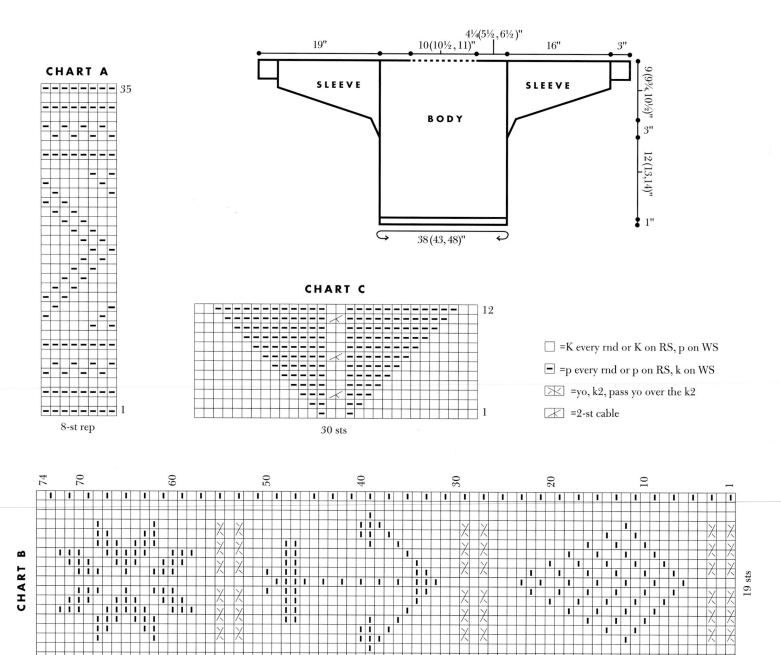

CHART A

35

1

8-st rep

CHART C

12

1

30 sts

□ =K every rnd or K on RS, p on WS

─ =p every rnd or p on RS, k on WS

=yo, k2, pass yo over the k2

=2-st cable

CHART B

19 sts

---

turn work. **Row 4:** Sl 1 purlwise wyif, p4, turn work. **Row 5:** Sl 1 knitwise wyib, k5, turn work. Cont working back and forth until all shoulder sts are used up and there are 15 neck gusset sts on third needle. Place these sts on a holder. Rep for other shoulder.

ROLLED COLLAR

(RS) Sl all sts of neck to 16" circular needle: 15 sts from each neck gusset, 56 (60, 64) sts each from front and back — 142 (150, 158) sts. Join yarn at back right shoulder, work around in St st for 3". Bind off loosely.

SLEEVE

Sl the gusset and seam sts to 16" circular needle, placing markers on either side of 15 center gusset sts. Join yarn and work across 23 sts in established pat. Pick up 127 (139, 151) sts evenly spaced around the armhole for a total of 150 (162, 174) sts. **Rnd 1:** Work 23 gusset and seam sts in pat, 20 (26, 26) garter rib, p1, k2 for 2-st cable, p1, k2 for St st, work 18 (18, 24) sts in double seed st, work between *'s (39 sts) of "Establish Pat" on Main Body, work 18 (18, 24) sts in double seed st, k2 for St st, p1, k2 for 2-st cable, p1, work 20 (26, 26) sts in garter rib. Cont as established for 2 rnds. **Rnd 4:** Work gusset and seam sts, dec gusset by SKP (sl 1, k1, psso) after first marker and k2tog 2 sts before second marker. Cont to

cable seam sts every 4th rnd and to dec at both sides on each side of the gusset every 5th rnd until 3 gusset sts rem between markers. Then dec as foll in the next rnd: Work 4 sts, remove marker, SK2P (sl 1, k2tog, psso), remove marker, work to end of rnd. Work 1 rnd even. **Next rnd:** Work 3 sts, p3tog, work to end of rnd — 134 (146, 158) sts. Place markers at either side of 7-st cable seam sts to mark for sleeve decs. Cont to work in pat, dec at markers (in sleeve sts) every 4th rnd as foll: work to 2 sts before first marker, SKP, work 7 sts, k2tog, finish rnd. Cont in this way until sleeve measures 10" from armhole, dec 4 sts in last rnd, 2 in each 8-st cable. Work chart A, and cont to dec at markers every 4th rnd, then work in St st, keeping the 7-st cable seam sts in pat, and cont to dec 2 sts every 4th rnd until 64 (76, 88) sts rem. Work even in St st, maintaining seam sts, until sleeve measures 16", or 3" less than desired length. CUFF **Dec Rnd:** Work seam sts in pat, then p across rem sts, dec 4 (10, 16) sts evenly for a total of 60 (66, 72) sts. CUFF PAT **Rnds 1, 2 and 4:** *P1, k2; rep from * around. **Rnd 3:** *P1, work 2-st cable; rep from * around. Rep rnds 1-4 for 3". Bind off. Work other sleeve in same way.

FINISHING

Block to measurements, being careful not to flatten cables. Do not block the rolled collar or cuffs.

COUNTERPANE PULLOVER

INTERMEDIATE

SIZES

To fit woman's Small/Medium (Large). Directions are for small/medium size with larger size in parentheses. If there is only one figure it applies to both sizes. Shown on page 32 in size Large.

KNITTED MEASUREMENTS

Bust at underarm 50 (54)"
Length 21 (23)"
Sleeve width at upper arm 24 (25)"

MATERIALS

19 (20) 1¾oz/50g skeins (each approx 126yd/115m) of Rowan DK Tweed in #851 Cricket (MC)
1 ¾oz/25g skeins (each approx 74yd/67m) of Rowan Lightweight DK in #71 Dk Rust (A), #77 Lt Rust (B), #606 Dk Green (C), #404 Lt Green (D), #11 Gold (E), #10 Lt Gold (F), and #54 Teal (G)
One pair size 4 (for Small/Medium) or 6 (for Large) knitting needles *or size needed to obtain gauge*
Sizes 4 or 6 circular needle 16" long

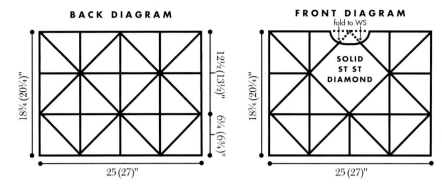

BACK DIAGRAM

18¾ (20¼)" 12½ (13½)" 6¼ (6¾)"
25 (27)"

FRONT DIAGRAM
fold to WS

SOLID
ST ST
DIAMOND

18¾ (20¼)"
25 (27)"

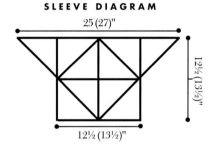

SLEEVE DIAGRAM
25 (27)"

12½ (13½)"

12½ (13½)"

GAUGE

For Size Small/Medium:
20 sts and 28 rows to 4" over St st using size 4 needles; 1 square (2 triangles sewn tog) = approx 6¼"square.
For Size Large:
18 sts and 26 rows to 4" over St st using size 6 needles. 1 square (2 triangles sewn tog) = approx 6¾" square.
To save time and ensure accurate sizing, check gauges.

STITCH GLOSSARY

Inc 1: K into front and back of st
Inc 1P: P into back and front of st
Bobble: Row 1 (RS): K into front, back, front and back of st (4 sts), turn. **Row 2:** K 4, turn. **Row 3:** K2tog twice; sl 2nd st on RH needle over first st.

TRIANGLES (4 triangles = 1 diamond)

Make 24 for back, 18 for front and 10 for each sleeve. With size 4 (6) needles and MC, cast on 1 st. **Row 1 (RS):** Inc 1 — 2 sts. **Row 2:** K 1, inc 1 — 3 sts. **Row 3:** K 2, inc 1 — 4 sts. **Row 4:** K 3, inc 1 — 5 sts. **Rows 5-12:** K to last st, inc 1 — 13 sts at end of row 12. **Row 13:** K 12, inc 1 — 14 sts. **Row 14:** P 13, inc 1P — 15 sts. **Row 15:** K 14, inc 1 — 16 sts. **Row 16:** P 15, inc 1P — 17 sts. **Row 17:** [K 2, p 2] 4 times, inc 1 — 18 sts. **Row 18:** P 2, [k 2, p 2] 3 times, k 2, p 1, inc 1P — 19 sts. **Row 19:** P 1, [k 2, p 2] 4 times, k 1, inc 1 — 20 sts. **Row 20:** K 1, [p 2, k 2] 4 times, p 2, inc 1 — 21 sts. **Row 21:** [P 2, k 2] 5 times, inc 1 — 22 sts. **Row 22:** P 21, inc 1P — 23 sts. **Row 23:** K 22, inc 1 — 24 sts. **Row 24:** P 23, inc 1P — 25 sts. **Row 25:** K 24, inc 1 — 26 sts. **Row 26:** K 25, inc 1 — 27 sts. **Row 27:** K 26, inc 1 — 28 sts. **Row 28:** K 27, inc 1 — 29 sts. **Row 29:** K 28, inc 1 — 30 sts. **Row 30:** K 29, inc 1 — 31 sts. **Row 31:** K 30, inc 1 — 32 sts. **Row 32:** P 31, inc 1P — 33 sts. **Row 33:** K 32, inc 1 — 34 sts. **Row 34:** K 33, inc 1 — 35 sts. **Row 35:** K 2, [yo, k2tog] 16 times, inc 1 — 36 sts. **Row 36:** K 35, inc 1 — 37 sts. **Row 37:** K 36, inc 1 — 38 sts. **Row 38:** P 37, inc 1P — 39 sts. **Row 39:** K 2, [bobble, k 4] 7 times, bobble, inc 1 — 40 sts. **Row 40:** P 39, inc 1P — 41 sts. **Row 41:** K 40, inc 1 — 42 sts. **Row 42:** K 41, inc 1 — 43 sts. **Row 43:** K 2, [yo, K2tog], 20 times, inc 1 — 44 sts. **Row 44:** K 43, inc 1 — 45 sts. **Row 45:** K 44, inc 1 — 46 sts. **Row 46:** P 45, inc 1P — 47 sts. **Row 47:** K 46, inc 1 — 48 sts. **Row 48:** Bind off.

ASSEMBLY

Sew triangles tog foll back, front, and sleeve diagrams.

SOLID FRONT DIAMOND (make 1)

INC ROWS **Row 1 (RS):** With size 4 (6) needles and MC, cast on 1 st; k into front, back and front of this st —3 sts. **Row 2:** Purl. **Row 3:** Inc 1, k 1, inc 1 — 5 sts. **Row 4:** Purl. **Row 5:** Inc 1, k to last st, inc 1 — 7 sts. **Row 6:** Purl. Rep rows 5 and 6 until there are 63 sts. DEC ROWS **Row 1 (RS):** K 1, k2tog, k to last 3 sts, SKP, k 1 — 61 sts. **Row 2:** Purl. Rep rows 1 and 2 until there are 29 sts. Bind off. Sew solid front diamond into front of pullover. Fold 2 triangles at each neck edge back 2" from edge and sew to back to form neck shaping.

FINISHING

Sew shoulder seams. Place markers 12½ (13½)" down front shoulder seams on front and back for armholes. Sew top of sleeve between markers. SLEEVE CUFF With RS facing, using size 4 (6) needles and MC, pick up and k 60 sts along lower edge of sleeve. Work in garter st for 1", end with a WS row dec 1 st each end of last row — 58 sts. Work in k2, p2 rib for 2½". Bind off in rib. FRONT LOWER EDGE With RS facing, using size 4 (6) needles and MC, pick up and k 120 sts along lower edge of front. Work in garter st for 1½", end with a WS row. Bind off. BACK LOWER EDGE Work as for front lower edge. NECKBAND With RS facing, using size 4 (6) circular needle and MC, pick up and k 116 sts around neck edge. Join and work around in k2, p2 rib for 6". Bind off in rib. Sew side and sleeve seams.

FOLIAGE

LEAVES Make 12 leaves combining 2 shades of same color for each leaf, beg with darker shade and changing to lighter shade when desired. With larger needles and darker shade, cast on 5 sts. **Row 1 (RS):** K 2, yo, k 1, yo, k 2 — 7 sts. **Rows 2, 4, 6, 10, 12, 16 and 18:** Purl. **Row 3:** K 3, yo, k 1, yo, k 3 — 9 sts. **Row 5:** K 4, yo, k 1, yo, k 4 — 11 sts. **Row 7:** Bind off 3 sts, k 1, yo, k 1, yo, k 5 — 10 sts. **Row 8:** Bind off 3 sts, p 6 — 7 sts. **Row 9:** K 3, yo, k 1, yo, k 3 — 9 sts. **Row 11:** K 4, yo, k 1, yo, k 4 — 11 sts. **Row 13:** Bind off 3 sts, k 1, yo, k 1, yo, k 5 — 10 sts. **Row 14:** Bind off 3 sts, p 6 — 7 sts. **Row 15:** K2tog, k 3, k2tog — 5 sts. **Row 17:** K2tog, k 1, k2tog — 3 sts. **Row 19:** Sl 1, k2tog, psso. Fasten off last st. BERRIES (make 3 each of B and E; 6 of A): With size 4 (6)needles and B, cast on 1 st; k in front and back of this st until there are 5 sts. [K 1 row, p 1 row] twice. **Next row (RS):** K2tog, k 1, k2tog — 3 sts. **Next row:** Sl 1 purlwise, p2tog, psso; bind off rem st. Turn to purl side. Sew foliage to center diamond on front of pullover. With A, stem st vines around leaves and berries.

CENTER CABLE AND RIB PULLOVER

INTERMEDIATE

SIZES
To fit sizes Small (Medium, Large). Directions are for smaller size with larger sizes in parentheses. If there is only one figure it applies to all sizes. Shown on page 36 in size Medium.

FINISHED MEASUREMENTS
Bust at underarm: 41 (44, 48)"
Length from shoulder: 19 (21, 22)"
Sleeve width at upper arm: 13½ (14½, 15¼)"

MATERIALS
12 (13, 14) 1¾oz/50g balls (each approx 104 yd/94m) of Reynolds Paloma in #305 Burgundy
Sizes 5 and 7 needles *or size needed to obtain gauge*
Size 5 circular needle 16" long
Cable needle (cn)
Stitch markers
Stitch holder

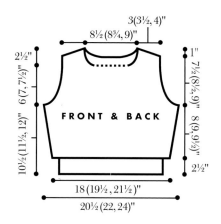

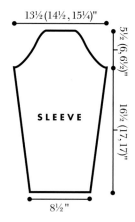

GAUGE
20 sts and 25 rows to 4" over rib pat using larger needles. *To save time and ensure accurate sizing, check gauge.*

CABLE PAT (over 34 sts)
Rows 1 and 3 (RS): K4, [p2, k2] 7 times, k2. **Row 2 and all WS rows:** K the knit sts and p the purl sts. **Row 5:** Sl 4 sts to cn and hold to *front,* (k 2, p 1), k 4 from cn, k1, [p2, k2] 4 times, p2, k1, sl 3 sts to cn and hold to *back,* k 4, (p 1, k 2) from cn. **Row 7:** Rep row 2. **Row 9:** K2, p1, sl 4 sts to cn and hold to *front,* (p1, k 2), k 4 from cn, [k2, p2] 3 times, k2, sl 3 sts to cn and hold to *back,* k 4, (k2, p 1) from cn, p1, k2. **Row 11:** Rep row 2. **Row 13:** K2, p2, k2, sl 4 sts to cn and hold to *front,* (p2, k 1), k 4 from cn, p1, k2, p2, k2, p1, sl 3 sts to cn and hold to *back,* k 4, (k 1, p 2) from cn, k2, p2, k2. **Row 15:** Rep row 2. **Row 17:** [K2, p2] twice, k1, sl 4 sts to cn and hold to *front,* (k 1, p 2), k 4 from cn, p2, sl 3 sts to cn and hold to *back,* k 4, (p 2, k 1) from cn, k1, [p2, k2] twice. **Rows 19 and 21:** Rep row 2. **Row 23:** M1-k (insert LH needle into horizontal strand between last st worked and next st on LH needle, k through back lp of this strand), [k2, p2] twice, k1, SKP (sl 1, k1, psso), p1, k4, p2, k4, p1, k2tog, k1, [p2, k2] twice, M1-k. **Row 25:** K1, M1-k, [k2, p2] twice, k1, SKP, k4, p2, k4, k2tog, k1, [p2, k2] twice, M1-k, k1. **Row 27:** K2, M1-k, [k2, p2] twice, k1, SKP, k3, p2, k3, k2tog, k1, [p2, k2] twice, M1-k, k2. **Row 29:** K3, M1-k, [k2, p2] twice, k1, SKP, k2, p2, k2, k2tog, k1, [p2, k2] twice, M1-k, k3. **Row 31:** K4, M1-p (work as for M1-k, but p through back lp of strand), [k2, p2] twice, k1, SKP, k1, p2, k1, k2tog, k1, [p2, k2] twice, M1-p, k4. **Row 33:** K4, p1, M1-p, [k2, p2] twice, k1, SKP, p2, k2tog, k1, [p2, k2] twice, M1-p, p1, k4. **Row 34:** Rep row 2. Rep rows 1-34 for cable pat.

RIB PAT (multiple of 10 sts)
Row 1 (RS): *K4, p2, k2, p2; rep from * to end. **Row 2** K the knit sts and p the purl sts. Rep row 2 for rib pat.

BACK
With smaller needles, cast on 98 (106, 114) sts. **Beg k2, p2 rib: Row 1 (RS):** *K 2, p 2; rep from *, end k 2. **Row 2:** K the knit sts and p the purl sts. Rep rows 1 and 2 for k2, p2 rib for 2½", end with a RS row. Change to larger needles. Purl one row. **Beg rib and cable pats: Row 1 (RS):** K2 (4, 0), p0 (2, 0), [k4, p2, k2, p2] 3 (3, 4) times, work 34 sts cable pat, [p2, k2,

p2, k4] 3 (3, 4) times, p0 (2, 0), k2 (4, 0). Cont in pat as established, working sts either side of cable in rib pat as est, and inc 1 st each side (keeping first and last 2 sts in St st and working inc sts inside of these 2 sts and into rib pat) every 8th row 6 times — 110 (118, 126) sts. Work even until piece measures 10½ (11½, 12)" from beg. ARMHOLE SHAPING Bind off 4 sts at beg of next 2 rows, 3 sts at beg of next 2 rows, 2 sts at beg of next 8 rows, 1 st at beg of next 6 rows — 74 (82, 90) sts. Work even until armholes measure 7½ (8½, 9)", end with a RS row. SHOULDER AND NECK SHAPING Bind off 6 (7, 8) sts at beg of next 2 rows, 5 (6, 7) sts at beg of next 4 rows, AT SAME TIME, bind off center 22 (24, 26) sts for neck and working both sides at once, bind off from each neck edge 5 sts twice.

FRONT
Work same as back until armholes measure 6 (7, 7½)", end with a WS row. NECK AND SHOULDER SHAPING **Next row (RS):** Work 20 (24, 28) sts, join 2nd ball of yarn and work center 34 sts placing them on a holder, work to end. Working both sides at once, work one row even. **Next row (RS):** Work to last 4 sts of left front, k2tog, p 2; on right front, p 2, SSK, work to end. Cont in this way to dec 1 st at each neck edge every other row 3 (4, 5) times more — 16 (19, 22) sts each side. Work until same length as back to shoulders. Work shoulder shaping as on back.

SLEEVES
With smaller needles, cast on 42 sts. Work rib pat as foll: [K2, p2, k4, p2] 4 times, k2. Cont in rib as est for 2". Change to larger needles. Cont in rib pat, inc 1 st each side as for back every 6th row 13 (15, 17) times — 68 (72, 76) sts. Work even until piece measures 16½ (17, 17)" from beg, end with a WS row. CAP SHAPING Bind off 4 sts at beg of next 2 rows, 3 sts at beg of next 2 rows, 2 sts at beg of next 2 rows. Dec 1 st each side every other row twice, every 4th row 4 (5, 6) times, every other row twice. Bind off 2 sts at beg of next 2 rows, 3 sts at beg of next 2 rows. Bind off rem 24 (26, 28) sts.

FINISHING
Block pieces to measurements. Sew shoulder seams. NECKBAND With RS facing and circular needle, beg at center back neck, pick up and k31 (33, 35) sts, place marker, work cable pat across 34 sts from front holder, place marker, pick up and k31 (33, 35) sts to center back neck — 96 (100, 104) sts. Join. **Next rnd:** K1 (0, 1), p2 (1, 2), [k2, p2] 7 (8, 8) times, sl marker, cont cable pat across 34 sts of front, sl marker, [p 2, k 2] 7 (8, 8) times, p 2 (1, 2), k1 (0, 1). Cont to work center front 34 sts in cable pat and rem sts in k2, p2 rib as est, until neckband measures 3½". Bind off in pat. Set in sleeves. Sew side and sleeve seams.

MOREHOUSE FAMILY CARDIGAN & PULLOVER

EASY

SIZES
To fit child's (8, 10, 12); woman's or man's [Small, Medium, Large, X-Large]. Directions for child's sizes are in parentheses ( )'s; woman's or man's sizes are in [ ]'s. If there is only one figure given it applies to all sizes. Shown on page 41 in child's sizes 8 and 10 and adult size X-Large.

FINISHED MEASUREMENTS
Chest/bust at underarm: (29½, 31, 34)"; [41, 45½, 50, 52½]"
Length from shoulder: (18, 19½, 21)"; [25, 26, 26½, 27]"
Sleeve width at upper arm: (14, 15, 16)"; [17½, 18, 19, 20]"

MATERIALS
A total of (12); [15] approx 2oz/60g skeins (each approx 145yd/130m) of 3-strand Morehouse Merino as foll: (4); [5] skeins of three different shades; Main color, or A, should be middle shade, B should be close to main color, C should be either darkest or lightest color of the three). This yarn is available in five natural shades: Soft White, Oatmeal, Silver, Charcoal (brownish gray), and Chocolate. (Silver - A, Soft White - B, Chocolate - C); [Silver - A, Oatmeal - B, Charcoal - C].
One pair each size 5 and 7 needles *or size needed to obtain gauge*
Size 5 circular needle 16" long
(7); [9] buttons for cardigan

GAUGE
22 sts and 32 rows to 4" over pat st using larger needles. *To save time and ensure accurate sizing, check gauge.*

PATTERN STITCH (multiple of 4 sts plus 3)
Row 1 (RS): With B, k1 (edge st), k1, *sl 1 wyib, k1; rep from * to last st, k1 (edge st).
Row 2: With B, k1 (edge st), p to last st, k1 (egde st).
Row 3: With C, k1 (edge st), *k3, sl 1 wyib; rep from * to last 2 sts, k 1, k1 (edge st).
Row 4: With C, k1 (edge st), p1, *sl 1 wyif, p1; rep from * to last st, k1 (edge st).
Row 5: With A, k1 (edge st), k 1, *sl 1 wyib, k3; rep from * to last st, k1 (edge st).
Row 6: With A, k1 (edge st), p to last st, k1 (edge st).
Rep Rows 1-6 for pat st.

CARDIGAN

BACK
With smaller needles and A, cast on (71, 75, 81); [97, 111, 121, 127] sts. Work k 1, p 1 rib for (1½)"; [2¼]". **Next row (WS):** K1 (edge st), p across, inc (12, 12, 14); [18, 16, 18, 20] sts evenly spaced, k1 (edge st) —(83, 87, 95); [115, 127, 139, 147] sts. Change to larger needles. Work in pat st until piece measures (18, 19½, 21)"; [24, 25, 25½, 26]" from beg. NECK SHAPING **Next row:** Keeping to pat, work (23, 25, 29); [46, 51, 56, 59] sts, join 2nd ball of yarn, bind off center (37); [23, 25, 27, 29] sts, work to end. Working both sides at once, bind off from each neck edge (0); [6] sts twice. Cont, if necessary, until piece measures (18, 19½, 21)"; [25, 26, 26½, 27]" from beg. Bind off rem (23, 25, 29); [34, 39, 44, 47] sts each side for shoulders.

LEFT FRONT
With smaller needles and A, cast on (31, 35, 39); [45, 53, 57, 61] sts. Work k 1, p 1 rib as for back. **Next row (WS):** K1, p across, inc (8); [10] sts evenly spaced, k1 — (39, 43, 47); [55, 63, 67, 71] sts. Change to larger needles. Work in pat st until piece measures (16, 17½, 19)"; [22, 23,

23½, 24]" from beg, end with a RS row. NECK SHAPING Keeping to pat, bind off from neck edge (5 sts once, 3 sts twice, 2 sts twice, 1 st (1, 3, 3) times) — (23, 25, 29) sts; [6 sts once, 4 sts twice, 3 sts (1, 2, 2, 2) times, 2 sts once, 1 st (2, 2, 1, 2) times] — [34, 39, 44, 47] sts. Work even until same length as back. Bind off rem sts for shoulder.

RIGHT FRONT
Work to correspond to left front, reversing neck shaping.

SLEEVES
With smaller needles and A, cast on (38); [46, 46, 50, 50] sts. Work k 1, p 1 rib for (2½)"; [3½]". P next row on WS, inc (19); [23, 23, 25, 25] sts evenly across — (57); [69, 69, 75, 75] sts. Change to larger needles. Work in pat st, inc 1 st each side (working inc sts into pat) every (6th) row (11, 13, 17) times — (79, 83, 91) sts; every [8th, 6th, 8th, 6th] row [15, 17, 16, 19] times — [99, 103, 107, 113] sts. Work even until piece measures (13, 14½, 16)"; [19, 19½, 19½, 20]" for woman's or [21, 21½, 21½, 22]" for man's from beg. Bind off.

FINISHING
Block pieces to measurements. Sew shoulder seams. NECKBAND With RS facing, smaller needles and A, pick up and k (79); [95, 99, 101, 109] sts evenly around neck edge. Work k 1, p 1 rib for (6); [8] rows. Bind off in rib. LEFT FRONT BAND (for girls or women); RIGHT FRONT BAND (for boys or men): With RS facing, smaller needles and A, pick up and k (91, 99, 109); [125, 131, 133, 137] sts along front edge, including side of neckband. Work k 1, p 1 rib for (6); [8] rows. Bind off in rib. Place markers on band for (7); [9] buttons, the first one ½" from lower edge, the last ½" from neck edge and the others evenly spaced between. RIGHT FRONT BAND (for girls or women); LEFT FRONT BAND (for boys or men): Work to correspond to button band, working buttonholes opposite markers on (3rd); [4th] row as foll: **Buttonhole row:** *Rib to marker, bind off 3 sts, rep from * across all markers, rib to end. On next row, rib casting on 3 sts over each set of bound-off sts. Rib (2); [4] more rows. Bind off in rib. Place markers (7, 7½, 8)"; [8¾, 9, 9½, 10]" down from shoulders on front and back for armholes. Sew top of sleeve between markers. Sew side and sleeve seams. Sew on buttons.

PULLOVER

BACK
Work as for Cardigan back.

FRONT
Work same as Cardigan back until piece measures (16, 17½, 19)"; [22, 23, 23½, 24]" from beg, end with a RS row. NECK SHAPING **Next row:** Keeping to pat, work (39, 41, 44); [55, 60, 66, 69] sts, join 2nd ball of yarn, bind off center (5, 5, 7); [5, 7, 7, 9] sts, work to end. Working both sides at once, bind off from each neck edge (4 sts once, 3 sts twice, 2 sts (2, 2, 1) times, 1 st (2, 2, 3) times); [4 sts once, 3 sts 3 times, 2 sts 3 times, 1 st (2, 2, 3, 3) times]. Work until same length as back. Bind off rem (23, 25, 29); [34, 39, 44, 47] sts each side for shoulders.

SLEEVES
Work as for Cardigan sleeves.

FINISHING
Block pieces to measurements. Sew shoulder seams. NECKBAND With RS facing, circular needle and A, pick up and k (84); [102, 104, 110, 116] sts evenly around neck edge. Join and work in k 1, p 1 rib for 7 rnds. Bind off in rib. Place markers (7, 7½, 8)"; [8¾, 9, 9½, 10]" down from shoulders on front and back for armholes. Sew top of sleeve between markers. Sew side and sleeve seams.

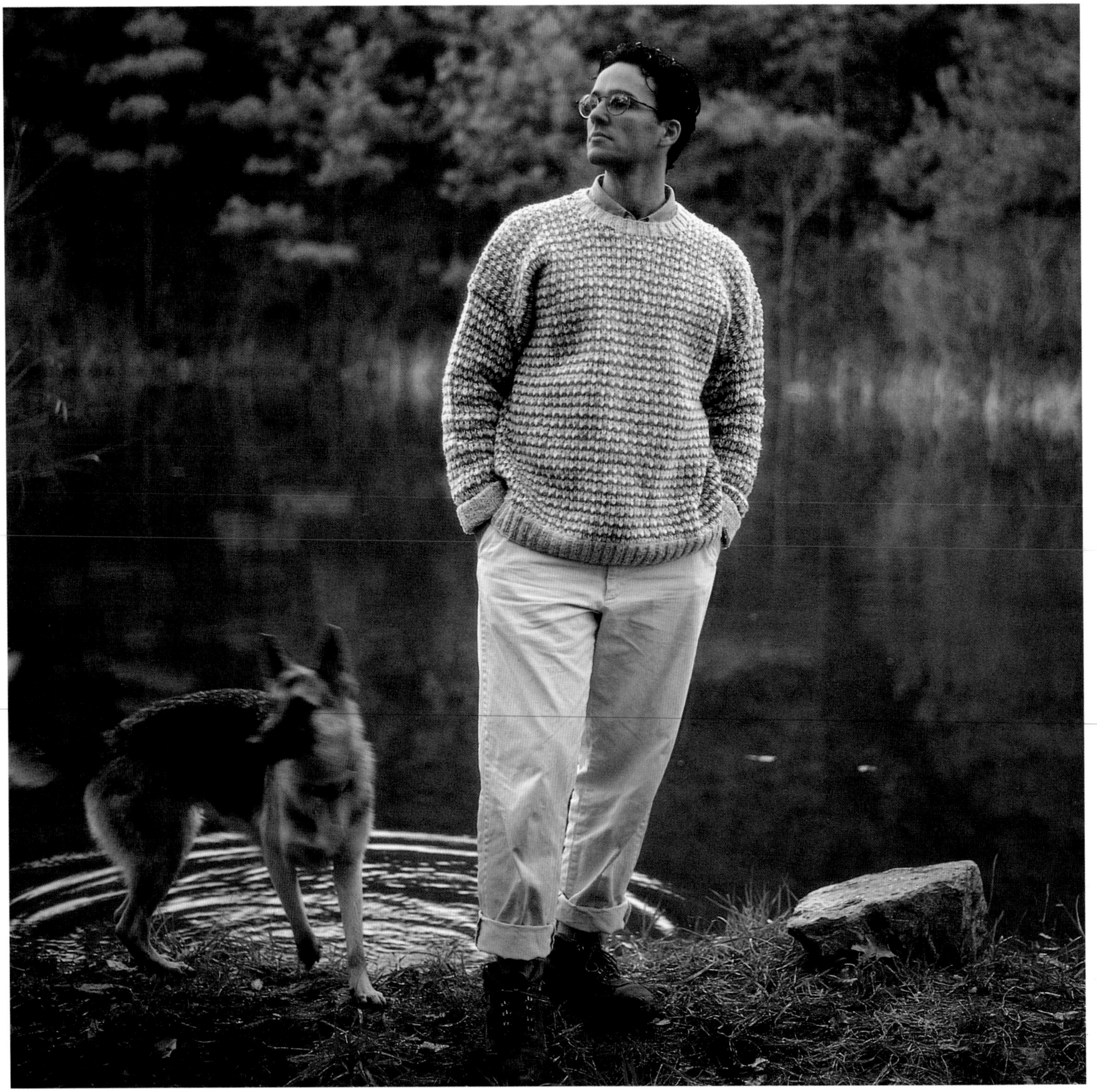

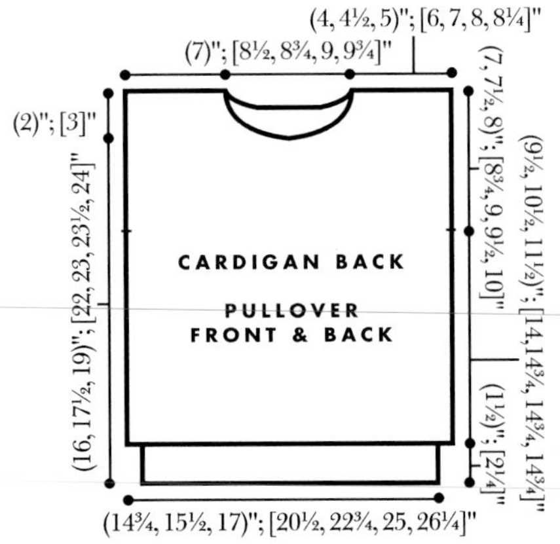
(4, 4½, 5)"; [6, 7, 8, 8¼]"
(7)"; [8½, 8¾, 9, 9¾]"
(2)"; [3]"
(7, 7½, 8)"; [8¾, 9, 9½, 10]"
(9½, 10½, 11½)"; [14, 14¾, 14¾, 14¾]"
(16, 17½, 19)"; [22, 23, 23½, 24]"
CARDIGAN BACK
PULLOVER FRONT & BACK
(1½)"; [2¼]"
(14¾, 15½, 17)"; [20½, 22¾, 25, 26¼]"

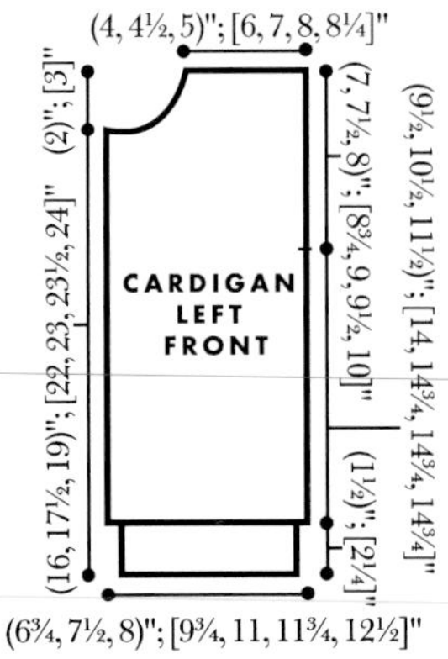
(4, 4½, 5)"; [6, 7, 8, 8¼]"
(2)"; [3]"
(7, 7½, 8)"; [8¾, 9, 9½, 10]"
(9½, 10½, 11½)"; [14, 14¾, 14¾, 14¾]"
(16, 17½, 19)"; [22, 23, 23½, 24]"
CARDIGAN LEFT FRONT
(1½)"; [2¼]"
(6¾, 7½, 8)"; [9¾, 11, 11¾, 12½]"

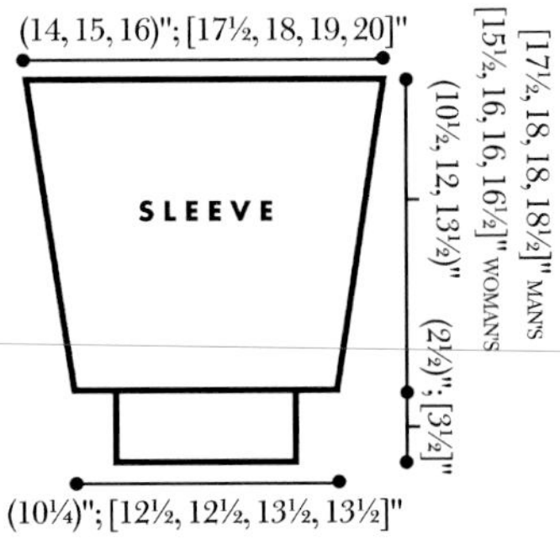
(14, 15, 16)"; [17½, 18, 19, 20]"
[17½, 18, 18, 18½]" MAN'S
[15½, 16, 16, 16½]" WOMAN'S
(10½, 12, 13½)"
SLEEVE
(2½)"; [3½]"
(10¼)"; [12½, 12½, 13½, 13½]"

MOTHER-DAUGHTER HARVEST FRUIT PULLOVER

EXPERIENCED

SIZES

To fit girl's (10, 12); woman's [Small, Medium, Large]. Directions for girl's sizes are in parentheses ( )'s; woman's sizes are in brackets [ ]'s. If there is only one figure it applies to all sizes. Shown on pages 43 and 47 in girl's size 10 and woman's size Medium.

FINISHED MEASUREMENTS

Chest/bust at underarm: (40, 43)"; [47, 50, 53]"
Length from shoulder: (22, 24)"; [28, 28½, 29]"
Sleeve width at upper arm: (16, 17)"; [19, 19½, 20]"

MATERIALS

(10, 11); [15, 15, 16] 1¾oz/50g skeins (each approx 126yd/115m) of Rowan Yarns DK Tweed in (#850 Wren (MC); [#853 Hare (MC)]
1 ¾oz/25g skein (each approx 70yd/64m) of Kid/Silk each in #994 Goat Brown (A), #989 Old Gold (B)
1 1¾oz/50g skein (each approx 75yd/68m) of Fine Cotton Chenille each in #388 Lacquer (C), #386 Plum (D), #399 Ink (E), #394 Privet (F), #400 Oasis (G), #395 Willow (H)
1 1¾oz/50g skein (each approx 126yd/115m) of DK Tweed each in #657 (I)and #691 (J)
1 ¾oz/25g skein (each approx 110yd/100m) of Donegal Lambswool Tweed each in #480 Roseberry (K),#479 Cinnamon (L), #481 Leaf (M), #485 Bay (N)
One pair each sizes 4 and 5 needles *or size needed to obtain gauge*
Cable needle (cn)
Size 4 circular needle 16" long
2 buttons

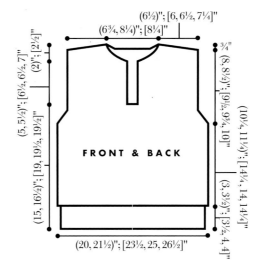

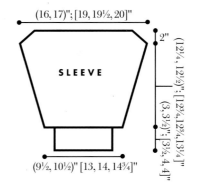

GAUGE

21 sts and 32 rows to 4" over basketweave pat using larger needles. *To save time and to ensure accurate sizing, check gauge.*

STITCH GLOSSARY

3-st Right Cable (RC): Sl 1 st to cn and hold to *back* of work, k2, k 1 from cn.
3-st Left Cable (LC): Sl 2 sts to cn and hold to *front* of work, k1, k2 from cn.
3-st Right Purl Cable (RPC): Sl 1 st to cn and hold to *back* of work, k2, p1 from cn.
3-st Left Purl Cable (LPC): Sl 2 sts to cn and hold to *front* of work, p1, k2 from cn.
4-st Right Cable (RC): Sl 2 sts to cn and hold to *back* of work, k2, k2 from cn.
4-st Left Cable (LC): Sl 2 sts to cn and hold to *front* of work, k2, k2 from cn.

CABLE #1 (over 12 sts)
Row 1 (RS): P2, k8, p2. **Row 2 and all WS rows:** K the knit sts and p the purl sts. **Row 3:** P2, 4-st RC, k4, p2. **Row 5:** Rep row 1. **Row 7:** Rep row 3. **Row 9:** P2, k4, 4-st LC, p2. **Row 11:** Rep row 1. **Row 13:** Rep row 9. Rep rows 2-13 for cable #1.

CABLE #2 (over 12 sts)
Row 1 (RS): P4, 4-st RC, p4. **Row 2 and all WS rows:** K the knit sts and p the purl sts. **Row 3:** P3, 3-st RC, 3-st LC, p3. **Row 5:** P2, 3-st RC, k2, 3-st LC, p2. **Row 7:** P1, 3-st RC, k4, 3-st LC, p1. **Row 8:** Rep row 2. Rep rows 1-8 for cable #2.

CABLE #3 (over 13 sts)
Row 1 (RS): P2, k2, p2, k4, p3. **Row 2 and all WS rows:** K the knit sts and p the purl sts. **Row 3:** P2, 3-st LPC, 3-st RPC, 3-st LPC, p2. **Row

5:** P3, 4-st RC, p2, k2, p2. **Row 7:** P2, 3-st RPC, 3-st LPC, 3-st RPC, p2. **Row 9:** P2, k2, p2, 4-st LC, p3. Rep rows 2-9 for cable #3.

CABLE #4 (over 12 sts)
Row 1 (RS): P2, k8, p2. **Row 2 and all WS rows:** K the knit sts and p the purl sts. **Row 3:** P2, 4-st RC, 4-stLC, p2. **Row 5:** Rep row 1. **Row 7:** P2, 4-st LC, 4-st RC, p2. **Row 9:** Rep row 1. **Row 11:** Rep row 7. **Row 13:** Rep row 1. **Row 15:** Rep row 3. **Row 16:** Rep row 2. Rep rows 1-16 for cable #4.

CABLE #5 (over 12 sts)
Row 1 (RS): P2, k8, p2. **Row 2 and all WS rows:** K the knit sts and p the purl sts. **Row 3:** P2, k4, 4-st RC, p2. **Row 5:** P2, k2, 4-st RC, k2, p2. **Row 7:** P2, 4-st RC, k4, p2. Rep rows 2-7 for cable #5.

BACK

With smaller needles and color K, cast on (111, 119); [135, 143, 151] sts. **Next row (RS):** Purl. Change to MC and purl 1 row. **Next row (RS):** K 1 (salvage st), work (0); [12] sts cable #1, work(18, 20); [18, 20, 22] sts in k2, p2 rib as foll: k2, p (2, 1); [2, 1, 2], *k2, p2; rep from * to last (6,5); [6, 5, 6] sts, k2, p (2, 1); [2, 1, 2], k2, 12 sts cable #2, (18, 20); [18, 20, 22] sts k2, p2 rib as before, 13 sts cable #3, (18, 20); [18, 20, 22] sts k2, p2 rib as before, 12 sts cable #4, (18, 20); [18, 20, 22] sts k2, p2 rib as before, (0); [12] sts cable #5, k 1 (salvage st). Cont in pats as established until piece measures (3, 3½)"; [3½, 4, 4]" from beg, end with a WS row and inc 1 st in center of each of the 4 rib panels on last row — (115, 123); [139, 147, 155] sts. Change to larger needles. Using the photos and suggestions that follow as a guide, or placing fruit motifs as desired: **Next row (RS)** Work (0); [12] sts cable #1, (19, 21); [19, 21, 23] sts chart #1, 12 sts cable #2, (19, 21); [19, 21, 23] sts chart #2, 13 sts cable #3, (19, 21); [19, 21, 23] sts chart #1, 12 sts cable #4, (19, 21); [19, 21, 23] sts

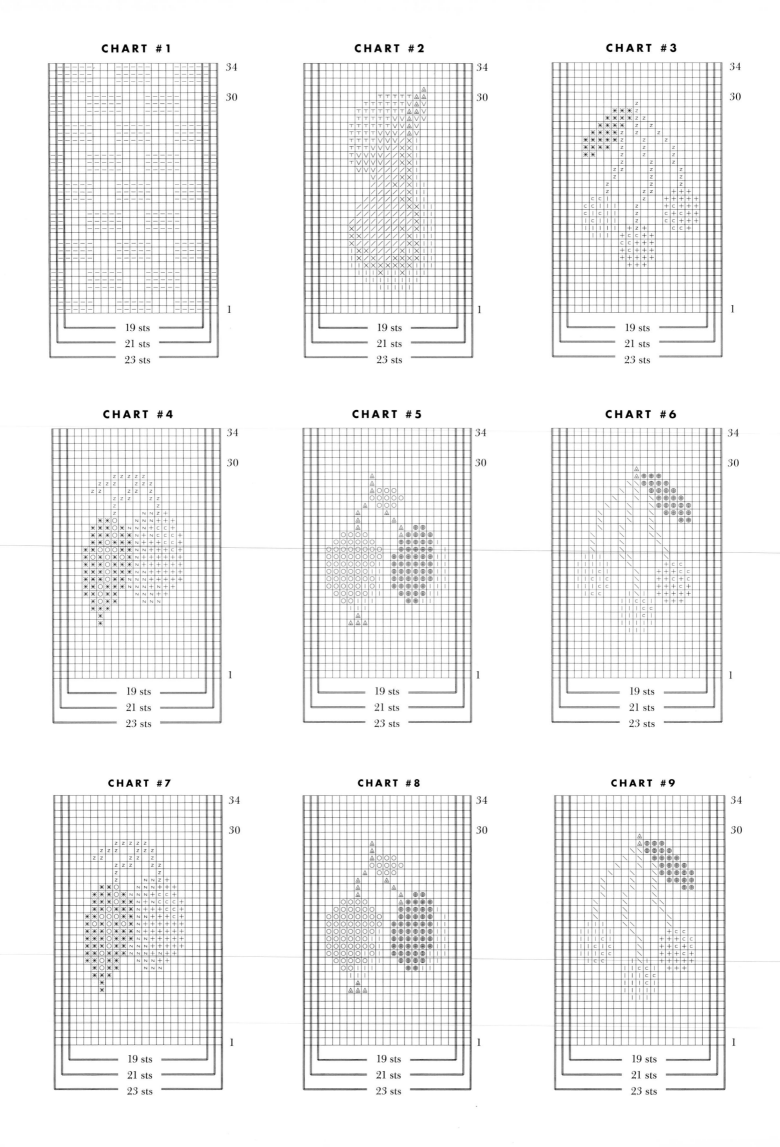

chart #3, (0); [12] sts cable #5. Cont in pats as established, working (19, 21); [19, 21, 23] sts and (30, 34); [30, 34, 34] rows for each chart, alternating as desired, AT THE SAME TIME, when woman's pullover **only** measures [17¾, 18, 18¼]" from beg, ARMHOLE SHAPING Keeping to pat, bind off 4 sts at beg of next 6 rows. Cont all sizes of girl's and woman's pullover on (115, 123); [115, 123, 131] sts until piece measures (21¼, 23¼)"; [27¼, 27¾, 28¼]" from beg. SHOULDER AND NECK SHAPING Bind off (13); [11, 12, 14] sts at beg of next 4 rows, (12); [12, 14, 14] at beg of next 2 rows, AT THE SAME TIME, after 2 rows have been worked, bind off center (27, 35); [35] sts. Working both sides at once, bind off from each neck edge 6 sts once.

FRONT
Work as for back until piece measures (15, 16½)"; [19, 19½, 19½]" from beg. PLACKET SHAPING **Next row:** Work (52, 56); [52, 56, 60] sts, join 2nd ball of yarn and bind off center 11 sts, work to end. Work both sides at once until placket measures (5, 5½)"; [6½, 6½, 7]". NECK SHAPING Bind off from each neck edge (4, 5); [5] sts once, (3); [3] sts once, (2); [2] sts (3, 5); [5] times, (1,0); [0] st once — (38); [34, 38, 42] sts at each side. Work until same length as back to shoulders. Shape shoulders as for back.

SLEEVES
With smaller needles and L, cast on (41, 45); [51, 55, 59] sts. **Next row (RS):** Purl 1 row. Change to MC and purl 1 row. **Next row (RS):** Work (13, 15); [18, 20, 22] sts as foll: k 1 (selvage st), p (0, 1); [0, 1, 0], k (1, 2); [1, 2, 1], p (1, 2); [2], *k2, p2; rep from * to last 2 sts, k2, 13 sts of cable #3, beg with k2, work (13, 15); [18, 20, 22] sts in k2, p2 rib, k 1 (selvage st). Cont in established rib pat until piece measures (3, 3½)"; [3½, 4, 4]" from beg, inc (6, 7); [11] sts evenly spaced across each rib panel — (53, 59); [73, 77, 81]sts. Change to larger needles. Work pats as for back, working charts as in photo or as desired either side of cable, AT THE SAME TIME, inc 1 st each side every 4th row (21, 20); [7, 4, 0] times, every 6th row (0, 0); [11, 13, 16] times (working added sts into established pat when there are enough sts to complete a fruit chart or cable) — (95, 99); [109, 111, 113] sts. Work until sleeve measures (15¼, 16)";

[16¼, 16¾, 17¼]" from beg. For girl's pullover: Bind off all sts. For woman's pullover: Bind off 8 sts at beg of next 2 rows, 5 sts at beg of next 8 rows, 8 sts at beg of next 2 rows. Bind off rem [37, 39, 41] sts.

FINISHING
Block pieces to measurements. LEFT FRONT PLACKET With RS facing, smaller needles and MC, pick up and k (29, 33); [39, 39, 43] sts along left front placket edge. **Next row (WS):** P (2); [3], * k 2, p 2, rep from * across, end p (1); [2]. Work in established rib for (9); [11] more rows, slipping the first st of each row, end with a WS row. Change to N and knit 1 row. **Next row:** Bind off knitwise with N. Mark position of 2 buttons on left front ribbing: first one (1)"; [1]" below neck edge; second one (2)"; [3]" from bottom edge. RIGHT FRONT PLACKET With RS facing, using smaller needle and MC, pick up and k (29, 33); [39, 39, 43] sts along right front placket edge. **Next row:** P (1); [2], * k 2, p 2; rep from * across, end p (2); [3]. Work in established rib for 3 rows. **Next row:** *Rib to marker, bind off 2 sts; rep from * once, rib to end. **Next row:** Work rib, casting on 2 sts over each set of bound-off sts. Rib for (3); [5] more rows. Change to N and knit 1 row. Bind off knitwise with N. Sew shoulder seams. COLLAR With RS facing, smaller needles and MC, pick up and k 2 sts from left front placket edge, (20, 23); [24] sts from left front, (38, 44); [46] sts from back neck, (20, 23); [24] sts from right front, 2 sts from right front placket edge — (82, 94); [98] sts. Cont in k 2, p 2 rib for (4, 4½)"; [4¾]" slipping the first st of every row, end with a RS row. Change to color K and knit 1 row on WS. Bind off knitwise with color K. Sew bottom edge of front plackets to pullover. Sew in sleeves. Sew side and sleeve seams. Sew on buttons.

☐ =St st with MC

⊟ =rev St st with MC

Foll colors in St st

z =A	+ =D	T =G	◣ =J	◉ =M
⟋ =B	N =E	O =H	c =K	V =N
I =C	✳ =F	◭ =I	✕ =L	

SELMA MIRIAM
KOUSA DOGWOOD SHAWL
EXPERIENCED

STITCH GLOSSARY
SSK: Sl 2 sts knitwise, one at a time, to RH needle; insert LH needle into fronts of these 2 sts and k them tog.
SK2P: Sl 1 st, k2tog, psso.
M1: Insert LH needle from front to back under strand between last st worked and next st on needle; k this strand tbl.
Yarn over (yo): Wyif, k next st.

BEETON'S FLOWER (make 3 squares):
Cast on 8 sts. Distribute sts evenly on 4 needles. Join, place marker, and work in rnds as foll: (**Note:** Rep all rnds 4 times, once on each needle.) **Rnd 1 and all odd-numbered rnds:** Knit. **Rnd 2:** K1, yo, k1. **Rnd 4:** [K1, yo] twice, k1. **Rnd 6:** K1, yo, k3, yo, k1. **Rnd 8:** K1, yo, k5, yo, k1. **Rnd 10:** K1, yo, k7, yo, k1. **Rnd 12:** K1, yo, k9, yo, k1. **Rnd 14:** K1, yo, k11, yo, k1. **Rnd 16:** K1, yo, k13, yo, k1. **Rnd 18:** K1, yo, k15, yo, k1. **Rnd 20:** [K1, yo] twice, k5, SSK, k1, k2tog, k5, [yo, k1] twice. **Rnd 22:** [K1, yo] twice, SSK, yo, k4, SSK, k1, k2tog, k4, yo, k2tog, [yo, k1] twice. **Rnd 24:**[K1, yo] twice, [SSK, yo] twice, k3, SSK, k1, k2tog, k3, [yo, k2tog] twice, [yo, k1] twice. **Rnd 26:** [K1, yo] twice, [SSK, yo] 3 times, k2, SSK, k1, k2tog, k2, [yo, k2tog] 3 times, [yo, k1] twice. **Rnd 28:** [K1, yo] twice, [SSK, yo] 4 times, k1, SSK, k1, k2tog, k1, [yo, k2tog] 4 times, [yo, k1] twice. **Rnd 30:** [K1, yo] twice, [SSK, yo] 5 times, SSK, k1, k2tog, [yo, k2tog] 5 times, [yo, k1] twice. **Rnd 32:** [K1, yo] twice, [SSK, yo] 6 times, SK2P, [yo, k2tog] 6 times, [yo, k1] twice. **Rnd 34:** [K1, yo] twice, [SSK, yo] 6 times, SSK, k1, k2tog, [yo, k2tog] 6 times, [yo, k1] twice. **Rnd 36:** [K1, yo] twice, [SSK, yo] 7 times, SK2P, [yo, k2tog] 7 times, [yo, k1] twice. **Rnd 38:** [K1, yo] twice, [SSK, yo] 7 times, SSK, k1, k2tog, [yo, k2tog] 7 times, [yo, k1] twice. **Rnd 40:** [K1, yo] twice, [SSK, yo] 8 times, SK2P, [yo, k2tog] 8 times, [yo, k1] twice. **Rnd 41:** Knit. Place 41 sts each side of square on CC

yarn to hold. When all 3 squares have been completed, graft sts of one square to sts of another square. Then graft sts of 3rd square to sts on top of one of the 2 squares already grafted tog (forming a V with the 3 squares). Center square, now diamond-shaped, is the back, while the other 2 squares form the right and left shoulders.

LEFT FRONT

Pick up and work 41 sts of left shoulder as foll: **Row 1 (WS)** Knit. **Row 2:** Purl. **Row 3:** K2tog, k to end. **Row 4:** Knit. **Row 5:** Purl. **Row 6:** K1, *yo, k2tog; rep from * to last st, k1. **Row 7:** P2tog, p to end. **Rows 8 and 9:** Knit. **Row 10:** Purl. **Row 11:** K2tog, k to end—38 sts. **Row 12:** K2, *yo, SK2P, yo, k1; rep from * 8 times more. **Rows 13, 19, 23, 25, 35, 39, 41, 43, 45, 47, 49, 51, 53, 57, 59, 61, 63, 67 and 69:** P2tog, p to end. **Row 14:** SSK, yo, *k1, yo, SK2P, yo; rep from * to last 3 sts, end k1, yo, k2tog. **Rows 15, 17, 21, 27, 29, 31, 33, 37 and 55:** Purl. **Row 16:** K1, SSK, yo, *k1, yo, SK2P, yo; rep from * to last 2 sts, end k2tog. **Row 18:** K2, SSK, yo, *k1, yo, SK2P, yo; rep from * to last 4 sts, end k1, yo, k3tog. **Row 20:** K2, *yo, SK2P, yo, k1; rep from * to end. **Row 22:** SSK, yo, *k1, yo, SK2P, yo; rep from * to last 4 sts, end k1, yo, k3tog—34 sts. **Row 24:** K1, SSK, yo *k1, yo, SK2P, yo; rep from * to last st, end k1. **Row 26:** *K1, yo, SK2P, yo; rep from * to last 3 sts, end k1, yo, k2tog. **Row 28:** K1, k2tog, yo, *k1, yo, k3tog, yo; rep from * to last 4 sts, end k1, yo, k3tog. **Row 30:** K2tog, yo, *k1, yo, k3tog, yo; rep from * to last 4 sts, end k1, yo, k3tog. **Row 32:** K1, *k1, yo, k3tog, yo; rep from * to last 4 sts, end k1, yo, k2tog, k1. **Row 34:** *K1, yo, k3tog, yo; rep from * to last 4 sts, end k1, yo, k2tog, k1. **Row 36:** K1, k2tog, yo, *k1, yo, k3tog, yo; rep from * to last 4 sts, end k1, yo, k2tog, k1. **Row 38:** K2tog, yo, *k1, yo, k3tog, yo; rep from * to last st, end k1. **Row 40:** K1, *k1, yo, k3tog, yo; rep from * to last st, end k1. **Row 42:** *K1, yo, k3tog, yo; rep from * to last st, end k1. **Row 44:** K1, k2tog, yo, *k1, yo, k3tog, yo; rep from * to last st, end k1. **Row 46:** K2tog, yo, *k1, yo, k3tog, yo; rep from * to last st, end k1—23 sts. **Row 48:** K1, *k1, yo, k3tog, yo; rep from * to last st, end k1. **Row 50:** K1, k2tog, yo, *k1, yo, k3tog, yo; rep from * to last 4 sts, end k1, yo, k3tog—20 sts. **Row 52:** K1, *k1, yo, k3tog, yo; rep from * to last 2 sts, end k2. **Row 54:** K1, k2tog, yo, *k1, yo, k3tog, yo; rep from * to last 3 sts, end k1, k2tog. **Row 56:** K1, *k1, yo, k3tog, yo; rep from * to last 3 sts, end k1, k2tog—15 sts. **Row 58:** K1, k2tog, yo, [k1, yo, k3tog, yo] twice, k1, yo, k3tog—14 sts. **Row 60:** K1, [k1, yo, k3tog, yo] twice, k1, yo, k3tog—12 sts. **Row 62:** K1, k2tog, yo, k1, yo, k3tog, yo, k1, yo, k3tog. **Row 64:** K2, yo, k3tog, yo, k1, yo, k3tog. **Row 65:** P2tog, p to end—7 sts. **Row 66:** K1, k2tog, yo, k1, yo, k3tog. **Row 68:** K1, yo, k3tog, k1. **Row 70:** K3tog. Pull yarn through. Fasten off.

RIGHT FRONT

Pick up and work 41 sts of right shoulder as foll: **Row 1 (WS):** Knit. **Row 2:** Purl. **Row 3:** k to last 2 sts, k2tog tbl. **Row 4:** Knit. **Row 5:** Purl. **Row 6:** K1, *k2tog, yo; rep from * to last st, k1. **Row 7:** P to last 2 sts, p2tog tbl. **Rows 8 and 9:** Knit. **Row 10:** Purl. **Row 11:** K to last 2 sts, k2tog tbl—38 sts. **Row 12:** K1, *yo, k3tog, yo, k1; rep from * 8 times more, end last rep k2, instead of k1. **Rows 13, 19, 23, 25, 35, 39, 41, 43, 45, 47, 49, 51, 53, 57, 59, 61, 63, 65, 67 and 69:** P to last 2 sts, p2tog tbl. **Row 14:** SSK, yo, *k1, yo, k3tog, yo; rep from * to last 3 sts, end k1, yo, k2tog. **Rows 15, 17, 21, 27, 29, 31, 33, 37 and 55:** Purl. **Row 16:** SSK, *yo, k3tog, yo, k1; rep from * to last 3 sts, end yo, k2tog, k1. **Row 18:** SK2P, yo, *k1, yo, k3tog, yo; rep from * to last 5 sts, end k1, yo, k2tog, k2. **Row 20:** *K1, yo, k3tog, yo; rep from * to last 2 sts, end k2. **Row 22:** SK2P, yo, *k1, yo, k3tog, yo; rep from * to last 3 sts, end k1, yo, k2tog—34 sts. **Row 24:** *K1, yo, k3tog, yo; rep from * to last 4 sts, end k1, yo, k2tog, k1. **Row 26:** SSK, yo, *k1, yo, k3tog, yo; rep from * to last st, end k1. **Row 28:** SK2P, yo, *k1, yo, SK2P, yo; rep from * to last 4 sts, end k1, yo, k2tog, k1. **Row 30:** SK2P, yo, *k1, yo, SK2P, yo; rep from * to last 3 sts, end k1, yo, k2tog. **Row 32:** SK2P, yo, *k1, yo, SK2P, yo; rep from * to last 2 sts, end k2. **Row 34:** K1, SSK, yo, *k1, yo, SK2P, yo; rep from * to last st, end k1. **Row 36:** K1, SSK, yo, *k1, yo, SK2P, yo; rep from * to last 4 sts, end k1, yo, SSK, k1. **Row 38:** *K1, yo, SK2P, yo; rep from * to last 3 sts, end k1, yo, SSK. **Row 40:** *K1, yo, SK2P, yo; rep from * to last 2 sts, end k2. **Row 42:** *K1, yo, SK2P, yo; rep from * to last st, end k1. **Row 44:** *K1, yo, SK2P, yo; rep from * to last 4 sts, end k1, yo, SSK, k1. **Row 46:** *K1, yo, SK2P, yo; rep from * to last 3 sts, end k1, yo, SSK—23 sts. **Row 48:** *K1, yo, SK2P, yo; rep from * to last 2 sts, end k2. **Row 50:** SSK, *yo, SK2P, yo, k1; rep from * to last 3 sts, end yo, SSK, k1. **Row 52:** K1, *k1, yo, SK2P, yo; rep from * to last 2 sts, end k2. **Row 54:** SSK, *k1, yo, SK2P, yo; rep from * to last 4 sts, end k1, yo, SSK, k1. **Row 56:** SK2P, yo, *k1, yo, SK2P, yo; rep from * to last 2 sts, end k2. **Row 58:** SK2P, yo, [k1, yo, SK2P, yo] twice, k1, yo, SSK, k1. **Row 60:** SK2P, yo, [k1, yo, SK2P, yo] twice, k2—12 sts. **Row 62:** [SK2P, yo, k1, yo] twice, SSK, k1. **Row 64:** SK2P, yo, k1, yo, SK2P, yo, k2. **Row 66:** SK2P, yo, k1, yo, SSK, k1. **Row 68:** K1, SK2P, yo, k1. **Row 70:** SK2P. Pull yarn through. Fasten off.

LOWER BORDER

With RS facing and circular needle, pick up 48 sts along curved edge of lower left front; sl 41 sts from contrasting color thread on to circular needle; pick up 2 sts where the squares join, then pick up 41 sts from one side of back square. Place marker for center back. Cont in same way around to right front—264 sts. EYELET BORDER Work back and forth on circular needle as foll: **Row 1 (WS):** K to 1 st before center marker, p2 center back sts, k to end. **Row 2:** Purl to 1 st before center back marker, yo, k2 sts of center back, yo, p to end. **Row 3:** Rep row 1. **Row 4:** Knit to 1 st before center back marker, yo, k2, yo, k to end. **Row 5:** Purl. **Row 6:** K1, *yo, k2tog; rep from * to 1 st before center marker, yo, k2, yo, *k2tog, yo; rep from * to last st, k1. **Row 7:** Purl. **Row 8:** K2, m1, k to center 2 sts, yo, k2, yo, k to last 2 sts, m1, k2. **Row 9:** Rep row 1. **Row 10:** P1, m1, p to center 2 sts, yo, k2, yo, p to last st, m1, p1. **Row 11:** Rep row 1. LACE RUFFLED EDGING With dpn, cast on 16 sts. **Foundation row:** K15, SSK (last st tog with 1st border st from circular needle), turn. **Row 1:** Sl 1, k9, [yo, k2tog] twice, yo, k2, turn. **Row 2:** K9, p5, turn. **Row 3:** K8, [yo, k2tog] twice, yo, k2, turn. **Row 4:** K10, p5, k2, SSK (last st with one from circular needle), turn. **Row 5:** Sl 1, k11, [yo, k2tog] twice, yo, k2, turn. **Row 6:** K11, p5, turn. **Row 7:** P5, k5, [yo, k2tog] twice, yo, k2, turn. **Row 8:** K19, SSK (last st with one from circular needle), turn. **Row 9:** Sl 1, k2, p5, k6, [yo, k2tog] twice, yo, k2, turn. **Row 10:** K18, turn. **Row 11:** P5, k13, turn. **Row 12:** Bind off 5 sts, k14, SSK (last st with one from circular needle). Rep around. I-CORD EDGING With 2 dpns, beg at lower right front edge, cast on 3 sts. Insert needle into an edge thread. K2, SSK (last st with picked-up edge st). Cont, always sliding sts to RH end of needle, do not turn work. Pull yarn firmly to make cord rounded. Pick up a few loops at a time with LH needle. When square with CC yarn is reached, use these sts to SSK. You will pick up approximately 42 sts before the 41 on the square, 2 at center back, 41 on other square, and about 42 on left front.

FINISHING

Wash shawl in mild soap. Rinse twice, adding a little vinegar to 2nd rinse water. Roll in towel and squeeze to remove excess moisture. Lay shawl flat on dry towel and pin to shape. Neck edges should be straight and side fronts should curve gently.

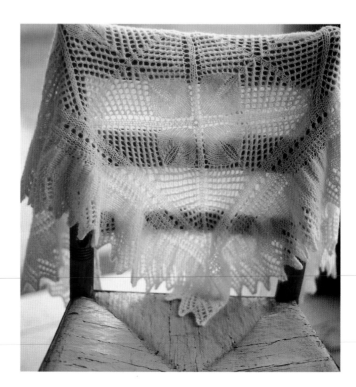

SIZES
To fit Woman's or Man's Small (Medium, Large). Directions are for smallest size with larger sizes in parentheses. If there is only one figure it applies to all sizes. Shown on page 52 in size Medium.

FINISHED MEASUREMENTS
Bust/chest at underarm: 46 (48, 50)"
Length from shoulder: 28½ (28¾, 30¼)" for woman's; 26½ (26¾, 27¼)" for man's
Sleeve width at upper arm: 19½ (20, 20½)"

MATERIALS
3 (3, 4) 3½ oz/100g skeins (each approx 170yd/153m) of Reynolds Candide in #72 Windward (A), 2 (2, 3) skeins each #64 Horizon (B) and #70 Duck Egg (C), 3 (3, 4) skeins #56 Blue/Green Mix (D), 1 skein each #104 Lt Teal (E) and #8 Denim Blue (F).
One pair size 10 needles *or size needed to obtain gauge*
Size 8 (9, 9) circular needle 16"
Cable needle (cn)
Stitch markers

GAUGE
16 sts and 20 rows to 4" over St st using size 10 needles. *To save time and to ensure accurate sizing, check gauge.*

STITCH GLOSSARY
make 1 (M1) Insert LH needle from front to back under horizontal strand between last st worked and next st on LH needle, forming loop on LH needle, k in back loop of this st.
Right Twist (RT): Skip next st on LH needle and k 2nd st in front of skipped st, k skipped st, sl both sts from LH needle.
Left Twist (LT): Skip next st on LH needle and k 2nd st in back of skipped st, k skipped st, sl both sts from LH needle.
4-st Right Cable (RC): Sl 2 sts to cn and hold to *back* of work, k2, k2 from cn.
4-st Left Cable (LC): Sl 2 sts to cn and hold to *front* of work, k2, k2 from cn.
4-st Right Purl Cable (RPC): Sl 2 sts to cn and hold to *back* of work, k2, p2 from cn.
5-st Right Cross (RC): Sl 3 sts to cn and hold to *back* of work, k2, k3 from cn.
5-st Left Cross (LC): Sl 2 sts to cn and hold to *front* of work, k3, k2 from cn.
6-st Right Cable (RC): Sl 3 sts to cn and hold to *back* of work, k3, k3 from cn.
6-st Left Cable (LC): Sl 3 sts to cn and hold to *front* of work, k3, k3 from cn.
10-st Right Cable (RC): Sl 5 sts to cn and hold to *back* of work, k5, k5 from cn.
10-st Left Cable (LC): Sl 5 sts to cn and hold to *front* of work, k5, k5 from cn.

STRIPE PATTERN
*8 rows A, 1 row E, 7 rows D, 4 rows B, 8 rows C, 6 rows A, 10 rows D, 1 row F, 7 rows B, 4 rows C; rep from * (56 rows) for stripe pat.

PATTERN STITCHES
Garter Rib (multiple of 6 sts) **Rows 1, 3 and 5 (WS):** *K1, p4, k1; rep from * to end. **Row 2:** *P1, k4, p1; rep from * to end. **Row 4:** Purl. **Row 6:** Rep row 2. Rep rows 1-6 for garter rib.
Irregular Braid (worked over 8 sts, see chart)
Twisted Panel (worked over 4 sts) **Row 1 (WS):** K1, p2, k1. **Row 2:** P1, RT, p1. **Rows 3-8:** Rep rows 1 and 2 three times. **Row 9:** K1, p2, k1. **Row 10:** P1, LT, p1. **Rows 11-16:** Rep rows 9 and 10 three times. Rep rows 1-16 for twisted panel.

Ribbed Panel (worked over 7 sts)
Rows 1, 3 and 5 (WS): [K1, p1] 3 times, k1. **Rows 2 and 4:** [P1, k1] 3 times, p1. **Rows 6-9:** Knit. **Row 10:** P1, k5, p1. Rep rows 1-10 for ribbed panel.
Large Cable #1 (worked over 17 sts, see chart)
Large Cable #2 (worked over 19 sts, see chart)
Smooth Cable (worked over 8 sts) **Rows 1, 3 and 5 (WS):** K1, p6, k1. **Row 2:** P1, 6-st RC, p1. **Rows 4 and 6:** P1, k6, p1. Rep rows 1-6 for smooth cable.
Seed St Row 1 (WS): *K1, p1; rep from * to end. **Row 2:** K the purl sts and p the knit sts. Rep row 2 for seed st.
Textured Band (sleeves only) *10 rows seed st, 1 row St st, 8 rows rev St st, 1 row St st, 6 rows seed st, 1 row St st, 6 rows rev St st, 1 row St st; rep from * (34 rows) for textured band.

BACK
With larger needles and A, cast on 126 sts. **Row 1 (WS):** P 2 (selvage sts), place marker (pm), work 18 sts garter rib, pm, 8 sts irregular braid, pm, 6 sts garter rib, pm, 4 sts twisted panel, pm, 18 sts garter rib, pm, 7 sts ribbed panel, pm, 17 sts large cable #1, pm, 24 sts garter rib, pm, 8 sts smooth cable, pm, 12 sts garter rib, pm, p 2 (selvage sts). **Rows 2-26:** Cont in pats as established and work in stripe pat, slipping markers every row. **Row 27 (WS):** P 2 (selvage sts), p 18 sts dec 6 (4, 2) sts evenly spaced, 8 sts irregular braid, p6, 4 sts twisted panel, p18 sts inc 1 st in center, 7 sts ribbed panel, 17 sts large cable #1, p 24, 8 sts smooth cable, p 12 sts dec 2 (0, inc 2) sts evenly spaced, p 2 (selvage sts) — 119 (123, 127) sts. **Rows 28 and 30 (RS):** K 2 (selvage sts), p 10 (12, 14), 8 sts smooth cable, p 24, 17 sts large cable #1, 7 sts ribbed panel, p19, 4 sts twisted panel, p6, 8 sts irregular braid, p 12 (14, 16), k 2 (selvage sts). **Rows 29 and 31:** P 2 (selvage sts), p 12 (14, 16), 8 sts irregular braid, p6, 4 sts twisted panel, p19, 7 sts ribbed panel, 17 sts large cable #1, p24, 8 sts smooth cable, p 10 (12, 14), p 2 (selvage sts). **Row 32 (RS):** K 2 (selvage sts), k 10 (12, 14), 8 sts smooth cable, k24, 17 sts large cable #1, 7 sts ribbed panel, k19, 4 sts twisted panel, k6, 8 sts irregular braid, k 12 (14, 16), k2 (selvage sts). **Row 33 (WS):** P2 (selvage sts), k 12 (14, 16) for rev St st, 8 sts irregular braid, 6 seed sts, 4 sts twisted panel, 19 sts Row 1 of large cable #2, 7 sts ribbed panel, 17 sts large cable #1, 8 sts Row 1 of irregular braid, pm, 4 sts Row 1 of twisted panel, pm, 12 seed sts, 8 sts smooth cable, k 10 (12, 14) sts for rev St st, p2 (selvage sts). Cont in pats as established in stripe pat until piece measures 9" from beg, end with a WS row. **Next row (RS):** K2 (selvage sts), k 10 (12, 14), 8 sts smooth cable, k12, 4 sts twisted panel, 8 sts irregular braid, 17 sts large cable #1, 7 sts ribbed panel, 19 sts large cable #2, 4 sts twisted panel, k6, 8 sts irregular braid, k 12 (14, 16), k2 (selvage sts). **Next row (WS):** P2 (selvage sts), 12 (14, 16) seed sts, 8 sts irregular braid, k6 for rev St st, 4 sts twisted panel, 19 sts large cable #2, 7 sts ribbed panel, 17 sts large cable #1, 8 sts irregular braid, 4 sts twisted panel, k12 for rev St st, 8 sts smooth cable, 10 (12, 14) seed sts, p2 (selvage sts). Cont in pats as established and stripe pat for 4", end with a WS row. **Next row (RS):** K2 (selvage sts), k10 (12, 14), 8 sts smooth cable, k12, 4 sts twisted panel, 8 sts irregular braid, 17 sts large cable #1, 7 sts ribbed panel, 19 sts large cable #2, 4 sts twisted panel, k6, 8 sts irregular braid, k 12 (14, 16), k2 (selvage sts). **Next row (WS):** P2 (selvage sts), k 12 (14, 16) for rev St st, 8 sts irregular braid, 6 seed sts, 4 sts twisted panel, 19 sts large cable #2, 7 sts ribbed panel, 17 sts large cable #1, 8 sts irregular braid, 4 sts twisted panel, 12 seed sts, 8 sts smooth cable, k 10 (12, 14) for rev St st, p2 (selvage sts). Cont in pats as established and stripe pat for 4", end with a WS row. Rep last 8", changing from seed st section to rev St st section and reverse St st section to seed st section every 4" by working a knit RS row first, then beg new pat on next row for these sections; AT THE SAME TIME, cont pats already established in other sections. Work until piece measures 16 (16, 17)" from beg for woman's or 14" from beg for man's, end with a WS row. RAGLAN ARMHOLE SHAPING Keeping in pats and stripe pat as established, work as foll: **Next row (RS):** Bind off 4 sts (1 st rem on RH needle to become edge st in St st), k8, pm, work to last 12 sts, p12. **Next row (WS):** Bind off 4 sts (1 st rem on RH needle to become edge st in St st), pm, work 7 sts Row 1 of ribbed panel, work

IRREGULAR BRAID

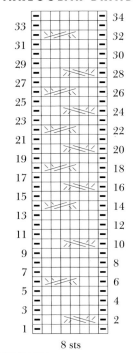

8 sts

LARGE CABLE #1

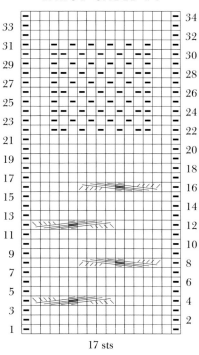

17 sts

LARGE CABLE #2

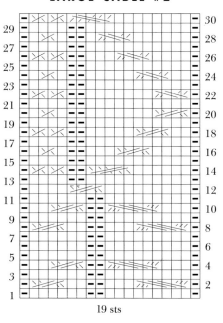

19 sts

to last 9 sts, work 8 sts Row 1 of irregular braid, p1 (selvage st). Work even for 2 rows. **Next row (RS):** K1 (selvage st), working pats as established, pat 7 sts, p2tog (this is last p st of irregular braid purled tog with next st), pat to last 10 sts, p2tog tbl, pat 7 sts, k1 (selvage st). **Next row (WS):** Work in pat as established, with no decs, knitting the dec sts of previous row. Rep last 2 rows 9 (10, 11) times, end with a WS row — 91 (93, 95) sts. **Note:** As decs are worked, keep in adjacent pats as long as possible even if there are not enough sts for a full panel. **Row 1 (RS):** K1 (selvage st), keeping pats as established, pat 7 sts, p2tog, pas as to last 10 sts, p2tog tbl, pat 7 sts, k1 (selvage st). **Row 2:** P1 (selvage st), keeping pats as established, pat 7 sts, SSK, pat to last 9 sts, k2tog, pat 6 sts, p1 (selvage st). **Row 3:** Rep Row 1. **Row 4:** Work in pats as established with no decs, knitting the dec sts of previous row. Rep last 4 rows, cont stripe pat, until 43 (45, 47) sts rem, end with a WS row. Bind off all sts.

FRONT
Work same as Back.

RIGHT SLEEVE
With larger needles and A, cast on 48 sts. **Row 1 (WS):** P2, k1, 4 sts twisted panel, 12 sts garter rib, 8 sts smooth cable, 6 sts garter rib, 4 sts twisted panel, 8 sts smooth cable, k1, p2. Cont in pats as established and stripe pat for 26 rows. P 5 rows. K next RS row inc 3 sts evenly across — 51 sts. **Next row (WS):** P2 (selvage sts), 15 seed sts (textured band pat), pm, 17 sts large cable #1, pm, 15 seed sts (textured band pat), p2 (selvage sts). **Next**

row (RS): K2 (selvage sts), M1, pat as established to last 2 sts, M1, k2 (selvage sts). Keeping pats as established and maintaining stripe pat, cont to inc 1 st each side (working inc sts into textured band pat) every 2nd and 4th row alternately until there are 81 (83, 85) sts. Work even in pats as established until piece measures 15½ (15½, 16)" from beg for woman's or 17½ (17½, 18)" from beg for man's, end with a WS row. RAGLAN CAP SHAPING Keeping in pat and stripe pat, bind off 4 sts at beg of next 2 rows — 73 (75, 77) sts. Keeping first and last st every row in St st, work 2 rows even. **Dec row (RS):** K1, SSK, pat as established to last 3 sts, k2tog, k1. Work 3 rows even. Rep last 4 rows 4 times more — 63 (65, 67) sts. Rep dec row every RS row 15 (16, 17) times. Bind off rem 33 sts.

LEFT SLEEVE
Work as for Right Sleeve, but work Large Cable #2 over center 19 sts instead of Large Cable #1 on center 17 sts and work rem sts in seed st.

FINISHING
Block pieces to measurements. Sew raglan sleeve caps to raglan armholes. Sew side and sleeve seams. NECKBAND With RS facing and size 8 (9, 9) circular needle, beg at right back raglan seam and cont in stripe pat from neck edge, pick up and k 126 sts evenly spaced around neck edge. Join, place a marker at beg of rnd. **Rnds 1 and 2:** Knit. **Rnd 3:** *6-st LC; rep from * around. **Rnds 4-6:** Knit. **Rnd 7:** K3, *6-st RC; rep from *, end k3. **Rnds 8-10:** *K4, p2; rep from * around. **Rnd 11:** Purl. **Rnds 12-19:** Rep rnds 8-11 twice. **Rnd 20:** Knit. Work in k 1, p 1 rib for 4 rnds. Bind off in rib.

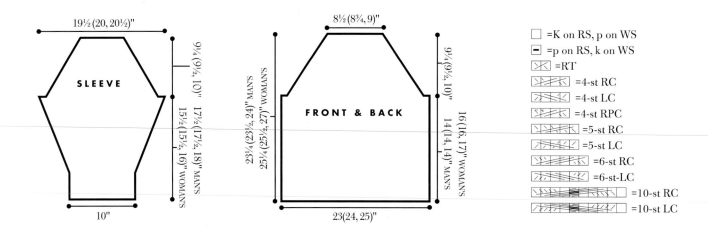

	=K on RS, p on WS
	=p on RS, k on WS
	=RT
	=4-st RC
	=4-st LC
	=4-st RPC
	=5-st RC
	=5-st LC
	=6-st RC
	=6-st LC
	=10-st RC
	=10-st LC

MOSS STITCH AND CABLE CARDIGAN & PULLOVER

EXPERIENCED

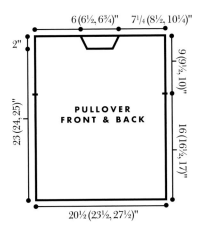

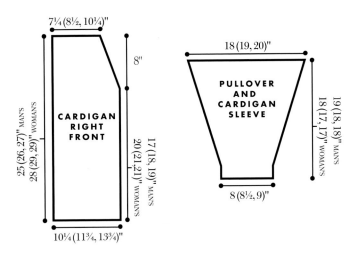

SIZES
To fit Woman's or Man's Small, Medium, Large. Directions for "Kelso Wool Tweed" are in parentheses ( )'s; for "Nature's Palette Cotton" are in brackets [ ]'s. If there is only one number, it applies to both yarns. Shown on pages 58, 63, and 184 in size Medium.

FINISHED MEASUREMENTS (for both yarns)
Bust/chest at underarm: 41 (47, 55)"
PULLOVER: Length from shoulder: 25 (26, 27)"
CARDIGAN: Length from shoulder: 28 (29, 29)" for woman's or 25 (26, 27)" for man's
Sleeve width at upperarm: 18 (19, 20)"

MATERIALS
PULLOVER:
8 (8, 9) 3½oz/100g hanks (each approx 176yd/158m) of Classic Elite Kelso Wool Tweed in #9250 Wensleydale Olive or
20 (21, 22) 1¾oz/50g hanks (each approx 93yd/84m) of Classic Elite Nature's Palette Worsted-Weight Cotton (50% Buffalo Fox Fibre, 50% Ecru Cotton) in #7325
Sizes 4 and 5 knitting needles, *or size needed to obtain gauge*
Size 4 circular needle 16" long
Cable needle (cn)
CARDIGAN:
9 (9, 10) 3½oz/100 g hanks (each approx 176yd/158m) of Classic Elite Mackenzie Silk Wool in #4275 Jacob
Needle sizes and gauge as for pullover, wool version
Nine buttons for woman's; 8 buttons for man's
Stitch markers

GAUGE
20 sts and 28 rows to 4" over cable pats using larger needles and Kelso Wool Tweed; 23 sts and 30 rows to 4" over cable pats and 20 sts and 30 rows to 4" over moss st using larger needles and Nature's Palette Cotton. *To save time and to ensure accurate sizing, check gauges.*

STITCH GLOSSARY
6-st Left Cable (LC): Slip 3 sts to cn and hold in *front*, k3, k3 from cn.
4-st Right Purl Cable (RPC): Sl 1 to cn and hold in *back*, k3, p1 from cn.
4-st Left Purl Cable (LPC): Sl 3 to cn and hold in *front*, p1, k3 from cn.
4-st Right Cable (RC): Sl 1 to cn and hold in *back*, k3, k1 from cn.
4-st Left Cable (LC): Sl 3 to cn and hold in *front*, k1, k3 from cn

MOSS STITCH (over any number of sts)
Row 1 (RS): *K1, p1; rep from *. **Rows 2 and 4:** K the knit sts and p the purl sts. **Row 3:** *P1, k1; rep from *. Rep rows 1-4 for moss st.

LEFT CABLE PAT (over 8 sts)
Row 1 and all WS rows: K1, p6, k1. **Row 2 (RS):** P1, 6-st LC, p1. **Rows 4 and 6:** P1, k6, p1. Rep rows 1-6 for left cable pat.

PULLOVER—BACK
With smaller needles, cast on (102, 118, 138); [118, 138, 154] sts. ESTABLISH CABLE PATS—WOOL VERSION: **Size Small:** Work 1 st in St st (selvage st), work [28 sts chart, 8 sts left cable pat] twice, 28 sts chart, 1 st in St st (selvage st). **Size Medium:** Work 1 st in St st (selvage st), work [8 sts left cable pat, 28 sts chart] 3 times, 8 sts left cable pat, 1 st in St st (selvage st). **Size Large:** Work 1 st in St st (selvage st), work [28 sts chart, 8 sts left cable pat] 3 times, 28 sts chart, 1 st in St st (selvage st). ESTABLISH

CABLE PATS—COTTON VERSION: **Size Small:** Work same as size Medium in wool version. **Size Medium:** Work same as size Large in wool version. **Size Large:** Work 1 st in St st (selvage st), work [8 sts left cable pat, 28 sts chart] 4 times, 8 sts left cable pat, 1 st in St st (selvage st). Cont as est, and rep rows 1-6 of chart twice. Change to larger needles. Cont to work chart Rows 7 to 46, then rep Rows 1 to 46, and keep rem sts as est, until piece meas 25 (26, 27)" for all versions. Bind off all sts.

FRONT
Work same as back until piece meas 23 (24, 25)", end with a WS row. NECK SHAPING **Next row (RS):** Work (40, 47, 56); [46, 55, 62] sts in pat, join 2nd ball of yarn and bind off center (22, 24, 26); [26, 28, 30] sts, work to end. Working both sides at once, dec 1 st at each neck edge every other row 4 times—(36, 43, 52); [42, 51, 58] sts. When same length as back, bind off rem sts each side for shoulders.

SLEEVES (all versions)
With smaller needles, cast on (40, 42, 44); [44, 46, 50] sts. ESTABLISH CABLE AND MOSS ST PATS Work (6, 7, 8); [8, 9, 11] sts in Moss st, place marker, work 28 sts chart pat, place marker, work (6, 7, 8); [8, 9, 11] sts in moss st. Work chart rows 1 to 6 twice. Change to larger needles and cont to work rows 7 to 46; then rep rows 1 to 46, AT THE SAME TIME, inc 1 st each side (working inc sts into moss st) every 4th row (25, 25, 24); [18, 25, 25] times, every (2nd); [6th] row (0, 2, 4); [8, 2, 2] times—(90, 96, 100); [96, 100, 104] sts. Work even until piece measures for woman's version: 18 (17, 17)" from beg; for man's version: 19 (18, 18)" from beg. Bind off all sts.

Block pieces to measurements. Sew shoulder seams. COLLAR .With RS facing and circular needle, pick up and k 96 (96, 104); [104, 104, 112] sts evenly around neck. Join and work in rnds as foll: **Rnds 1, 2, 4, 5, 6:** P2, k6. **Rnd 3:** *P2, 6-st LC; rep from * around. Rep rnds 1-6 for cable pat for 3". Bind off in pat. Place markers 9 (9½, 10)" down from shoulder seams on front and back for armholes. Sew top of sleeves between markers. Sew side and sleeve seams.

CARDIGAN

BACK

Work same as for pullover until piece meas 28 (29, 29)" for woman's or 25 (26, 27)" for man's. Bind off all sts.

RIGHT FRONT

With smaller needles, cast on 51 (59, 68) sts. ESTABLISH CABLE PATS **Size Small:** Work 1 selv st, work 8 sts left cable pat, 28 sts chart, 8 sts left cable pat, 5 sts in Moss St, work 1 selv st. **Size Medium:** Work 1 selv st, work 8 sts left cable pat, 28 sts chart, 8 sts left cable pat, 13 sts in Moss St, work 1 selv st. **Size Large:** Work 1 selv st, work 28 sts chart, 8 sts left cable pat, 28 sts chart, 2 sts in moss st, work 1 selv st. Cont in pats as established, change to larger needles as for back, until piece measures 8" from beg, end with a RS row. POCKET OPENING **Next row (WS):** Work 23 (31, 40) sts in pat, place marker (pm), work 20 sts, pm, slip 20 sts just knit back to left needle and work 20 sts with scrap yarn for pocket opening, pick up Main Color and cont working as est. When piece measures 20 (21, 21)" for woman's sweater or 17 (18, 19)" for man's sweater, end with a WS row. NECK SHAPING Dec 1 st at beg of next row (neck edge), then every 2nd row 3 (5, 5) times more, every 4th row 11 (10, 10) times—36 (43, 52) sts. When piece measures same as back, bind off rem sts for shoulder.

LEFT FRONT

Work same as right front, reversing placement of cables as foll: **Size Small:** Work 1 selv st, 5 sts in Moss St, work 8 sts left cable pat, 28 sts chart, 8 sts left cable pat, 1 selv st. **Size Medium:** Work 1 selv st, 13 sts in Moss St, work 8 sts left cable pat, 28 sts chart, 8 sts left cable pat, 1 selv st. **Size Large:** Work 1 selv st, 2 sts in Moss st, work 28 sts chart, 8 sts left cable pat, 28 sts chart, 1 selv st. Reverse pocket placement as foll: When piece measures 8" from beg, work next WS row as foll: work 8 sts, pm, work 20 sts, pm, slip 20 sts just knit back to left needle and work 20 sts with scrap yarn for pocket opening, pick up Main Color and cont working as est. Work as for right front, reversing shaping.

Block pieces to measurements. Sew shoulder seams. POCKET BORDER AND LINING Unravel contrast yarn. Pick up bottom sts and work in k1, p1 rib for 1". Bind off in rib. Pick up top sts and work in St st until piece measures 5" for lining. Bind off. Sew to WS of garment to complete pocket. FRONT AND NECK BAND - BUTTON BAND With smaller needles, cast on 10 sts. Work as foll: **Next row (RS):** P2, *k1 tbl (through back loop), p1; rep from *, end k1 tbl, slip 1 knitwise. **Next row:** P2, *k1, p1; rep from *, end k2. Rep these 2 rows until piece fits along front edge to center back of neck. Place sts on a holder. Sew band in place, (to left front for woman, right front for man) adjusting length if necessary. Place markers on band for nine buttons for woman's; 8 buttons for man's, the first one ¾" from lower edge, that last one just below first neck dec, and the others spaced evenly between. BUTTONHOLE BAND With smaller needles, cast on 10 sts. Work as foll: **Next row (WS):** K2, *p1, k1 tbl; rep from *, end p2. **Next row:** K2, *p1, k1; rep from *, end p1, sl 1 purlwise wyif. Rep these 2 rows, working buttonholes opposite markers (by yo, k2tog for buttonhole). Complete as for button band. Weave sts tog at center back neck. Place markers 9 (9½, 10)" down from shoulder seams on front and back for armholes. Sew top of sleeve between markers. Sew side and sleeve seams. Sew on buttons.

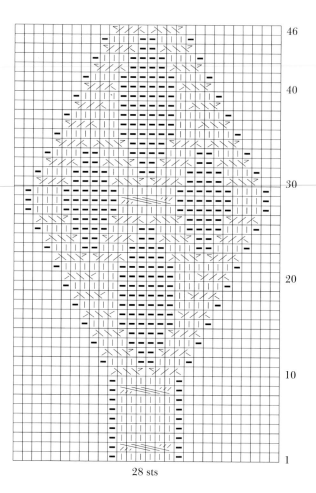

46

40

30

20

10

1

28 sts

	=moss st
	=k on RS, p on WS
	=p on RS, k on WS
	=4-st RPC
	=4-st LPC
	=4-st RC
	=4-st LC
	=6-st LC

LEAF KIMONO & PULLOVER

INTERMEDIATE

SIZES
One size. Shown on pages 66 and 69.

FINISHED MEASUREMENTS
KIMONO:
Bust at underarm (closed): 53"
Length (from turning ridge to shoulder): 21"
Sleeve width at upper arm: 23"
PULLOVER:
Bust at underarm: 53"
Length from shoulder: 27"
Sleeve width at upper arm: 24½"

MATERIALS
KIMONO:
8 1¾oz/50g skeins (each approx 130yd/117m) of On the Inca Trail light
    worsted-weight alpaca in #237 Dancing Moon (MC)
1 skein each in #211 Canyon Land (A), #212 Red Ochre (B), #235 Camel
    (C), #226 Green Fire (D), #227 Sage (E), #230 Blue Mist (F), #225
    Granite Grey (G), #201 Eclipse (H), #236 Cocoa (II), #221 Taupe
    (J), #210 El Dorado (K), #243 Indian Mulberry (L), #213 High Sierra
    (M), and #238 Cactus Flower (Note: On the Inca Trail has been dis-
    continued. Classic Elite Inca alpaca can be substituted, though colors
    are not identical.)
3 coat hooks
7 long metal beads (sweater in photograph made with 1 1/8" long Nepalese
    metal beads)
Small round glass beads
Sizes 3 and 5 circular needles 24" long *or size needed to obtain gauge*
Size C crochet hook
#1 sewing or beading needle
D beading thread
PULLOVER:
12 skeins in #234 Mystic Blue (MC)
1 skein each in #229 Night Shadow (A), #215 Azure (B), #231 Del Mar
    (C), #243 Indian Mulberry (D), #232 Peacock (E), #227 Sage (F),
    #230 Blue Mist (G), #233 Charcoal Grey (H), #216 Teal Lake (II),
    #223 Silver Grey (J), and #225 Granite Grey (K)
Size G crochet hook
One pair each sizes 3 and 5 needles *or size needed to obtain gauge*

GAUGE
18 sts and 24 rows to 4" over St st and MC using larger needle; 20 sts
and 24 rows to 4" over St st and color pat using larger needles. *To save
time and to ensure accurate sizing, check gauges.*

TEXTURED PAT #1 (over a multiple of 4 sts, plus 2)
Row 1 (RS): *P2, k2; rep from *, end p2.
Rows 2 and 4: K the knit sts, p the purl sts.
Row 3: *K2, p2; rep from *, end k2. Rep rows 1 - 4 for Textured
    Pat #1.

TEXTURED PAT #2 (over a multiple of 4 sts, plus 2)
Row 1 (RS): *P2, k2; rep from *, end p2. **Row 2:** K the purl sts,
    p the knit sts. Rep rows 1and 2 for Textured Pat #2.

KIMONO

BACK
With smaller needle and MC, cast on 132 sts. Work back and forth in St
st for 8 rows. **Next row (RS):** Purl across row for turning ridge. Change
to larger needle. **Next row (WS):** With MC, purl. Work Chart for Back
through row 126. Bind off.

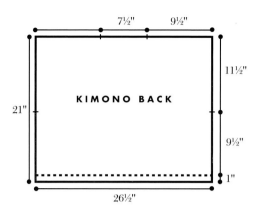

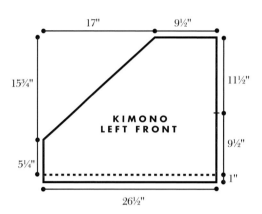

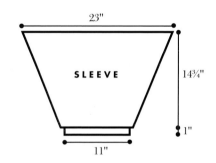

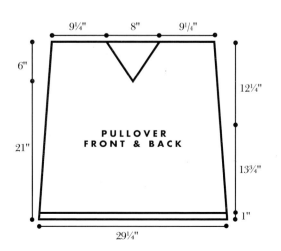

LEFT FRONT

Work as for back through chart row 32. NECK SHAPING **Next (dec) row (RS):** Work in pat to last 2 sts, k2tog. Work dec row every other row 8 times more, then every row 76 times — 47 sts. Work 1 row even. Bind off.

RIGHT FRONT

Work to correspond to left front, reversing neck shaping by working dec row at beg of RS rows (by SSK).

SLEEVES

With smaller needle and color K, cast on 46 sts. Work back and forth in Textured Pat #1 and in stripe pat as foll:1 row color K, 1 row B, 2 rows G, 2 rows N, 2 rows G, 1 row II, 2 rows color K, 1 row MC (12 rows). Change to larger needle. Beg chart for sleeve on next (RS) row, inc 10 sts evenly across first row — 56 sts. Cont in chart pat, AT SAME TIME, inc 1 st each side (working inc sts into chart pat) every other row 7 times, every 4th row 17 times — 104 sts. When chart is completed, cont in St st with MC only until piece measures 15¾" from beg. Bind off.

FINISHING

Block pieces to measurements. With RS facing, crochet hook and MC, sl st shoulder seams tog as foll: insert hook into one st on front shoulder and corresponding st on back shoulder, yo hook and pull yarn through both sts, cont in this way until all shoulder sts are seamed. Place markers 11½" down from shoulders on front and back for armholes. With RS facing, crochet hook and color K, sl st sleeves in place between markers. With color K, sl st side and sleeve seams, then work a sl st edge along right and left front edges, and along back neck edge. With D, beading thread and #1 needle, sew glass beads along front and back neck edges, just inside crochet edge. Sew metals beads along left front edge at even intervals, as desired. Fold hem to WS at turning ridge and sl st in place. Sew coat hooks to WS of fabric just inside right and left front edges (so that they do not show), with the first 13½" down from shoulders, the last 9" below first, and the third coat hook evenly between.

PULLOVER

BACK

With smaller needles and MC, cast on 130 sts. Work in Textured Pat #2 and in stripe pat as foll: 1 row each MC, C, E, J, II, F, E and 2 rows C. Change to larger needles. With MC, p next row on WS, inc 2 sts — 132 sts. Work in St st until piece measures 16" from beg, end with a WS row. Work chart for back, in desired colors, beg with row 62, omitting stems of flowers between main flower motifs. Work through chart row 126. Bind off.

FRONT

Work as for back until piece measures 20" from beg. V-NECK SHAPING **Next row (RS):** Work in pat across 64 sts, k2tog, join 2nd skein of yarn, SSK, work to end. Working both sides at once, dec 1 st at each neck edge on next row, then every other row 18 times more. Work even through chart row 126. Work 1 row even. Bind off rem 46 sts each side.

SLEEVES

With smaller needles and MC, cast on 62 sts. Work in textured pat #1 and stripes as foll: 2 rows MC, 2 rows H, inc 1 st in last row-63 sts. Change to larger needles and work in St st and colorwork pat as foll: **Beg Diamond Pat - Row 1 (RS):** *4E, 1CC (contrasting color as desired), 4E; rep from * to end. **Row 2:** *3E, 3CC, 3E; rep from * to end. **Row 3:** *2E, 5CC, 2E; rep from * to end. **Row 4:** Rep row 2. **Row 5:** Rep row 1. Cont in St st with MC only, inc 1 st each side every 4th row 20 times. Work even on 103 sts until piece measures 15¾" from beg. Bind off all sts.

FINISHING

Block pieces. With RS facing, crochet hook and E, sl st shoulder seams tog. Place markers 11½" down from shoulders on front and back for armholes. With RS facing, crochet hook and E, sl st sleeves in place between markers. With E, sl st side and sleeve seams. With J, work a sl st edge along lower edge of sleeves. With RS facing and crochet hook, work sc evenly around V-neck edge as foll: 1 rnd E, 1 rnd H, 1 rnd MC, 1 rnd J.

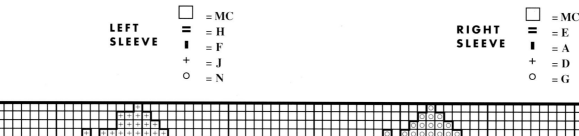

LEFT SLEEVE

□ = MC
= = H
▮ = F
+ = J
○ = N

RIGHT SLEEVE

□ = MC
= = E
▮ = A
+ = D
○ = G

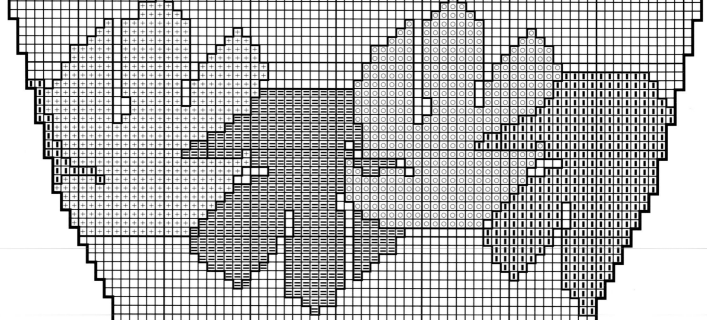

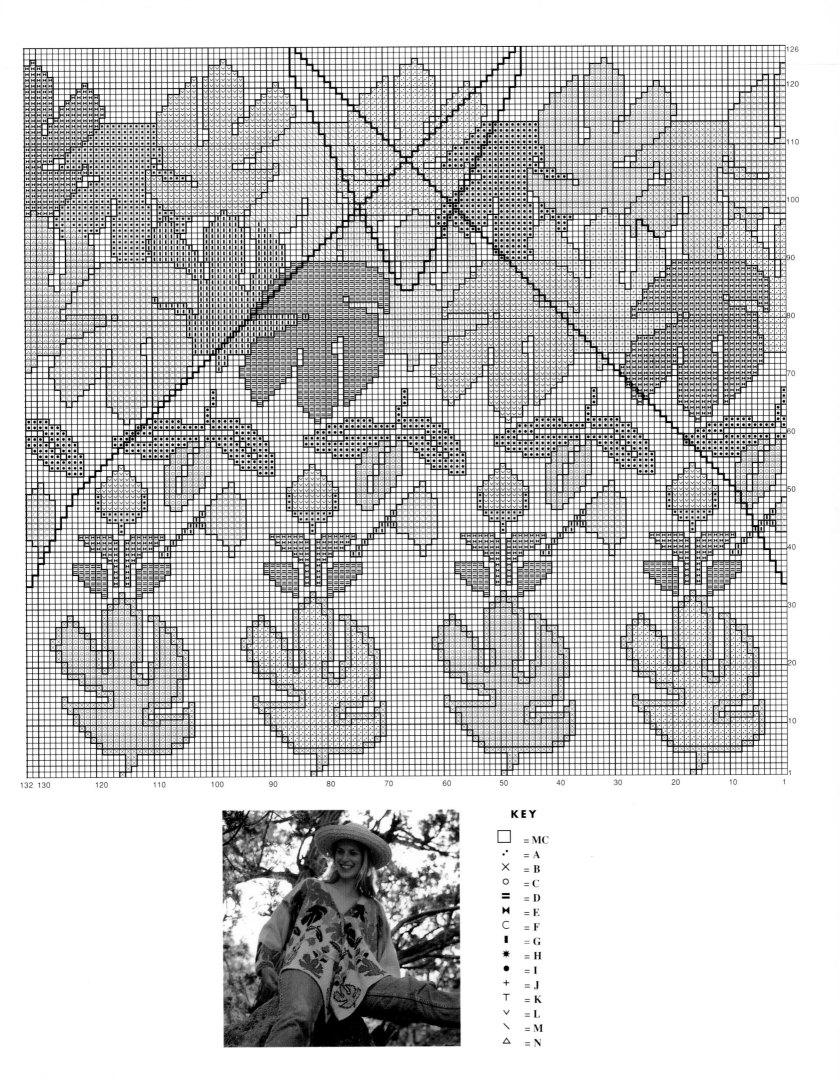

KEY

Symbol	Color
□	= MC
∴	= A
✕	= B
○	= C
=	= D
⋈	= E
C	= F
❙	= G
✳	= H
●	= I
+	= J
T	= K
∨	= L
＼	= M
△	= N

PRE-COLUMBIAN SHAWL

INTERMEDIATE

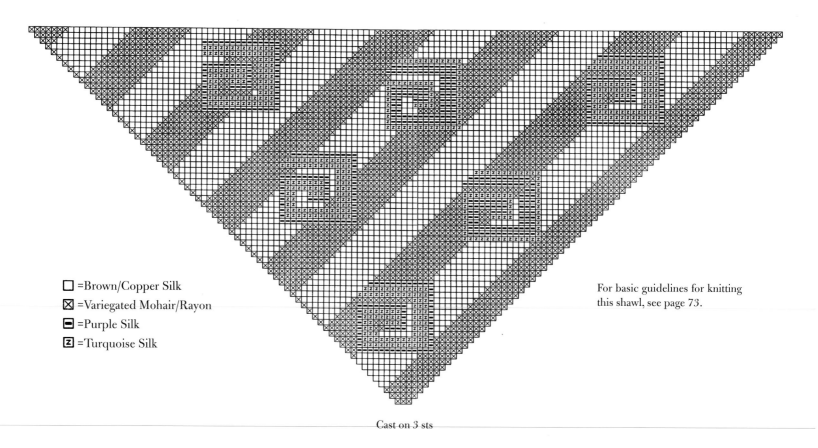

□ =Brown/Copper Silk

☒ =Variegated Mohair/Rayon

▬ =Purple Silk

☑ =Turquoise Silk

For basic guidelines for knitting this shawl, see page 73.

Cast on 3 sts

SOUTHWESTERN GEOMETRIC JACKET

EXPERT

SIZES
One size. Shown on pages 78 and 189.

FINISHED MEASUREMENTS
Bust at underarm: 52½"
Length from shoulder: 29¾"
Sleeve width at upper arm: 25"

MATERIALS
12 ¾oz/25g skeins (each approx 74yd/67m) of Rowan Yarns Lightweight DK in #62 Black (A)

7 skeins #77 Dark Rust (B)

3 skeins #89 Light Green (C)

2 skeins each #602 Red Brown (D), #663 Brown Red (E), and #27 Rust (F)

1 skein each #45 Red (G), #70 Dusty Rose (H), #69 Light Rose (I), #92 Pink (J), #125 Turquoise (K), #91 Spruce Green (L), #100 Medium Green (M), #123 Light Blue (N), #9 Olive Gold (O), #72 Gold (P), #14 Bright Gold (Q), #8 Pale Yellow (R), #99 Purple (S), #94 Mauve (T), #149 Dusty Violet (U), #611 Red Violet (V), #127 Violet (W), #121 Lavender (X), #104 Ochre (Y), #24 Salmon (Z), #424 Pink (a), #82 Tan (b), and #615 Beige (c)

1 1¾oz/50g skeins (each approx 187yd/170m) of Rowan Yarns 4-Ply Botany in #659 Purple (d) and #631 Fuchsia (e)

1 ¾oz/25g skeins (each approx 110yd/100m) of Rowan Yarns Donegal Lambswool in #484 Heathered Purple (f)

2 ¾oz/25g skeins (each approx 126yd/115m) of Rowan Yarns Designer DK in #688 Dark Pink (g)

2 3½oz/100g skeins (each approx 154yd/140m) of Rowan Yarns Aran Weight Magpie in #305 Ocean (h)

1 ¾oz/25g skeins (each approx 70yd/64m) of Kaffe Fassett Kid Silk in #993 Berry (i) and #976 Opal (j)

Sizes 6 and 8 knitting needles *or size needed to obtain gauge*

Size 6 circular needle 29"

Size 8 circular needle 39"

Size H crochet hook

5 coat hooks

GAUGE

16 sts and 22 rows to 4" over chart pat using larger needles. *To save time and to ensure accurate sizing, check gauge.*

Note: When changing colors on same row, bring new color under old color to twist strands and prevent holes. Carry yarn not in use loosely along WS of work.

LEFT BACK

With larger needles and 2 strands A, cast on 3 sts (row 1 of chart). **Row 2 (WS):** Cast on 2 sts, p3. **Next row (RS):** Inc 1 st, k to end. Cont to work Chart for Left Back, inc 1 st at beg of RS rows, and casting on 2 sts at beg of WS rows, through chart row 56. Cont to cast on 2 sts at beg of WS rows, bind off 2 sts at beg of RS rows through chart row 80. Cont to bind off 2 sts at beg of RS rows, work even on WS rows for 4 rows more. **Next row (RS):** Bind off 2 sts, work to last 2 sts of row, k2tog. Cont to bind off 2 sts at beg and dec 1 st at end of RS rows, while working WS rows even, through row 135. Work 1 row even. Dec 1 st at beg of next row. Work 1 row even. Bind off 3 sts.

RIGHT BACK

With larger needles and 2 strands A, cast on 3 sts (row 1 of chart). Work Chart for Right Back, casting on 2 sts at beg and inc 1 st at end of RS rows, and working WS rows even, through chart row 56. Cont to cast on 2 sts at beg of RS rows, bind off 2 sts at beg of WS rows, through row 80. Cont to bind off 2 sts at beg of WS rows, on RS rows work even for 4 rows more, then dec 1 st at beg of RS rows (by SKP), through chart row 136. Dec 1 st at end of next row. Work 1 row even. Bind off 3 sts.

LEFT FRONT

With larger needles and 2 strands A, cast on 3 sts (row 1 of chart). Work Chart for Left Front, working shaping as for right back through chart row 109. Cont to dec 1 st at beg of RS rows, bind off 3 sts at beg of WS rows, through row 120. Bind off 22 sts.

RIGHT FRONT

With larger needles and 2 strands A, cast on 3 sts (row 1 of chart). Work Chart for Right Front, working shaping as for left back through chart row 80. Cont to bind off 2 sts at beg of RS rows, work even on WS rows for 2 rows more. **Next row (RS):** Bind off 2 sts, work to last 2 sts of row, k2tog. Cont to bind off 2 sts at beg and dec 1 st at end of RS rows, while working WS rows even, through row 108. Bind off 3 sts at beg and dec 1 st at end of RS rows through row 118. **Next row (RS):** Bind off 3 sts, work to end. Bind off 22 sts.

FINISHING

Block pieces to measurements. Sew right and left backs tog at center seam. Sew shoulder seams.

SLEEVES

Place markers 12½" down on front and back for armholes. With larger needles and 1 strand h, pick up 100 sts between markers. Work Chart for Right or Left Sleeve, dec 1 st each side every other row 8 times, every 4th row 14 times—56 sts. Work even through chart row 82. K next row with 2 strands A, dec 18 sts evenly across—38 sts. Change to smaller needles. P 1 row on WS. CUFF **Row 1 (RS):** *K1, p1; rep from * to end. **Row 2:** With 2 strands A, k the knit sts, p the purl sts. **Row 3:** With 2 strands of each color, work as foll: *K1 with A, p1 with B; rep from * to end. **Row 4:** K the knit sts, p the purl sts, matching colors. **Rows 5 and 6:** Rep rows 3 and 4. **Row 7:** Rep row 3. **Row 8:** *K1 with 1 strand h, p1 with 2 strands A; rep from * to end. **Row 9:** K the knit sts, p the purl sts, matching colors. **Row 10:** *K1B, p1A; rep from * to end. **Row 11:** K the knit sts, p the purl sts, matching colors. **Rows 12 and 14:** Rep row 10. **Rows 13 and 15:** Rep row 11. Bind off in rib, using 2 strands A. Block sleeves to measurements.

RIGHT FRONT POCKET

With RS facing, larger needles and h, pick up 16 sts between rows 12 and 28 along right back side seam edge. Work in st st with h, work pocket shaping as foll: Cast on at beg of RS rows 6 sts once, 2 sts 3 times. Work 18 rows even. Bind off at beg of RS rows 2 sts 4 times, AT SAME

TIME, after 2 rows have been worked, bind off at beg of WS rows 2 sts times. Bind off rem sts. On front edge of pocket, pick up and k 18 sts with 2 strands A and size 6 needles. Extend sts slightly past pocket lining edges, work in k1, p1 rib for 2 rows. Bind off in rib.

LEFT FRONT POCKET

Work as for right front pocket, reversing shaping.

LOWER EDGE RIB

Sew side and sleeve seams, securing edges of pockets and leaving pocket openings. Sl st pocket linings to inside front of piece. With RS facing, smaller needles and 2 strands A, pick up 216 sts evenly along lower edge of piece. **Row 1 (RS):** *K1, p1; rep from * to end. **Row 2:** With 2 strands A, k the knit sts, p the purl sts. **Rows 3, 5, 7 and 9:** With 2 strands of each color, work as foll: *K1 with A, p1 with B; rep from * to end. **Rows 4, 6, 8 and 10:** K the knit sts, p the purl sts, matching colors. **Rows 11 and 13:** *K1 with 2 strands A, p1 with 1 strand h; rep from * to end. **Rows 12 and 14:** K the knit sts, p the purl sts, matching colors. **Rows 15–22:** Rep rows 3–10. **Rows 22 and 23:** With 2 strands A, k the knit sts, and p the purl sts. Bind off in rib, using 2 strands A. With crochet hook, work 1 row sc with 2 strands A.

FRONT BAND

With RS facing, larger needles and h, pick up 136 sts along right front edge, 40 sts along back neck from shoulder seam to shoulder seam, 136 sts along left front edge—312 sts. **Row 1 (WS):** With h, purl. **Row 2:** With 2 strands A, knit. **Rows 3–8:** Work 7 rows in charts for corresponding bands. **Row 9:** With 2 strands A, purl. **Row 10:** With 1 strand h, knit. **Row 11:** Knit on WS with h to form turning ridge. **Rows 12–19:** Work in st st with 2 strands A. **Row 20:** With h, purl. Bind off with h. Fold band to WS and sl st in place. Run 1 strand h through inside of band to keep it from stretching. Sew coat hooks to inside of bands as fasteners.

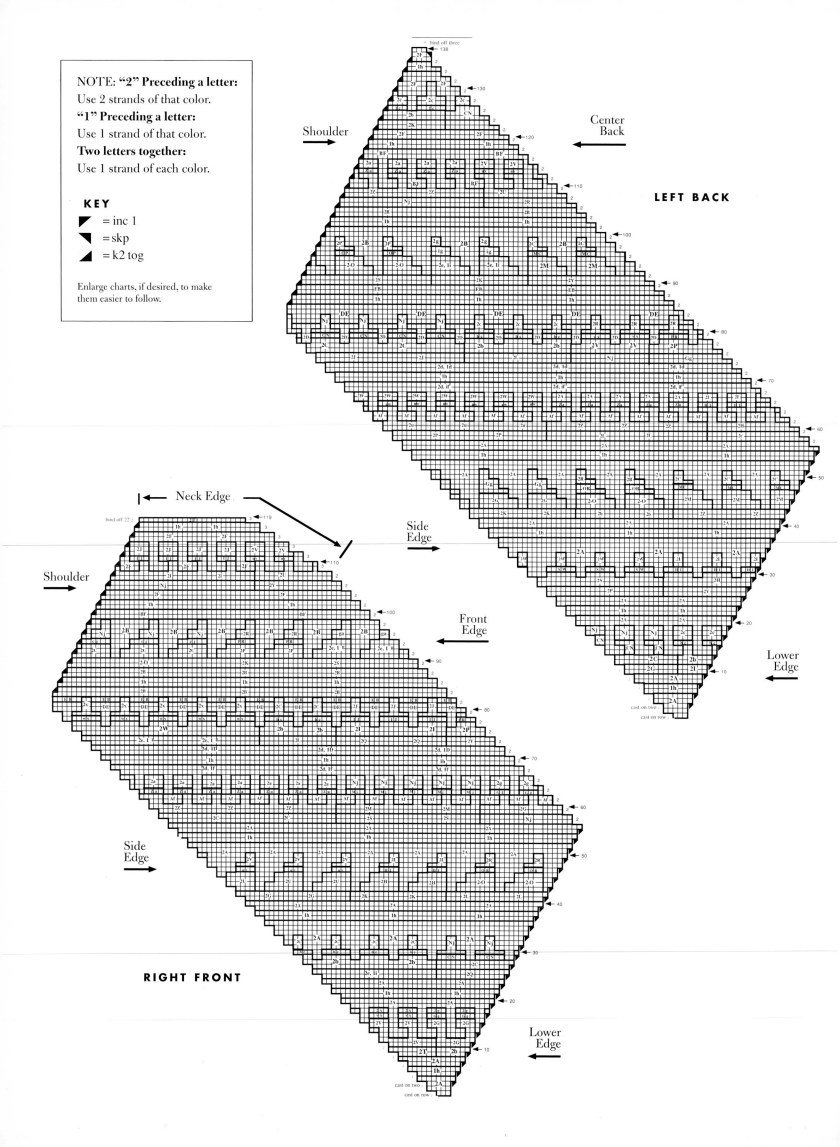

NOTE: "2" Preceding a letter:
Use 2 strands of that color.
"1" Preceding a letter:
Use 1 strand of that color.
Two letters together:
Use 1 strand of each color.

KEY

◣ = inc 1

◥ = skp

◢ = k2 tog

Enlarge charts, if desired, to make
them easier to follow.

Shoulder →

Center
Back

LEFT BACK

← Neck Edge

Shoulder →

Side
Edge →

Front
Edge

Side
Edge →

Lower
Edge

Lower
Edge

RIGHT FRONT

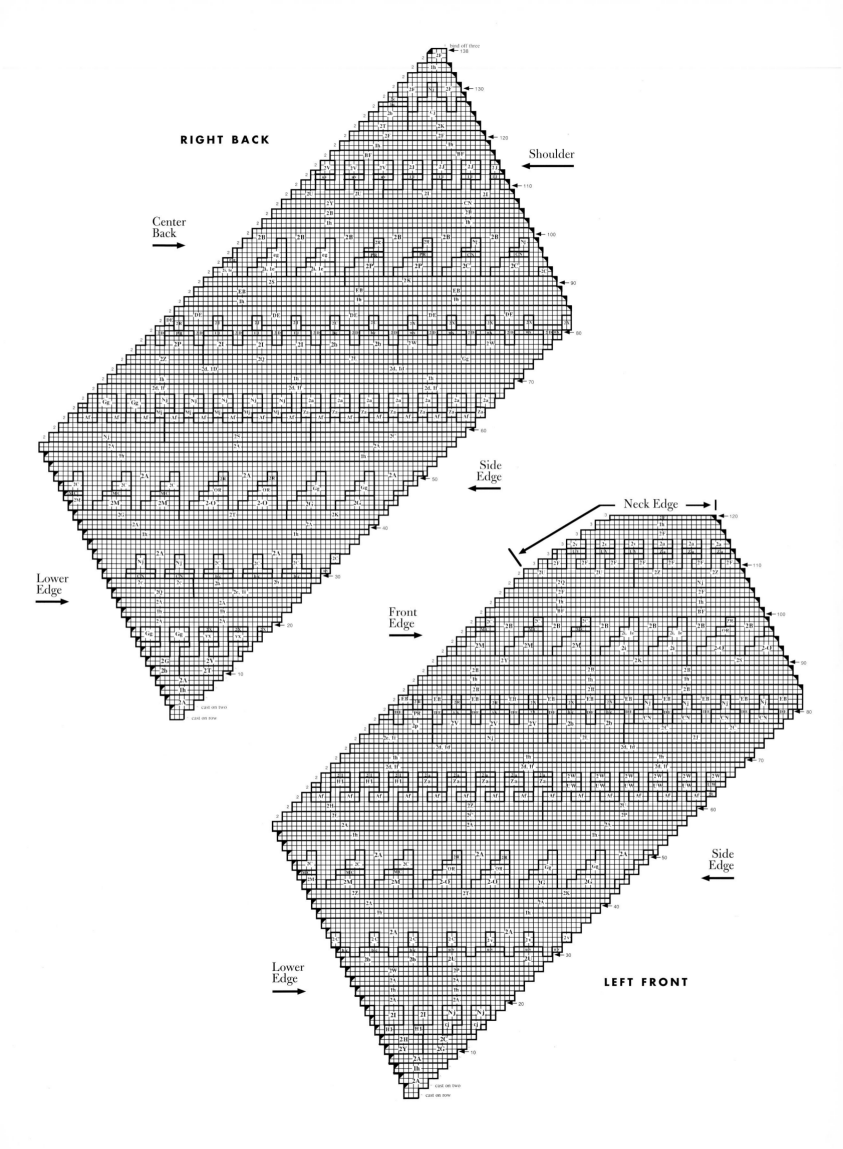

RIGHT BACK

Center Back →

Shoulder ←

Side Edge ←

Lower Edge →

Neck Edge →

Front Edge →

Side Edge ←

Lower Edge →

LEFT FRONT

LEFT SLEEVE

← 56 sts →

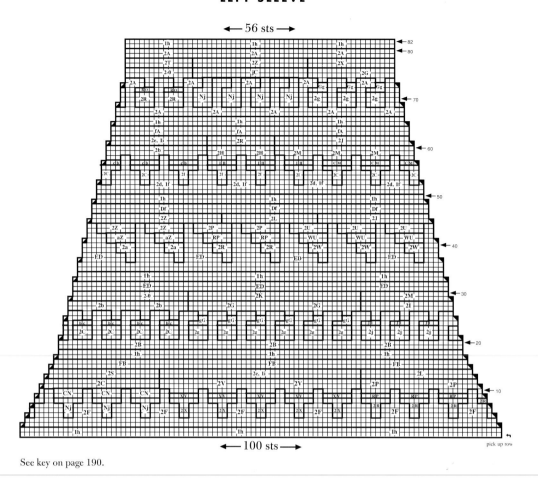

See key on page 190.

RIGHT SLEEVE

← 56 sts →

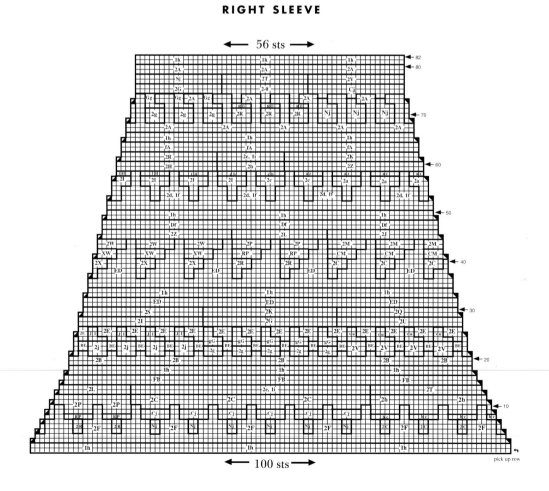

← 100 sts →

pick up row

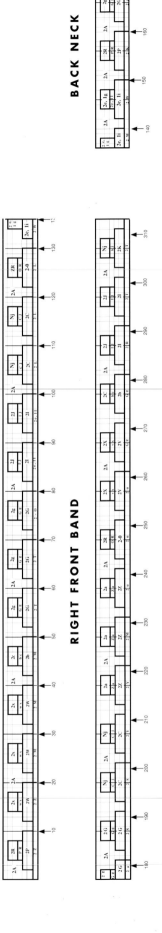

BACK NECK

LEFT FRONT BAND

RIGHT FRONT BAND

COLORADO CASHMERE WIMPLES

INTERMEDIATE

SIZES
Wimple #1 is loose-fitting; wimple #2 fits snugly around the head. Shown on pages 82 and 85.

FINISHED MEASUREMENTS
Circumference:
Wimple #1: 23”; Wimple #2: 20½”

MATERIALS (for one wimple)
5 oz fine 2-ply laceweight cashmere yarn (undyed) or 2½oz each cleaned white and brown cashmere down (available from Cashmere America)
One pair size 3 needles *or size needed to obtain gauge*
Size 3 circular needle 16” long
Gaywool dye in Pumpkin and/or Tomato

GAUGE
28 sts and 42 rows to 4” over St st using size 3 needles. ***To save time and to ensure accurate sizing, check gauge.***

Note: After working inc sts on rows 22, 26, 32, 36 and 40 of chart #2, work these new sts in St st.

SPINNING AND DYEING NOTES
Priscilla lightly teased together by hand white and brown cashmere down, then spun "Z" and plied "S" to create the laceweight yarn for the wimples. She did not thoroughly blend the two different shades of down, which allowed for a natural color variation in the yarn when she dyed it. For a similar effect in commercial yarn, use natural light gray or light brown (instead of white) yarn. She dyed her yarn according to the package instructions. She used Gaywool's Pumpkin dye for the loose-fitting wimple (wimple #1). For the snug-fitting wimple, she dyed the yarn with Pumpkin first, then top-dyed it with Tomato. She did not mix the two dyes into one solution.

WIMPLE #1
Beg at top of wimple with circular needle and double strand of Pumpkin, cast on 160 sts. Join, mark beg of rnd. Cut one strand. Work in St st (k every rnd) for 1½". Work Chart 1 through Rnd 18. Cont in St st until 11" from beg, inc 20 sts evenly spaced across last rnd — 180 sts. Cont in St st for 1". Work Chart 2 through Rnd 41, AT SAME TIME, on Rnds 22, 26, 32, 36 and 40 inc 1 st in each of the 12 St st sections (60 sts total incs)— 240 sts. Work Chart 3 through Rnd 8. Purl 1 rnd for base of wimple. EDGING With straight needles and double strand of Pumpkin, cast on 12 sts. Cut one strand. Work Rows 1-16 of Chart 4 for 30 reps, slipping first st of all odd-numbered rows and joining last st of edging with next st of wimple base on all even-numbered rows. Graft last 12 sts of edging to close. Weave in yarn ends. Block with steam.

WIMPLE #2
Beg at top of wimple, with circular needle and double strand of Tomato, cast on 144 sts. Join, mark beg of rnd. Cut one strand. Work in St st (k every rnd) for 12". **Next rnd:** K, inc 1 st in every 4th st around — 180 sts. Work in St st for 1½". **Next rnd:** K, inc 1 st in every 5th st around — 216 sts. Work in St st for 1½". **Next rnd:** K, inc 1 st in every 6th st around — 252 sts. **Next rnd:** K, inc 4 sts evenly spaced around — 256 sts. Work Chart 1 through Rnd 18. Work in St st for 4 rnds. **Next rnd:** K, inc 12 sts evenly spaced around — 264 sts. P next rnd for base of wimple. EDGING With straight needles and double strand of Tomato, cast on 12 sts. Cut one strand. Work Rows 1-16 of Chart 4 for 33 reps, slipping first st of all odd-numbered rows and joining last st of edging with next st of wimple base on all even-numbered rows. Graft last 12 sts of edging to close. Weave in yarn ends. Block with steam.

CHART #1

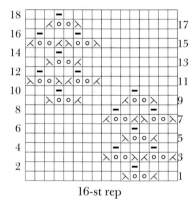

16-st rep

CHART #2

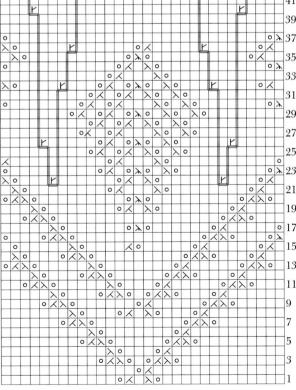

30-st rep

CHART #3

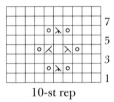

10-st rep

CHART #4

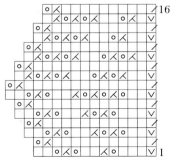

*note: open square=garter st (k every row)

☐ = k on RS, p on WS
− = p on RS, k on WS
○ = yarn over (yo)
○○ = yo twice
⋌ = k2tog
⋋ = ssk
⋏ = sl 1 knitwise, k2tog, psso
∨ = sl 1 st
⟋ = k2tog, joining last st of edging and next st of wimple
⌐ = inc 1 st

PATCHWORK-SUNFLOWER JACKET

INTERMEDIATE

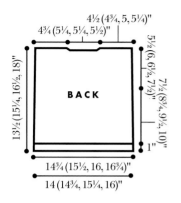

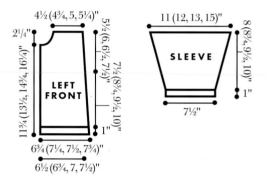

SIZES

To fit sizes 2 (4, 6, 8) or chest sizes 21 (23, 24½, 26½)". Directions are for smallest size with larger sizes in parentheses. If there is only one number, it applies to all sizes. Shown on page 93 in size 4.

FINISHED MEASUREMENTS

Chest at underarm (buttoned): 28 (29¼, 30¼, 32)"
Length from shoulder: 14 (15¾, 17, 18½)"
Sleeve width at upperarm: 11 (12, 13, 15)"

MATERIALS

3(3, 4, 4) 1¾oz/50g balls (each approx 109yd/99m) of Dale of
    Norway Heilo in #5563 Navy(A)
2(2, 3, 3) balls in #7562 Olive (B)
1 ball each in #5144 Lavender (C), #6545 Jade (D), #5545
    Periwinkle(E), #8152 Sea Foam(F), #2537 Dark Gold (G),
    #2427 Light Gold (H), #3418 Orange (I), #5036 Fuchsia(J)
Size 4 needles *or size needed to obtain gauge*
Size 4 circular needle 16" long
5 (5, 5, 6) ¾" drapery rings for buttons
Size E crochet hook
Tapestry needle
Stitch markers

GAUGE

20 sts and 27 rows to 4" over St st using size 4 needles. *To save time and to ensure accurate sizing, check gauge.*

BACK

With size 4 needles and A, cast on 74 (78, 80, 84) sts. Work in garter st (k every row) for 8 rows. Work in St st and chart for body, beg and end as indicated, dec 1 st each side after 14 rows, work 28 rows more and dec 1 st each side on next row—70 (74, 76, 80) sts. When piece measures 8½ (9¾, 10½, 11)" from beg, place marker each side for armholes. Work even until piece measures 5 (5½, 6, 7)" above markers, end with a WS row. NECK SHAPING **Next row (RS):** Work 24 (25, 26, 27) sts, join 2nd ball of yarn and bind off center 22 (24, 24, 26) sts, work to end. Working both sides at once, work 1 row even, dec 1 st at each neck edge on next row, work 1 row even. Bind off rem 23 (24, 25, 26) sts each side for shoulders.

LEFT FRONT

With size 4 needles and A, cast on 34 (36, 37, 39) sts. Work in garter st for 8 rows. Work in St st and chart for body, beg as for back and end as indicated for left front. Work decs and place armhole marker at side edge (beg of RS rows) as for back—32 (34, 35, 37) sts. Work even until piece measures 11¾ (13½, 14¾, 16¼)" from beg, end with a RS row. NECK SHAPING **Next row (WS):** Bind off 2 sts (neck edge), work to end. Cont to bind off from neck edge 2 sts 2 (3, 3, 4) times, then dec 1 st at neck edge 3 (2, 2, 1) times. Work even until piece measures same as back to shoulders. Bind off rem 23 (24, 25, 26) sts.

RIGHT FRONT

Work as for left front, reversing shaping. Beg body chart as indicated for right front, end as for back.

SLEEVES

With size 4 needles and A, cast on 39 sts. Work in garter st for 8 rows. Work in St st and chart for sleeve, beg and end as indicated. Inc 1 st each side every other row 0 (0, 0, 5) times, every 4th row 3 (6, 13, 13) times, every 6th row 6 (5, 1, 0) times—57 (61, 67, 75) sts. Work even until piece measures 9 (9¾, 10½, 11)" from beg. Bind off.

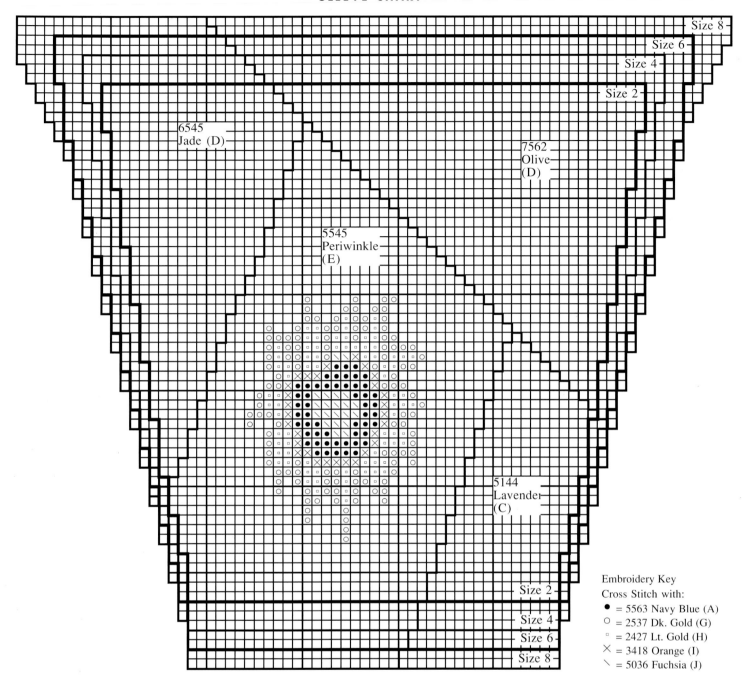

Size 8
Size 6
Size 4
Size 2

6545
Jade (D)

7562
Olive
(D)

5545
Periwinkle
(E)

5144
Lavender
(C)

Size 2
Size 4
Size 6
Size 8

Embroidery Key
Cross Stitch with:
● = 5563 Navy Blue (A)
○ = 2537 Dk. Gold (G)
▫ = 2427 Lt. Gold (H)
✕ = 3418 Orange (I)
╲ = 5036 Fuchsia (J)

FINISHING

Block pieces to measurements. EMBROIDERY Divide yarn into 2 strands. With tapestry needle, work feather st, fern st, spine ch st, and wheat ear st in colors as desired along color changes of all pieces. Cross st sunflowers on front, back, and sleeves, foll charts for placement and colors. Sew shoulder seams. Sew sleeves between markers. COLLAR With RS facing, circular needle and A, and beg at right front neck edge, pick up and k 61 (65, 65, 69) sts evenly around neck edge. Working in garter st, work 3 rows even. **Next (inc) row:** K3 (5, 5, 7), *inc 1 st in next st (by k into top of st below next st, then k next st), place marker (pm), k5; rep from * 8 times more, inc 1 st in next st, pm, end k3 (5, 5, 7)—71 (75, 75, 79) sts. Work 3 rows even. **Next (inc) row:** *Work to 1 st before marker, inc 1, sl marker; rep from *, end k3 (5, 5, 7). Rep last row every 4th row 4 times more—121 (125, 125, 129) sts. Bind off loosely. With crochet hook and A, work 1 row backwards sc (from left to right) along entire edge of collar. LEFT FRONT BUTTON BAND With RS facing, circular needle and A, pick up and k 55 (63, 69, 75) sts evenly

along left front edge to neck. Work in garter st for 7 rows. Bind off all sts on next row. RIGHT FRONT BUTTONHOLE BAND Pick up and work in garter st as for button band for 3 rows. **Next (buttonhole) row (RS):** K5 (5, 6, 4), *bind off 3 sts, k8 (10, 11, 10); rep from * 3 (3, 3, 4) times more, bind off 3 sts, k3 (3, 4, 3). Cont in garter st, on next row cast on 3 sts over each 3-st buttonhole. Work 2 rows even. Bind off. CROCHET BUTTONS With crochet hook and A, make a sl knot, then work sc into drapery ring until ring is completely filled. Cut yarn, leaving about 12". Thread this end through tapestry needle. Take needle through back of every other sc around ring, drawing yarn tightly so that edge draws in to form center of button. With rem yarn, sew button to button band, opposite a buttonhole. Work all buttons in same way. Sew side and sleeve seams. With crochet hook and J, work 1 row backwards sc around lower edge of each sleeve. Then work 1 row of backwards sc along right front edge (beg at top inside edge of buttonhole band), along lower edges of right front, back and left front, cont along left front edge, end at top inside edge of button band.

PATCHWORK-SUNFLOWER JACKET – BODY CHART

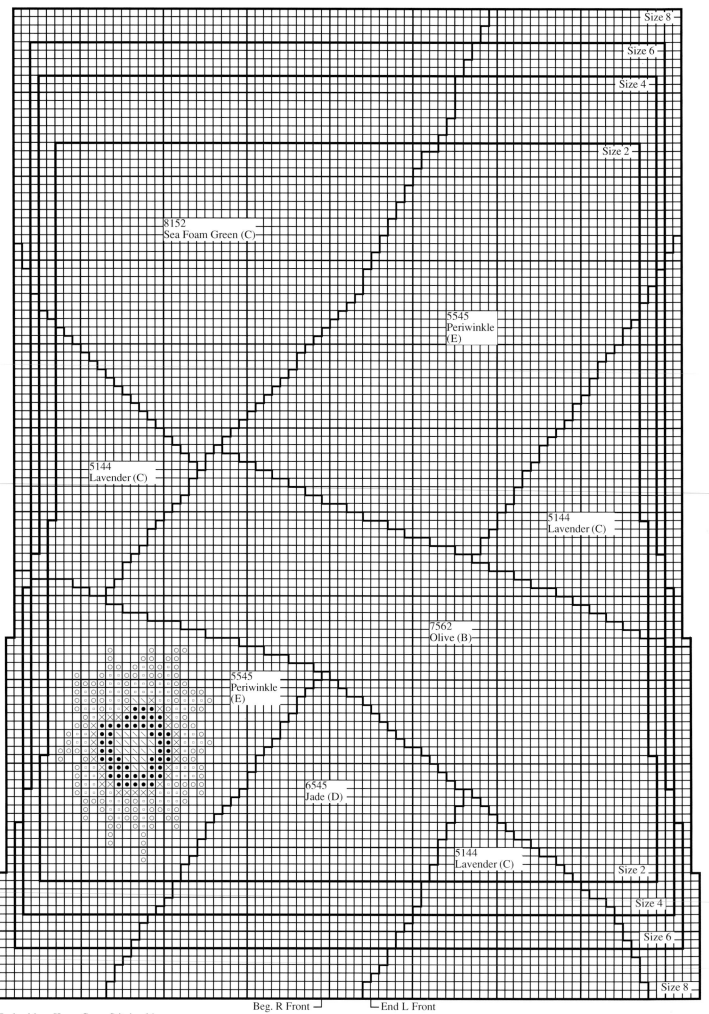

8152
Sea Foam Green (C)

5545
Periwinkle
(E)

5144
Lavender (C)

5144
Lavender (C)

7562
Olive (B)

5545
Periwinkle
(E)

6545
Jade (D)

5144
Lavender (C)

Size 8
Size 6
Size 4
Size 2
Size 2
Size 4
Size 6
Size 8

Beg. R Front   End L Front

Embroidery Key - Cross Stitch with:

● = 5563 Navy Blue (A)   ○ = 2537 Dk. Gold (G)   ▫ = 2427 Lt. Gold (H)   ✕ = 3418 Orange (I)   ╲ = 5036 Fuscia (J)

FAUX CABLE SAGE PULLOVER

SIZES

To fit sizes Woman's or Man's Small/Medium (Large). Directions are for smaller size with larger size in parentheses. If there is only one number, it applies to both sizes. Shown on pages 98 and 198 in size Small/Medium.

FINISHED MEASUREMENTS

Bust/chest at underarm: 44 (53)"
Length from shoulder: Woman's - 27 (28)"; Man's - 25 (26)"
Sleeve width at upper arm: 18"

MATERIALS

11 (12) 3½oz/100g skeins (each approx 110yd/101m) of Brown Sheep Company's Lamb's Pride Superwash Bulky in #002 Lichen
Sizes 6 and 9 knitting needles *or size needed to obtain gauge*
Size 6 circular needle 16" long
Cable needle (cn)

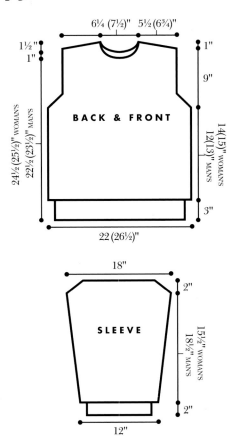

GAUGE

15 sts and 20 rows to 4" over rev St st using larger needles; 22 sts to 5" over Diamond Pat; 21 sts to 5" over Rib and Braid Pat. *To save time and to ensure accurate sizing, check gauges.*

STITCH GLOSSARY

2-st Left Twist (LT): Sl next st to cn and hold to *front,* k1, k1 from cn.
2-st Right Twist (RT): Sl next st to cn and hold to *back,* k1, k1 from cn.
2-st Left Purl Twist (LPT): Sl next st to cn and hold to *front,* p1, k1 from cn.
2-st Right Purl Twist (RPT): Sl next st to cn and hold to *back,* k1, p1 from cn.
2-st Left Slip Twist (LST): Sl next st to cn and hold to *front,* k1, sl 1 purlwise from cn.
2-st Right Slip Twist (RST): Sl next st to cn and hold to *back,* sl 1 purlwise, k1 from cn.
K1tbl: K1 st through back lp.
P1tbl: P1 st through back lp.

SL ST PAT (over 6 sts):

Rows 1 and 3 (WS): P6. **Row 2:** K1, RST, LST, k1. **Row 4:** RST, k2, LST. Rep rows 1 – 4 for sl st pat.

TWISTED V PAT (over 14 sts):

Row 1 (WS): P1tbl, k1, p1, k3, p2, k3, p1, k1, p1tbl. **Row 2:** K1tbl, RPT, p3, RT, p3, LPT, k1tbl. **Row 3:** [P2, k4] twice, p2. **Row 4:** RT, p3, RT, LT, p3, LT. **Row 5:** K5, p4, k5. **Row 6:** P4, RT, [k1tbl] twice, LT, p4. **Row 7:** K4, p1, k1, [p1tbl] twice, k1, p1, k4. **Row 8:** P3, RT, p1, [k1tbl] twice, p1, LT, p3. **Row 9:** K3, p2, k1, [p1tbl] twice, k1, p2, k3. **Row 10:** P2, RT, k1tbl, p1, [k1tbl] twice, p1, k1tbl, LT, p2. **Row 11:** K2, p1, k1, p1tbl, k1, [p1tbl] twice, k1, p1tbl, k1, p1, k2. **Row 12:** P1, RT, p1, k1tbl, p1, [k1tbl] twice, p1, k1tbl, p1, LT, p1. **Row 13:** K1, p2, k1, p1tbl, k1, p2, k1, p1tbl, k1, p2, k1. **Row 14:** RT, k1tbl, p1, k1tbl, RT, LT, k1tbl, p1, k1tbl, LT. **Row 15:** P1, k1, p1tbl, k1, p6, k1, p1tbl, k1, p1. **Row 16:** [K1tbl, p1] twice, RT, k2, LT, [p1, k1tbl] twice. **Row 17:** [P1tbl, k1] twice, p1, k1, p2, k1, p1, [k1, p1tbl] twice. **Row 18:** K1tbl, p1, k1tbl, [RT, p1] twice, LT, k1tbl, p1, k1tbl. **Row 19:** P1tbl, k1, [p2, k2] twice, p2, k1, p1tbl. **Row 20:** K1tbl, p1, RT, p2, k2, p2, LT, p1, k1tbl. Rep rows 1 – 20 for Twisted V Pat.

DIAMOND PAT (over 22 sts):

Row 1 (WS): K2, p2, k4, p6, k4, p2, k2. **Row 2:** P2, RT, p4, [LT] 3 times, p4, LT, p2. **Row 3:** Rep row 1. **Row 4:** P2, k2, p3, [RT] 3 times, LT, p3, k2, p2. **Row 5:** K2, p2, k3, p8, k3, p2, k2. **Row 6:** P2, RT, p2, RT, RPT, LT, LPT, [LT, p2] twice. **Row 7:** K2, p2, k2, p3, k1, p2, k1, p3, k2, p2, k2. **Row

8:** P2, k2, p1, RT, RPT, p1, k2, p1, LPT, LT, p1, k2, p2. **Row 9:** K2, p2, k1, p3, k2, p2, k2, p3, k1, p2, k2. **Row 10:** P2, [RT] twice, RPT, p2, LT, p2, LPT, [LT] twice, p2. **Row 11:** K2, p5, k3, p2, k3, p5, k2. **Row 12:** P1, [RT] twice, RPT, p3, k2, p3, LPT, [LT] twice, p1. **Row 13:** K1, p5, k4, p2, k4, p5, k1. **Row 14:** P1, k1, [RT] twice, p4, LT, p4, [LT] twice, k1, p1. **Row 15:** Rep row 13. **Row 16:** P1, LPT, RT, LT, p3, k2, p3, RT, LT, RPT, p1. **Row 17:** Rep row 11. **Row 18:** P2, RT, LPT, [LT, p2] twice, RT, RPT, LT, p2. **Row 19:** Rep row 9. **Row 20:** P2, k2, p1, LPT, LT, p1, k2, p1, RT, RPT, p1, k2, p2. **Row 21:** Rep row 7. **Row 22:** P2, RT, p2, LPT, [LT] twice, RT, RPT, p2, LT, p2. **Row 23:** Rep row 5. **Row 24:** P2, k2, p3, LPT, [RT] twice, RPT, p3, k2, p2. Rep rows 1 – 24 for Diamond Pat.

RIB AND BRAID PAT (over 21 sts):

Rows 1 and 3 (WS): K3, [p2, k2, p2, k3] twice. **Row 2:** P3, [RT, p2, RT, p3] twice. **Row 4:** P2, [RPT, LPT] twice, [p2, k2] twice, p3. **Rows 5 and 7:** K3, [p2, k2] twice, p1, k2, p2, k2, p1, k2. **Row 6:** P2, k1, p2, LT, p2, k1, [p2, k2] twice, p3. **Row 8:** P2, [LPT, RPT] twice, [p2, k2] twice, p3. **Row 9:** Rep row 1. **Row 10:** P3, RT, p2, RT, p3, k2, p2, k2, p3. **Rows 11 – 17:** Rep rows 3 – 9. **Rows 18 and 19:** Rep rows 2 and 3. **Row 20:** P3, [k2, p2] twice, [RPT, LPT] twice, p2. **Rows 21 and 23:** K2, [p1, k2, p2, k2] twice, p2, k3. **Row 22:** P3, [k2, p2] twice, k1, p2, LT, p2, k1, p2. **Row 24:** P3, [k2, p2] twice, [LPT, RPT] twice, p2. **Rows 25 and 27:** Rep row 1. **Row 26:** P3, k2, p2, k2, p3, RT, p2, RT, p3. **Rows 28 – 32:** Rep rows 20 – 24. Rep rows 1 – 32 for Rib and Braid Pat.

BACK

With smaller needles, cast on 78 (90) sts. Work in k2, p2 ribbing for 3", inc 19 (23) sts evenly across last (RS) row—97 (113) sts. Change to larger needles. ESTABLISH PATS **Next row (WS):** Work 4 (12) sts in rev St st, work Sl St Pat over 6 sts, Diamond Pat over 22 sts, Sl St Pat over 6 sts, Rib and Braid Pat over 21 sts, Sl St Pat over 6 sts, Diamond Pat over 22 sts, Sl St Pat over 6 sts, 4 (12) sts in rev St st. Cont in pats as est until piece measures 17 (18)" for Woman's; 15 (16)" for Man's from beg, end with a WS row. ARMHOLE SHAPING Dec 1 st each side *every* row 10 times—77 (93) sts. Cont in pats until armhole measures 8 ½", end with a WS row. NECK AND SHOULDER SHAPING **Next row (RS):** Work 29

(34) sts, join 2nd skein and bind off center 19 (25) sts, work to end. Working both sides at once, bind off from each neck edge 2 sts twice, AT SAME TIME, after 2 rows of neck shaping have been worked, bind off from each shoulder edge 8 (10) sts 2 (3) times, 9 sts 1 (0) time.

FRONT

Work as for back until armhole measures 7½", end with a WS row. NECK AND SHOULDER SHAPING **Next row (RS):** Work 31 (36) sts, join 2nd skein and bind off center 15 (21) sts, work to end. Working both sides at once, bind off from each neck edge 2 sts twice, dec 1 st each neck edge every other row twice, AT SAME TIME, when piece measures same as back to shoulders, shape shoulders as for back.

SLEEVES

With smaller needles, cast on 34 sts. Work in k2, p2 rib for 2", inc 20 sts evenly across last (RS) row—54 sts. Change to larger needles. ESTABLISH PATS **Next row (WS):** Work 2 sts in rev St st, work Twisted V Pat over 14 sts, Diamond Pat over 22 sts, Twisted V Pat over 14 sts, 2 sts rev St st. Cont in pats as est, inc 1 st each side (working inc sts into rev St st) every 8th row 4 times, every 10th row 3 times—68 sts. Work even until piece measures 17½" for Woman's; 20½" for Man's from beg, end with a WS row. CAP SHAPING Work shaping as for back armhole—48 sts. Bind off.

FINISHING

Block pieces to measurements. Sew shoulder seams. NECKBAND With RS facing and circular needle, beg at right shoulder, pick up 88 (96) sts evenly around neck edge. Join, place marker, and work in rnds of k2, p2 rib for 5". Bind off. Fold band in half to WS and sew to neck edge. Set in sleeves. Sew side and sleeve seams.

NAVAJO PULLOVER

INTERMEDIATE

SIZES

To fit woman's or man's Small (Medium, Large, X-Large). Directions are for smallest size with larger sizes in parentheses. If there is only one figure it applies to all sizes. Shown on page 97 in Small.

FINISHED MEASUREMENTS

Bust/chest at underarm: 44 (48, 52, 56)"
Length from shoulder: 24 (25, 26, 27)"
Sleeve width at upper arm: 17 (18, 19, 20)"

MATERIALS

22 (25, 28, 31) oz of La Lana Wools Machine-Spun Worsted-
    Weight Wool in Black (A)
4 oz each of La Lana Handspun in Apassionada (B), Zulu Prince
    (C), and Pastorale (D)
One pair each sizes 8 and 10½ needles *or size needed to obtain
    gauge*
Size 8 circular needle 24" long
Stitch markers

GAUGE

16 sts and 20 rows to 4" over St st using larger needles. ***To save time and to ensure accurate sizing, check gauge.***

Note: When working charts, use a separate ball or bobbin of yarn for each contrasting color carrying only background color across the center pattern.

STITCH GLOSSARY

Left Twist (LT): Skip next st on LH needle and k 2nd st in back loop, slip skipped st purlwise onto RH needle, drop 2nd st from LH needle.

RIBBING PATTERN (muliple of 6 sts plus 2)
Rows 1, 3 and 5 (WS): K 2, *p 4, k 2; rep from * to end.
Row 2: P 2, *LT, k 2, p 2; rep from * to end.
Row 4: P 2, *k 1, LT, k 1, p 2; rep from * to end.
Row 6: P 2, *k 2, LT, p 2; rep from * to end.
Rep Rows 1-6 for ribbing pat.

FRONT

With smaller needles and A, cast on 86 (92, 98, 104) sts. Work 6 rows of ribbing pat 3 times (18 rows), then rep row 1 once more. Change to larger needles. **Next row (RS):** K, inc 4 (6, 8, 10) sts evenly across row — 90 (98, 106, 114) sts. **Next row:** Purl. Work in St st as foll: **Beg chart #1:** Work 5 (9, 3, 7) sts A, work 20-st rep of chart #1 4 (4, 5, 5) times, work 5 (9, 3, 7) sts A. Cont as established through row 12. Cont in St st with A only until piece measures 8½ (9½, 10½, 11½)" from beg, end with a WS row. **Beg chart #2: Row 1 (RS):** K 2 (6, 10, 14) sts with A, place marker, work row 1 of chart #2 over next 86 sts as foll: work sts 1 - 43 of chart, then working from left to right, work chart back from sts 43 - 1, place marker, k 2 (6, 10, 14) sts A. Cont chart #2 in St st as established until chart row 56 has been completed. NECK SHAPING **Next row (RS):** Cont chart #2, k 36 (40, 44, 48) sts, join 2nd ball of yarn (or bobbin) and bind off center 18 sts, work to end. Working both sides at once, work 1 row even. **Dec row (RS):** K to 3 sts before end of first half, k2tog, k 1; with 2nd ball of yarn, k 1, sl 1, k 1, psso, k to end. Rep dec row every other row 9 times more. Bind off rem 26 (30, 34, 38) sts each side for shoulders.

BACK

Work as for front until chart #2 row 70 has been completed. NECK SHAPING **Next row (RS):** K 29 (33, 37, 41) sts, join 2nd ball of yarn (or bobbin) and work center 32 sts and place on holder, work to end. Working both sides at once, cont chart in St st, rep dec row as for front every other row 3 times. Bind off rem 26 (30, 34, 38) sts each side.

SLEEVES

With smaller needles and A, cast on 44 (50, 50, 56) sts. Work 6 rows of ribbing pat 3 times (18 rows), then rep row 1 once more. Change to larger needles. Cont in St st with A only, inc 1 st each side every 4th row 5 (0, 3, 0) times, every 6th row 7 (11, 10, 12) times — 68 (72, 76, 80) sts. Work even until piece measures 13 (14, 14½, 15)" from beg, end with a WS row. Work chart #1, beg with chart row 12, as foll: Work 4 (6, 8, 0) sts A, work 20-st rep of row 12 of chart #1 3 (3, 3, 4) times, work 4 (6, 8,

0) sts A. Cont as established, working down to chart row 1. Work with A only until piece measures 17 (18, 18½, 19)" from beg for woman's; 19 (20, 20½, 21)" from beg for man's. Bind off.

FINISHING

Block pieces to measurements. Sew shoulder seams. NECKBAND With RS facing, circular needle and A, pick up and k 32 sts along right front neck edge, k 32 sts from back holder, then pick up and k 32 sts along left front neck edge — 96 sts. Work back and forth as with straight needles as foll: **Rows 1, 3 and 5 (WS):** P 1 (edge st), *p 4, k 2; rep from * to last 5 sts, p 4, p 1 (edge st). **Row 2:** K 1 (edge st), *LT, k 2, p 2; rep from * to last 5 sts, LT, k 2, k 1 (edge st). **Row 4:** K 1 (edge st), *k 1, LT, k 1, p 2; rep from * to last 5 sts, k 1, LT, k 1 (edge st). **Row 6:** K 1 (edge st), *k 2, LT, p 2; rep from * to last 5 sts, k 2, LT, k 1 (edge st). Rep these 6 rows of ribbing pat 3 times more, then rep row 1 once more. Bind off. Sew ends of neckband to bound-off front neck edge, overlapping right front over left front for woman, left over right for man. Place markers 8½ (9, 9½, 10)" down from shoulder seams on front and back for armholes. Sew top of sleeves between markers. Sew side and sleeve seams.

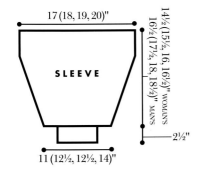

=Black (A)

⊠ =Apassionada (B)

□ =Zulu Prince (C)

z =Pastorale (D)

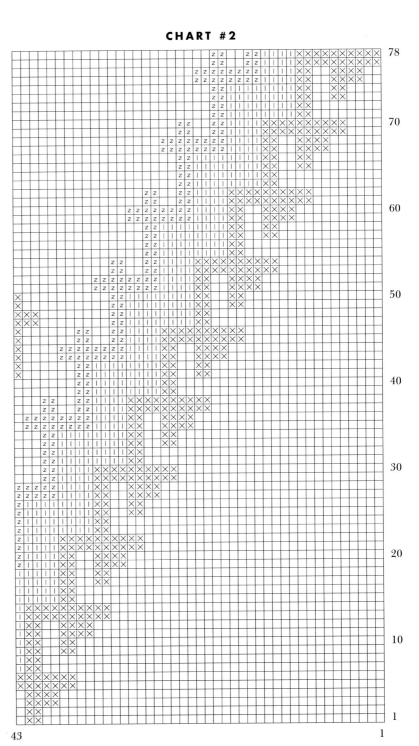

CHART #2

CHART #1

20-st rep

KESTRALS ALIGHT CROPPED KIMONO

SIZES

To fit sizes Petite (Small/Medium, Large). Directions are for smaller size with larger sizes in parentheses. If there is only one figure it applies to all sizes. Shown on page 104 in size Small/Medium.

FINISHED MEASUREMENTS

Bust at underarm (closed): 34½ (42½, 50½)"
Length from shoulder: 21 (22, 23)"
Sleeve width at upperarm: 19½ (20½, 21½)"

MATERIALS (see Spinning and Dyeing Notes if making handspun version)

8 (9, 10) 1¾oz/50 gm balls (each approx 143yd/129m) of Classic Elite Avalon in #5975 Mined Slate (MC)
7 (8, 9) balls in #5916 Natural (CC)
Small amounts in #5911 Young Girl's Blush, #5984 Sweet Butter, #5921 Lamb's Ear, #5923 Mellow Autumn, and #5958 Ravishing Red
Size 2 circular needle each 16" and 32" long *or size needed to obtain gauge*
Size 1 circular needle 32" long
One set dpn each sizes 1 and 2
Two ¾" buttons
Stitch markers
Sewing machine (optional)

GAUGE

32 sts and 36 rows to 4" over chart pat using larger needle. *To save time and ensure accurate sizing, check gauge.*

SPINNING AND DYEING NOTES

To make the yarn for the Kestrals Alight Cropped Kimono, Sarah spun a 3-ply yarn at approx 1300 yds per pound. Two plies are from Cormo fleece and one is from a Merino fleece. They are all spun "Z" by the worsted method and 3-plied "S". She made the sweater in a Small/Medium and used 450 grams blue yarn and 400 grams red/orange/magenta yarn. Blue yarn was dyed in an Indigo Hydrosulfite Vat. Yarn was divided into seven equal skeins and dyed in a 7 value progression. Value differences are achieved by both number and length of dips into bath. Red/Orange/Magenta yarn was dyed in a Cochineal/Madder dye bath. 8% WOG (Weight Of Goods) Cochineal was ground, soaked, and the dye extracted to make 15 cups of solution. 40% WOG Madder was ground, soaked, and the dye extracted to make 15 cups of solution. Into each of five half-gallon jars went combinations of the dye as foll: *1)* 5 cups madder and 1 cup cochineal; *2)* 4 cups madder and 2 cups cochineal; *3)* 3 cups madder and 3 cups cochineal; *4)* 2 cups madder and 4 cups cochineal; *5)* 1 cup madder and 5 cups cochineal. The yarn was divided into five equal skeins, premordanted with 10% alum and 5% Cream of Tartar, then rinsed thoroughly. It was placed in warm (100 degrees F) dye solutions in the five jars in a large canner filled with water. This method helps to maintain a constant even temperature. It was then slowly heated to 170 degrees F, held at temperature for one hour and allowed to cool in the bath. At high temperatures, madder tends to turn brown. All yarns were thoroughly washed and rinsed. While knitting the sweater, Sarah changed red/orange/magenta yarns every other round (2 rounds of each hue), moving evenly and consistently from the most orange to the most magenta and back. She changed blue yarns (from darkest to lightest) in the body approximately every 2 inches, working an inch of overlap (a gradual transition from one color to the next to avoid striping) after each 2-inch block of one color, as follows: knit 2 rounds of first (darkest) color, 1 round of second color, 3 rounds of the first color, 1 round of the second color, 2 rounds of the first color, 1 round of the second color, 1 round of the first color and one of the second color 3 times, and then the reverse, moving into the second color. Knit approximately 2 more inches, then transition into the next lightest shade. For the sleeves Sarah knit only 1 inch of each color before beginning the transition to the next color. All color changes in the body of the sweater took place within the steek and were later cut out. Blue (MC) was used as the background color (BC) and red (CC) was used for the vines and birds [design color (DC)] for the back of the sweater, the left sleeve, the right cuff, and the left front. Red (CC) was used as the background color (BC) for the right front, right sleeve, and left cuff.

BODY

With smaller circular needle and CC, cast on 202 (262, 322) sts using cable cast on as foll: cast on 2 sts using standard knitting-on method. Insert right needle between 2 sts on left needle, wrap yarn around right needle as if to knit and pull yarn through to make a new st, then transfer new st to left needle by inserting tip of left needle through top of st on right needle. Cont until desired number of sts are achieved, always inserting right needle between first 2 sts on left needle. Work back and forth in garter st (k every row) for 4 rows (2 ridges). **Next row (RS):** *K2 CC, k2 MC; rep from *, end k2 CC. **Next row (WS):** Rep last row, making sure that color is carried in front (WS of work). With CC, k 2 more rows (1 ridge), then k 1 row, inc 32 (36, 40) sts evenly across row, place marker and cast on 10 sts at end of row for steek alternating colors MC and CC. **Note:** All steek sts are worked in St st alternating 1 st MC and 1 st CC, forming a check pat, always working MC of previous row in CC and vice-versa — 244 (308, 372) sts. Change to larger 32" circular needle and work in rnds. **Beg pat - Next rnd:** Place marker for right front, *k1 BC, work 48 (64, 80) sts of Chart #1, k1 BC*, place marker for back, k3 MC, cont chart #1 over next 128 (160, 192) sts, k3 MC, place marker for left front; rep between *'s once, using (MC) as background (BC) work 10 steek sts. Cont to work in pat as established, rep rnds 1-10 only of chart #1, until piece measures 8 (8, 8 ½)" from beg. NECK SHAPING **Next (dec) rnd:** At either side of steek sts (front neck), dec 1 st as foll: on Right Front, k1, SKP; on Left Front, work to last 3 sts, k2 tog, k 1. Rep dec rnd every 12th (10th, 8th) rnd 2 (8, 5) times, every 14th (12th, 10th) rnd 6 (3, 8) times, AT THE SAME TIME, when piece measures 10 ½ (11, 11½)" from beg, make armhole steek as foll: work to 1 st before back marker, inc 1 st in next st for armhole edge st, sl marker, place next st on holder, cast on 8 sts in alternate colors for steek, place marker, inc 1 st in next st for armhole edge st, work across sts of back to last st, inc 1 st in next st for armhole edge st, place marker, put next st on holder, cast on 8 sts in alt colors for steek, sl marker, inc 1 st in next st for armhole edge st, finish rnd. Work armhole edge sts in BC on every row. Cont working Chart #1 (rnds 1-10 only) until piece measures 13½ (14 ½, 15½)" from beg. Work rnds 11 - 71 of Chart #1. Armhole measures approx 9¾ (10¼, 10¾)", end by binding off center steek. SHOULDER SHAPING On next row, work back and forth in St st with BC only, work 7 short rows on right front as foll to shape shoulder: K 31 (41, 51), turn, sl first st, p to neck edge. Turn, k 21 (28, 34), turn, sl first st, p to neck edge. Turn, k 11 (15, 17), turn, sl first st, p to neck. Turn, K across all sts and leave on needle, bind off steek in MC. Leave center 52 (58, 62) sts on holder for neck and work same short rows on left and right back shoulders. Bind off other steek and work short rows for left front. Graft front and back tog at shoulder.

SLEEVES

Baste down center of each steek. With a small st and loose tension, machine-stitch down one side of the basting, across the bottom, and up the other side, staying as close to the center st as possible while leaving enough space for the blade of the scissor. Cut on basting. (Alternatively, back-stitch by hand down each side of the center basting, then cut steek at center.) Using larger 16" circular needle and BC, slip st from holder and pick up and k 152 (160, 170) sts around armhole —153 (161, 171) sts. Join and work in rnds as foll: **Next rnd:** K 13 (17, 6) BC, beg with rnd 10, work 32-st rep of Chart #1 4 (4, 5) times, k 12 (16, 5) BC. (Carry DC across BC at underarm.) **Note:** Work 10 rnds of chart #1 backwards, by working rnd 10 through rnd 1. Cont to work in rnds of pat for 3 rnds more. **Next (dec) rnd:** K 1, SKP, k to last 2 sts, k2 tog. Cont to rep dec rnd every 4th rnd 31 (33, 27) times more, every other rnd 0 (0, 9) time times — 89 (93, 97) sts. Work even until sleeve measures 15½". Change to dpn when there are too few sts for circular needle. CUFF Note: reverse colors for chart #2 - BC will be worked with DC from sleeve. K 1 rnd with CC, dec 29 (23, 27) sts — 60 (70, 70) sts. P 1 rnd to make P ridge on RS. Work rnds 1 - 15 of Chart #2. K 1 rnd with CC, dec 8 (10, 10) sts — 52 (60, 60) sts. Change to smaller dpn. P 1 rnd for P ridge on RS. **Next rnd:** *K2 MC, k2 CC; rep from * around. **Next rnd:** *P2 MC, p2 CC; rep from * around, carrying color on WS of work. With CC, [k 1 rnd, p 1 rnd] 3 times. Bind off on last P rnd. Work other sleeve, reversing colors.

FRONT BAND AND COLLAR
Cut front steek as for armholes. With RS facing, larger needles and CC, beg at lower edge of right front, pick up and k 154 (161, 169) sts up front and across shoulder, k 52 (58, 62) back neck sts from holder, pick up 154 (161, 169) sts across left shoulder and down left front — 360 (380, 400) sts. **Next row (WS):** K5, place marker, k to last 5 sts, place marker, k5. Keeping first and last 5 sts in garter st with CC, work rem sts in St st and Chart #2 (CC as BC). After last row of chart, p next row with CC, dec 60 sts evenly spaced — 300 (320, 340) sts. Change to smaller needles and work in garter st for 2 rows. Change to MC, work 6 rows garter st. **Next 2 rows:** *K2 MC, K2 CC; rep from * to end. Cont to work in garter st with MC until band measures 5½" from beg, leave sts on needle.

I-CORD BIND OFF
With RS facing, beg at bottom edge of right front band, with CC and smaller needles, cast on 3 sts. *K2, sl 1, knit up 1 st from garter border (in garter ridge), pass slipped st over knit st. Slide sts to opposite end of needle; rep from *, knitting up 1 st from each garter ridge across to 1 ridge before the front edge corner. To turn corner: Work a row of I-cord (k3, slide sts to opposite end of needle) *without joining* to border, join next row, work a row without joining, join next row to corner st, work one more row without joining. Cont up the front as foll: *slip the 3 I-cord sts to needle holding the front band sts, k2, sl 1, k1 (next st on needle holding front band), psso; rep from * to 7½" above bottom edge of *right* front. MAKE BUTTONHOLE: Work I-cord *without joining* for ¾"; bind off 6 sts from front band as foll: slip next 2 sts of front band to spare needle, [pass first st over 2nd st (1 st bound off), slip next st from front band to spare needle] 5 times, then bind off 6th st in same way. Return st on spare needle to front band needle; rep from * to 8 (8, 8½)" from bottom of *left* front, make a buttonhole as before. Rep from * to 1 st from corner, turn corner as for right front, work across bottom edge as for right front band. Bind off.

FINISHING
If steeks were hand-stitched, trim and cross-stitch edges to secure. Sew buttons opposite buttonholes on outside of left front and inside of right front. Duplicate st details of birds and leaves with contrasting colors as desired (see photo).

CHART #1

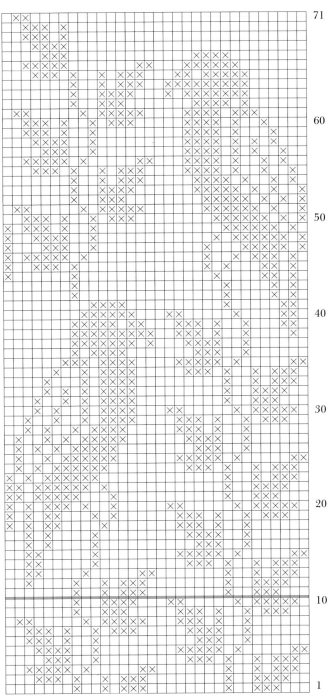

71

60

50

40

30

20

10

1

32 sts

CHART #2

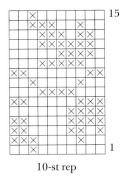

15

1

10-st rep

☐ Background color (BC)

☒ Design color (DC)

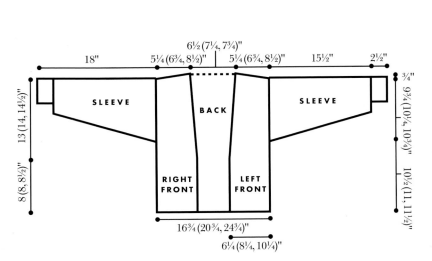

18"   5¼ (6¾, 8½)"   6½ (7¼, 7¾)"   5¼ (6¾, 8½)"   15½"   2½"

SLEEVE   BACK   SLEEVE

RIGHT FRONT   LEFT FRONT

13 (14, 14½)"

8 (8, 8½)"

16¾ (20¾, 24¾)"

6¼ (8¼, 10¼)"

¾"

9¾ (10¼, 10¾)"

10½ (11, 11½)"

SNOQUALMIE STRIPES JACKET

INTERMEDIATE

SIZES

To fit Small/Medium (Large/X-Large). Directions are for smallest size with larger size in parentheses. If there is only one figure it applies to both sizes. Shown on page 112 in size Large/X-Large.

FINISHED MEASUREMENTS

Bust at underarm (buttoned): 45 (53)"
Length from shoulder: 30¾"
Sleeve width at upper arm: 19 (20)"

MATERIALS

10 (10) skeins 3½oz/100g (each approx 166yd/152m) of Creative Yarns International BioSpun Merino 8-ply in #236 Deep Wood (A)
2 skeins each in #210 Thimbleberry (B), #211 Red Currant (D), #218 Indian Paintbrush (E), #242 Blueberry (F), and #213 Blackberry (G),
3 skeins each in #230 Yew (C), #250 Sage (H), and #251 Green Tea (I)
One pair each size 3, 6, 8 and 10 needles *or size needed to obtain gauge*
Sizes 6 and 10 circular needles 29" long
Stitch holders
3 buttons

GAUGE

18 sts and 27 rows to 4" over St st and chart pat using size 6 needles. *To save time and to ensure accurate sizing, check gauge.*

Note 1: When changing colors, twist yarns on WS to prevent holes. Use separate bobbins or balls of yarn for each rectangle. **Note 2.** For ease in knitting, use markers to separate various chart pats.

WOVEN STITCH (multiple of 2 + 1)

Row 1 (RS): *Skip first st, knit into back of 2nd st but leave on needle, knit into front of first st and let both drop off needle; rep from * across, end k 1.
Row 2: *Skip first st, purl into front of 2nd st but leave on needle, purl into front of first st and let both drop off needle; rep from * across, end p 1. Rep Rows 1 and 2 for woven st.

Rectangle A: 18 sts, see chart
Rectangle B: 18 sts, see chart
Rectangle C: 18 sts, worked in St st
Rows 1 and 2: 6 A, 6 H, 6 A. Rows 3 and 4: 6 C, 6 I, 6 C.
Rows 5-40: Work rows 1-4 nine times.
Rectangle D: 18 sts and 40 rows in St st with A

BACK

With size 3 needles and A, cast on 100 (116) sts. Work in k 1 p 1 rib in stripes as foll: 1 row B, 1 row D, 1 row C, 1 row F, 1 row G, inc 8 (10) sts evenly spaced across last row — 108 (126) sts. Change to size 6 needles and St st. Work rectangles foll back placement diagram. Piece measures approx 30¾" from beg. Place all sts on a holder.

RIGHT FRONT

POCKET LININGS (make 2) With size 6 needles and E, cast on 18 sts. Work in St st for 6½". Place sts on a holder. With size 3 needles and A, cast on 41 (49) sts. Rib as back for 5 rows, inc 4 (5) sts evenly spaced across

last row — 45 (54) sts. Change to size 6 needles and St st. Work rectangles foll right front placement diagram, until piece measures approx 9" (20 rows of 2nd rectangle) from beg, end with a WS row. POCKET PLACEMENT **Next row (RS):** Work 18 (18) sts, sl next 18 sts to a holder for pocket opening, work across 18 sts of one pocket lining holder, work to end. Work even in pats until 160 rows (4 rectangles) have been completed. Piece measures approx 24¾" from beg. NECK SHAPING Cont to foll diagram, dec 1 st at neck edge (beg of RS rows) on next row, then every 6th row 4 times more — 40 (49) sts. Work to end of diagram. Place sts on a holder.

LEFT FRONT

Work as for right front, foll left front placement diagram and reversing pocket placement and neck shaping.

SLEEVES

With size 10 needles and A, cast on 71 (75) sts. Work in woven st for 4". Change to size 8 needles and cont in woven st for 4" more, ending with a RS row of woven st completing cuff. Change to size 6 needles. Work rectangles foll sleeve placement diagram, beg with a k row on RS, which will be WS of cuff, inc 1 st at beg of first row, then inc 1 st each side every 10th row 7 times — 86 (90) sts. Work to end of diagram. Piece measures approx 20" from beg. Change to size 8 needles and bind off all sts loosely.

FINISHING

Block pieces to measurements. *Work knit tog bind off on 40 (49) sts* of right shoulder, bind off 28 sts across back of neck; rep between *'s for left front. Place markers 9½ (10)" down from shoulders on front and back for armholes. Sew top of sleeves between markers. Sew side and sleeve seams.

SHAWL COLLAR

With RS facing, using size 6 circular needle and A, pick up and k 164 sts along right front edge, 25 sts across back neck, 164 sts along left front edge skipping approx every 5th st — 353 sts. Change to size 10 circular needle. Do not join; work back and forth on circular needle. Beg on RS of collar with Row 1, work 2 rows of woven st. **Row 3 (dec):** Working Row 1 of woven st, knit 3rd and 4th sts tog through back of sts but do not drop off needle, then knit first and 2nd sts tog through front of sts and drop off needle tog, work to last 5 sts, knit 3rd and 4th sts together through back of sts but do not drop off needle, then knit first and 2nd sts tog through front of sts and drop off needle tog, k last st. Work short rows as foll: **Next row:** Work to last 61 sts, sl 1, turn. Rep last row. Cont to work 20 sts less at end of every row 4 times, then work 10 sts less at end of every row 6 times. **Next row:** Work 12 sts more, then turn. Rep this row 5 more times, then work 22 sts more on each row 4 times. **Next row (WS):** Work to end of row. **Next row (RS):** Rep Row 3 (dec) above. **Next row:** Working Row 2 of woven st, purl 3rd and 4th sts tog but do not drop off needle, then purl first and 2nd sts tog and drop off needle tog, work to last 5 sts, purl 3rd and 4th sts tog but do not drop off needle, then purl first and 2nd sts tog and drop off needle tog, p last st. Rep last 2 rows once more. Bind off all sts loosely. BUTTON BAND With RS facing, using size 3 circular needle and A, beg at right front lower edge, pick up and k4 sts in every 5 rows along inner edge of collar, ending at left front lower edge. Work in k 1, p 1 rib for 1 row. **Next row:** Work 3 buttonholes 2" apart, where desired, by binding off 2 sts for each buttonhole. On next row, cast on 2 sts over bound-off sts. Rib 2 rows more. Bind off in rib. POCKET BANDS With size 6 needles work in k 1, p 1 rib across pocket sts on holder as foll: 1 row F, 1 row A, 1 row E, 1 row C. Bind off with A. Sew pocket linings in place on WS.

RECTANGLE A

40

18 sts

1

RECTANGLE B

40

18 sts

1

☐ =Deep Wood (A)

| =Thimbleberry (B)

c =Yew (C)

— =Red Currant (D)

✳ =Indian Paintbrush (E)

\ =Blueberry (F)

O =Blackberry (G)

z =Sage (H)

X =Green Tea (I)

V =S1 1 wyib on RS
S1 wyif on WS

RIGHT FRONT PLACEMENT DIAGRAM

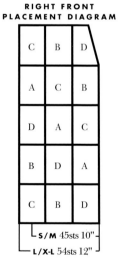

C	B	D
A	C	B
D	A	C
B	D	A
C	B	D

S/M 45sts 10"
L/X-L 54sts 12"

LEFT FRONT PLACEMENT DIAGRAM

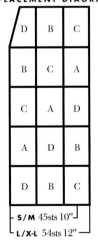

D	B	C
B	C	A
C	A	D
A	D	B
D	B	C

S/M 45sts 10"
L/X-L 54sts 12"

SLEEVE PLACEMENT DIAGRAM

(19, 20)"

A	C	B	C	A
D	A	C	A	D

12"

WOVEN ST WITH A

8"

15"

BACK PLACEMENT DIAGRAM

C	B	D	A	D	B	C
A	C	B	D	B	C	A
D	A	C	B	C	A	D
B	D	A	C	A	D	B
C	B	D	A	D	B	C

(9½, 10)"

(20½, 20)"

SMALL/MEDIUM 108sts 24"
LARGE/X-LARGE 126sts 28"

LA PLATA SOCKS

SIZES

To fit woman's(man's) size. Directions are for woman's size with man's size in parentheses. If there is only one figure, it applies to both sizes. Shown on pages 118-121.

MATERIALS

WOMAN'S SOCKS:

1 1¾oz/50 gm skein each of Happy Trails Sock Yarn for Buckskin Sock: Buckskin (A), Campfire (B), Bandana (C), Raspberry Jam (D), Larkspur (E) or for Green Sock: Sage (A), Cactus (B), Larkspur (C), Miss Kitty (D), Rabbit Rush (E)

One set (4) double-pointed needles size 3 *or size needed to obtain gauge*

Stitch marker

MAN'S SOCKS:

2 1¾oz/50 gm skeins of Stetson (black) or Cloud (white) (MC), 1 skein each of Cloud or Stetson (A) and Sagebrush (green/gray) (B)

One set (4) dpn size 4 *or size needed to obtain gauge*

Stitch marker

GAUGE

WOMAN'S SOCKS:

26 sts and 32 rnds to 4" over St st using size 3 needles.

MAN'S SOCKS:

24 sts and 30 rnds to 4" over St st using size 4 needles.

To save time and to ensure accurate sizing, check gauge.

Note: When changing colors, twist yarns on WS to prevent holes.

LEG

Using B and D (MC and A), and size 3 (4) dpns, cast on 58 sts by making a slip knot with both colors and cast on using the long tail method (with B (MC) over the index finger and D (A) over the thumb). The slip knot, with both colors, will be removed before the sts are joined and does not figure in the st count. Divide sts on 3 dpns. Join, being careful not to twist sts, place marker for beg of rnd. **Rnd 1:** With B (MC), work in k 1, p 1 rib. **Rnd 2:** * K 1 D (A), p 1 B (MC), rep from * across. **Rnds 3-5:** With B (MC), rib. **Rnd 6:** Rep rnd 2. **Rnds 7-14:** With B (MC), rib. **Rnd 15:** With B (MC), rib and k2tog at end of rnd — 57sts. FOR WOMAN'S SOCK: Work chart #1 as foll: beg with first st of chart, work to rep, work 20-st rep twice, work last 14 sts of chart. Cont as established, working rnds 1-18 twice, then work rnds 1-3 once more. FOR MAN'S SOCK Foll chart #2, rep rnds 1-18 twice, then work rnds 1-9 once. DIVIDE FOR HEEL Divide sts for heel by placing the first 15 sts and last 15 sts of the leg onto one dpn (these are the last 15 sts of the present rnd and the first 15 sts of the next rnd); sl the next 27 sts on a piece of scrap yarn (they will form the instep and are ignored while working the heel). With WS of heel sts facing, attach A and p the 30 heel sts. Turn, *sl 1, k 1; rep from * across. Turn, sl 1, p 29. Rep these 2 rows until you have 30 rows and 15 chain sts at the edges of the heel flap, ending with a WS row. TURN HEEL Turn the heel by working a series of "short rows" from the center of the heel flap as foll, slipping the first st of each short row. **Next row:** (Sl 1, k 1) in pat across 18 sts, SSK. *Turn, sl 1, p 6, p2tog. Turn, sl 1, pat across 6 sts as established, SSK*. Rep from * to * until all sts have been worked — 8 sts rem. SHAPE GUSSET With A, k across 8 heel sts, with the same dpn pick up and k 15 sts up right side of heel flap; with 2nd dpn k across 27 instep sts; with 3rd dpn pick up and k 15 sts down left side of heel flap, then k first 4 heel sts (19 sts on first and 3rd dpns, 27 instep sts on 2nd dpn). Place marker to indicate beg of rnd. **Next rnd:** On first dpn work to last 3 sts, k2tog, k 1; on 2nd dpn k across instep sts; on 3rd dpn k 1, SSK, work to end of rnd. **Next rnd:** Work even. Rep last 2 rnds until you have dec'd 7 sts at each side of heel flap (12 sts on first and 3rd dpns and 27 instep sts on 2nd dpn). Work 3 rnds even.

FOOT

WOMAN'S SOCK **Rnds 1 and 3:** *K1A, k1B, k1A; rep from * around. **Rnd 2:** *K2D, k1A; rep from * around. **Rnds 4-8:** Knit with A. **Rnds 9 and 11:** *K1A, k1C, k1A; rep from * around. **Rnd 10:** Rep rnd 2. **Rnds 12-16:** Knit with A. **Rnds 17-19:** Rep rnds 1-3. With A, k 1 rnd. MAN'S SOCK: **Rnds 1 and 3:** *K2MC, k1A; rep from * around. **Rnd 2:** *K1MC, k2B; rep from * around. **Rnds 4-8:** K with MC. **Rnds 9 and 11:** *K2MC, k1B; rep from * around. **Rnd 10:** *K1MC, k2A; rep from * around. **Rnds 12-16:** K with MC. **Rnds 17-27:** Rep rnds 1-11. With A, work 3 rnds. SHAPE TOE BOTH SOCKS **Dec rnd:** With A, on first dpn work all sts; on 2nd dpn k 1, ssk, work to last 3 sts, k2tog, k 1; on 3rd dpn k to end of rnd. **Next rnd:** Work even. **Next rnd:** On first dpn work to last 3 sts, k2tog, k 1; on 2nd dpn k 1, SSK, work to last 3 sts, k2tog, k 1; on 3rd dpn k 1, SSK, work to end of rnd. Rep last 2 rnds until there are 6 sts on first and 3rd dpns and 13 instep sts on 2nd dpn. Rep dec every rnd until 2 sts rem on first and 3rd dpns and 5 instep sts on 2nd dpn. Break off yarn and thread into a blunt point wool needle. Thread yarn through rem sts and draw up tightly. Weave in all ends and block socks under a damp towel or on sock blockers.

□ =D
◉ =A
○ =B
z =C
⊠ =E

CHART #1

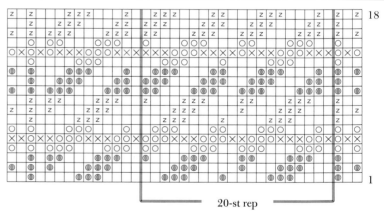

20-st rep

□ =A
⊠ =MC
◉ =B

CHART #2

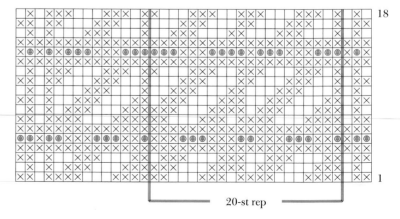

20-st rep

ENTRELAC CHRISTMAS SOCK

EXPERIENCED

FINISHED MEASUREMENTS

Leg: 13" long from cuff to turning point of heel, 13" around at cuff; Foot: 6" long (after heel shaping). Shown on page 125.

MATERIALS

Sportweight wool in seven shades of green, one shade of red, and one shade of gold, approx 30 yards of each color. It takes about 12 yards of one color to knit twelve 6-st rectangles One set (5) dpn sizes 1, 2, and 3 *or size needed to obtain gauge*

GAUGE

Since the sock will not be worn, the gauge is not critical. The gauge on the sock in the photograph is 7 sts and 8 rows to 1" over cuff pat using size 3 needles. Heavier yarn and larger needles will make a bigger sock; smaller yarn and smaller needles will make a smaller sock.

OPEN CAST ON

Cut a strand of contrasting waste yarn about four times the required width of cuff. With the working yarn, make a slip knot and place it on two needles. *Hold waste yarn beside the stitch on needle and take the working yarn under it and over the needles from front to back. Bring the working yarn in front of the waste yarn. Rep from * until all the sts are cast on. Take out one needle before working the first row. Remove waste yarn when you are ready to pick up sts along the edge.

CUFF

With size 3 needles and red yarn, using open cast on, cast on 90 sts. Divide sts evenly over 3 needles. Join, and place marker for beg of rnd. **Next 9 rnds:** *K2 red, k2 gold, k2 green; rep from * around. **Next 2 rnds:** *K2 gold, k2 green, k2 red; rep from * around. **Next 2 rnds:** *K2 green, k2 red, k2 gold; rep from * around. **Next 2 rnds:** *K2 red, k2 gold, k2 green; rep from * around. Pull out the thread from the invisible cast on and pick up 30 sts on each of 3 needles. Now the work is on 6 needles, 3 on the top of the work and 3 on the bottom. Turn the work so that the wrong sides are tog and the knit side of the fabric is facing. K the two edges tog, keeping in the pat of 2 red, 2 gold and 2 green. K 1 rnd using all 3 strands of red, gold and green. Cut red yarn and weave it in. Change to size 2 needles and work with 1 strand each of gold and green as foll: **Next rnd:** Dec 6 sts on each needle for a total of 18 decs and 72 sts. Change to size 3 needles. K 1 rnd with gold and green. Change to size 2 needles. Cut gold and weave in end. K 1 rnd green. Change to size 1 needles. K 1 rnd green. FIRST SET OF TRIANGLES **Note:** To purl from the knit side: with WS of work facing, insert needle purlwise and wrap yarn around. Turn work so the RS is facing, noting where and how the needle and yarn are positioned. Cont to purl from the knit side. To knit from the purl side: With RS facing, insert needle knitwise and wrap yarn around. Turn work so the WS is facing, noting where and how needle and yarn are positioned. Cont to knit from the purl side. To avoid constant turning of work, knit and purl from the same side. Each triangle is worked back and forth on a set of 6 sts. Turn work at end of each row, except row 9. There are 12 triangles in the circumference of the sock. **Row 1:** With RS facing and green of your choice, k2. **Row 2:** P2 (these are the same 2 sts you worked in row 1.) **Row 3:** K3. **Row 4:** P3. **Row 5:** K4. **Row 6:** P4. **Row 7:** K5. **Row 8:** P5. **Row 9:** K6. Rep these 9 rows around, ending with twelve 6-st triangles. You will need to rotate these triangles on your needles as you go so all the work doesn't end up on one needle. This sock has 7 rows of peaks. Two rows of entrelac rectangles need to be worked to form a row of peaks, or set. The first row is worked flat, the 2nd row of rectangles forces the peak out because you beg picking up sts in the opposite corner as for the flat rectangles. Change colors after each row as desired. ENTRELAC PEAKS SET 1 Beg these rectangles with WS facing. Pick up 5 sts purlwise along side of first triangle, working from tip to base; p1

from triangle on left needle (this st will be a different color). **Row 1:** K6. **Row 2:** P5, p2tog, using 1 st from LH needle triangle. Rep these 2 rows until all 6 sts from LH needle triangle have been used and the first rectangle is complete. Work along the foll triangles in the same way, creating entrelac rectangles as you knit. 2ND ROW OF RECTANGLES TO FORM PEAK With WS of work facing, with LH needle, pick up 5 sts purlwise along long edge of rectangle on LH needle, beg at bottom of rectangle next to RH needle and work up to LH needle. K 1 st from rectangle on LH needle to make a 6-st rectangle. Rep directions for first set of rectangles, pushing out the peak as you make the rectangles. ENTRELAC PEAKS SET 2 Beg these rectangle with RS facing and new green yarn. Pick up 6 sts along side of rectangle, beg at its tip. K 1 from LH needle, pass previous k st over this. **Row 1:** P6. **Row 2:** K5, sl 1, k1 from LH needle, psso. Rep these 2 rows until all sts from LH needle have been worked, and twelve 6-st rectangles have been made. 2ND ROW OF RECTANGLES TO FORM PEAK With RS of work facing, with LH needle, pick up 6 sts along long edge of rectangle on LH needle, beg at bottom of rectangle next to RH needle and work up to LH needle. K 1 st from LH needle, pass previous knit st over this. Rep directions for first set of rectangles of set 2. Those 2 sets, the 2 rows of rectangles that you pick up from the purl side (entrelac peaks set 1) and the 2 rows that you pick up from the knit side (entrelac peaks set 2), are the pat. Do these for 5 more sets, ending with a WS set. K one more row of rectangles, picking up sts with RS facing. LAST SET OF TRIANGLES Beg these at center back. With WS of work facing, pick up 5 sts purlwise, beg at the tip of the square, k1 from LH needle (this st will be a different color). **Row 1:** Sl 1 knitwise, k1. **Row 2:** Sl 1 purlwise, p2. **Row 3:** Sl 1 knitwise, k3. **Row 4:** Sl 1 purlwise, p4. **Row 5:** Sl 1 knitwise, k5. **Row 6:** Sl 1 purlwise, p6. **Row 7:** Sl 1 knitwise, k6, k2tog. **Row 8:** Sl 1 purlwise, p6, sl 1, p2tog, psso. Cont in this way until all spaced between entrelac rectangles have been filled in with 8-st triangles – a total of 96 sts. **Dec row:** Dec 12 sts evenly. Because you had a WS facing when you got around to the end of the last triangle, your thread is in the wrong place when you turn it around for RS facing. Take that last st on RH needle and pass it over to the LH needle. Now when you turn the work around for RS facing, the thread is coming from the right needle, so it's in the correct place to beg. You have a total of 84 sts, 21 sts on each of 4 needles. Work 10 rows of pat same as cuff of sock. DIVIDE FOR HEEL K 1 rnd with red. With red, k21 sts on needle 1, with waste yarn, k21 sts on needle 2 and needle 3 (heel sts to be worked later), with red, k21 sts on needle 4.

FOOT

Work on all 84 sts as foll: **Next 6 rnds:** *2 red, 2 green; rep from * around. **Next rnd:** *1 red, 2 green, 1 red; rep from * around. Cont to shift color over 1 st every rnd for 4 rnds. Cont working stripes, using 2 sts of 2 different colors each rnd and shifting colors as desired, until there are a total of 30 rnds from heel sts. SHAPE TOE **Dec rnd:** *K1 red, k1 green; rep from * to last 2 sts on needle 1, SKP; on needle 2, k2tog, cont alternating 1 green with 1 red to end of needle; cont red and green to last 2 sts on needle 3; SKP; on needle 4, k2tog, cont red and green to end. Rep dec rnd every other rnd for 13 rnds, (matching color of previous rnd) then work dec rnd every rnd until there are 2 sts on each needle. Run yarn through rem 8 sts, pull snug and weave in tail. SHAPE HEEL With RS facing, red and size 2 dpn, pick up 21 sts above waste yarn row, with a 2nd needle, pick up the rem 21 sts above waste yarn, with a 3rd needle, pick up 21 sts below waste yarn, with a 4th needle, pick up rem 21 sts below waste yarn. There are a total of 84 sts. Remove waste yarn. Join and work in St st with red, working decs and finish as for toe.

FINISHING

If desired, with all colors, make a braid or twisted cord and attach to cuff of sock as foll: Fold braid or cord in half. Insert fold between the 2 rows of sts at top edge of cuff (on heel side of sock). Make a slip knot, then knot

LEE'S CROW-BEAR CARDIGAN

EXPERIENCED

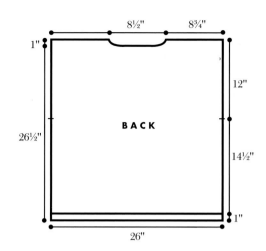

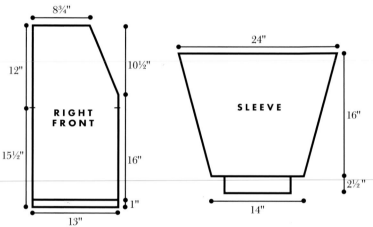

SIZES
One size. Shown on page 128.

FINISHED MEASUREMENTS
Chest at underarm (buttoned): 53"
Length from shoulder: 27½"
Sleeve width at upper arm: 24"

MATERIALS
7 4oz/113g skeins (each approx 190yd/171m) of Brown Sheep
    Company's Top of the Lamb Worsted in #103
    Brownstone(MC)
2 skeins each in #101 Stone (A) and #201 Burnt Red (B)
1 skein each in #210 Onyx (D), #100 Natural (E), #331 Mallard
    (F), #200 Russet (G)
1 4oz/113g skein (each approx 190yd/171m) of Brown Sheep
    Company's Lamb's Pride Worsted in #M15 Gold Glow (C)
Sizes 6 and 7 knitting needles *or size needed to obtain gauge*
Size G crochet hook
Five buttons

GAUGE
20 sts and 27 rows to 4" on larger needles in St st. *To save time and to ensure accurate sizing, check gauge.*

BACK
With larger needles and MC, cast on 131 sts. Work in k1, p1 rib for 1", end with a RS row. P next row on WS. Work Chart for Back through row 172. NECK SHAPING **Next row (RS):** Work 49 sts, join 2nd skein and bind off center 33 sts, work to end. Working both sides at once, bind off from each neck edge 2 sts once, 3 sts once. Work 1 row even. Bind off rem 44 sts each side for shoulders.

LEFT FRONT
With larger needles and MC, cast on 65 sts. Work rib as for back. P 1 row on WS. Work Chart for Left Front through chart row 108. NECK SHAPING **Next row (RS):** Work in pat to last 3 sts, k2tog, k1. Work 2 rows even; rep dec every 3rd row 20 times more (working k1, p2tog at beg of WS rows)—44 sts. Work even through chart row 178. Bind off.

RIGHT FRONT
Work to correspond to left front, working chart for Right Front and reversing neck shaping by working k1, SSK at beg of RS rows; SSP, k1 at end of WS rows.

SLEEVES
With smaller needles and MC, cast on 47 sts. Work in k1, p1 rib for 2½", inc 24 sts evenly across last (WS) row—71 sts. Change to larger needles. Work in St st for 22 rows, AT SAME TIME, inc 1 st each side every 4th row 5 times—81 sts. Mark center st. Beg Chart for Sleeve on next row, matching center st of chart to center st on needle. Work chart through row 98, then cont with MC to end of piece, AT SAME TIME, cont to inc 1 st each side every 4th row 10 times more, then every 6th row 10 times—121 sts. Bind off.

FINISHING
Block pieces to measurements. RIGHT FRONT BAND With smaller needles and MC, cast on 8 sts. Work in k1, p1 rib until band fits along right front edge to center back neck. Place sts on holder. Sew band in place. Sew buttons on right front, at inside edge of band, with the first ½" from lower edge, the last at neck dec, and 3 others spaced evenly between. LEFT FRONT BAND **Note:** Instructions do not include buttonholes; instructions for button loops follow. If desired, buttonholes may be worked in center of band by (yo, k2tog) opposite buttons. Work as for right front band. Sew band seam at center back neck. Set in sleeves. Sew side and sleeve seams. BUTTON LOOPS (make 5): With crochet hook, make a ch approx 10" long. Fold ch in half and insert loop end under a st on front edge directly opposite a button, at inside edge of band. Secure loop by making a knot on the loop side of the st. Then take loop through a knit st in center of left front band. Knot should keep loop from extending more than ½". Make another knot in ch to the right of first st entered. Work 4 other button loops in same way. Make 6 more chs approx 6—8" long and tie them to right and left fronts as shown in photo.

LEE'S CROW-BEAR CARDIGAN

BEAR CLAW: Introspection. Bear helps us to reach other levels of imagination so that our goals may become concrete realities.
CROW: Keeper of the sacred law (the higher law of honesty and truth that transcends the law of humans).
ARROWS: Male energy and power.
SNAKE: Transformation; the power of creation, cosmic consciousness, and wholeness.
TEEPEE OR SACRED MOUNTAIN, COYOTE TRACKS, CLOUDS, TRACKS, CORN, FEATHERS: See Danya's southwest Motif Jumper-Vest.
BUFFALO HORN BUTTONS: The appearance of buffalo is a sign of fulfilled prophecy and answered prayers and a time of abundance and plenty.

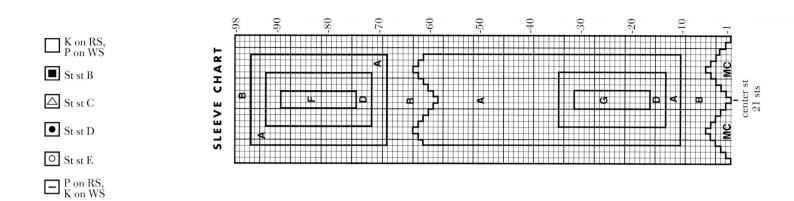

SLEEVE CHART

K on RS, P on WS
St st B
St st C
St st D
St st E
P on RS, K on WS

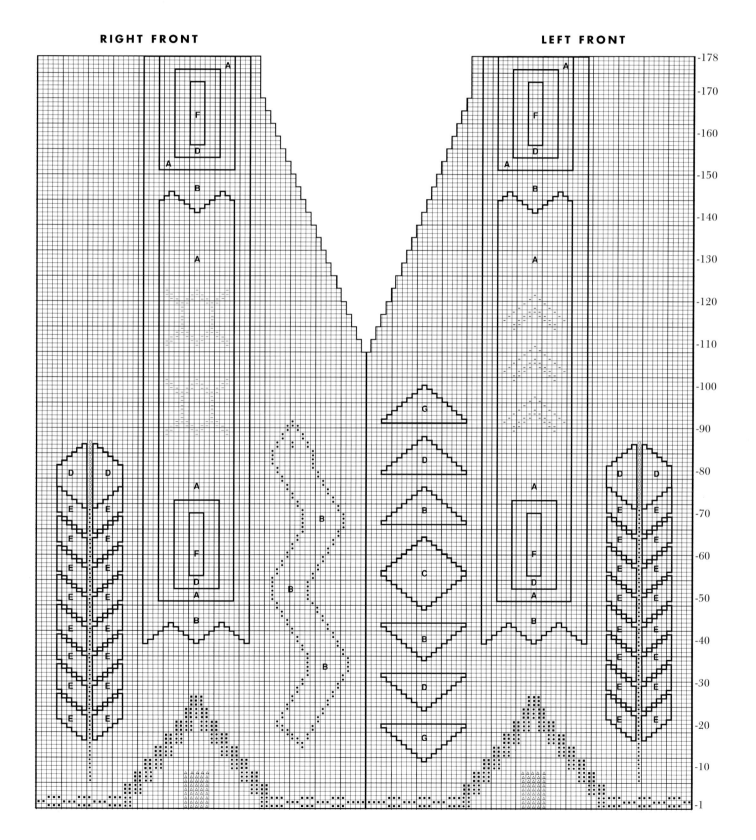

RIGHT FRONT

LEFT FRONT

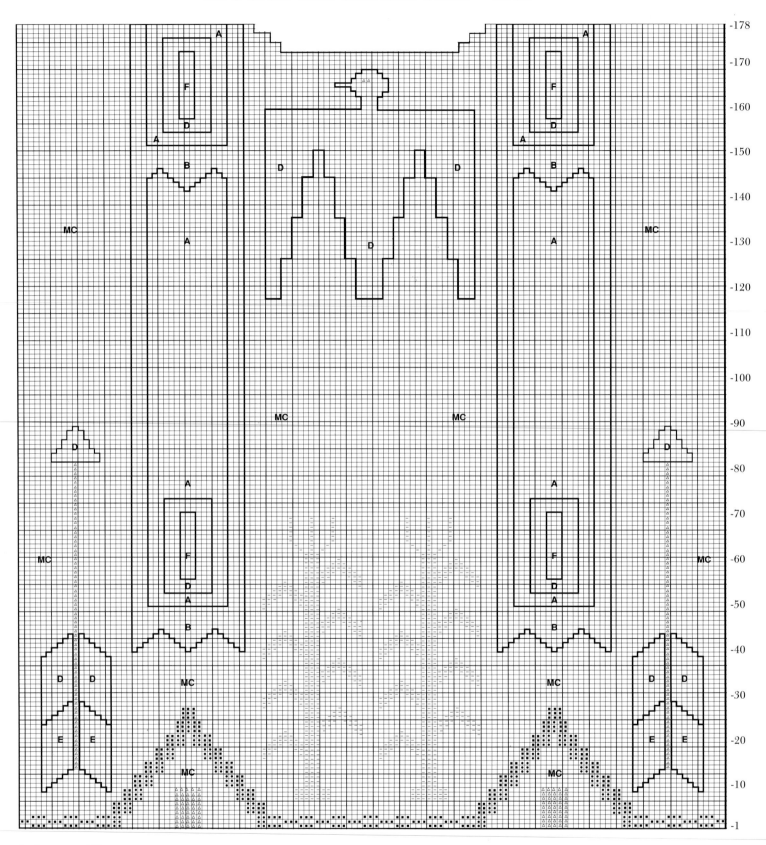

See key on page 207.

DANYA'S SOUTHWEST MOTIF JUMPER-VEST

INTERMEDIATE

SIZES
To fit child's size 2 through 6. Width is adustable.
Shown on page 128.

FINISHED MEASUREMENTS
Chest at underarm (fully closed at sides): 30"
Length from shoulder (above hem): 13"

MATERIALS
2 3½oz/100g skeins (each approx 215yd/194m) of Brown Sheep
    Company's Cotton Fleece in #150 Antique Lace (MC)
1 skein each in #005 Cavern (A), #340 Goldenrod (B), #930
    Candy Apple (C), #320 Roasted Coffee (D), and #480
    Navajo Turquoise (E)
One pair size 4 knitting needles *or size needed to obtain gauge*
Size E crochet hook
3 buttons

GAUGE
23 sts and 32 rows to 4" over St st using size 4 needles. *To save time and to ensure accurate sizing, check gauge.*

Note: When changing colors on same row, bring new color under old color to twist strands and prevent holes.

BACK
With size 4 needles, cast on 87 sts in foll color sequence: 14 sts with A, 7 with MC, 3 with B, 7 with MC, 25 with A, 7 with MC, 3 with B, 7 with MC, 14 with A. **Row 1 (WS):** Purl, matching colors. Cont in St st, matching colors, for 4 rows more. **Next (eyelet) row (RS):** Matching colors, work as foll: K1, *yo, k2tog; rep from * to end. Purl 1 row, matching colors. Beg chart pat on Row 1 (RS). Cont in chart pat through chart row 98. NECK SHAPING **Next row (WS):** P27 sts with MC, join skein of C (leave a 10" tail to work sts on this side of neck edge), p33 with C, with MC, p to end. **Next row:** With MC, k25, k2tog, k1 with C, join A (leaving about 10" tail), k1 with A, bind off center 29 sts with A; on 2nd side, k1 with A, k1 with C, with MC, SSK, k to end. Next row Purl, matching colors. **Next row:** K24 MC, k2tog, k1C, k1A; on 2nd side, k1A, k1C, with MC, SSK, k to end. **Next row:** Purl, matching colors. Place 27 sts each side on holders.

LEFT FRONT
With size 4 needles, cast on 43 sts in foll color sequence: 13 sts A, 7 sts MC, 3 sts B, 7 sts MC, 13 sts A. Work hem as for back. Work chart for Left Front through row 68. NECK SHAPING **Next row (RS):** Work in pat to last 4 sts, k2tog with MC, k1C, k1A. Cont to dec 1 st at neck edge with MC, 2 sts in from edge (1 st C and 1 st A) every other row 15 times more — 27 sts. Work even through chart row 103. Place sts on holder.

RIGHT FRONT
Cast on and work hem as for left front. Work chart for Right Front through chart row 68. Work neck shaping as for left front, but in reverse (at beg of RS rows, 2 sts in from edge, work SSK with MC). When chart is complete, place 27 sts on holder.

FINISHING
Block pieces to measurements. Graft shoulder seams tog. With crochet hook and MC, work 1 row sc along front and neck edges, working buttonhole loops on right front (by ch 4), with the first approx 3" from lower edge, the last at beg of neck dec, and 1 between these. Work 1 row sc along side and armhole edges. TIES (make 6): With crochet hook, make a ch approx 15" long. Run a tie from front to back in 1 sc at side edge of right front (at desired armhole depth), then run same end of tie from back to front through 1 sc opposite this (on side edge of back). Pull tog and tie a bow. Place another tie in same way approx halfway between armhole tie and lower edge. Place 2 more ties in same way on LH edge. Place rem 2 ties at shoulders as foll: Beg at armhole edge, run 1 end of tie over sc and under first 2 k sts, *over next 2 sts, under next 2 sts; rep from * 4 times more, run tie over next 2 sts, under last 3 sts and through 2 MC sts at WS of neck edge to secure, then turn and work back to armhole edge in same way, taking sts under or over at same places as before. Make sure ends of tie are equal, and gather shoulder sts by pulling ends of tie and securing. Work other shoulder in same way. Fold lower edge to WS on eyelet row. Sew in place.

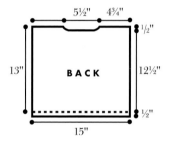

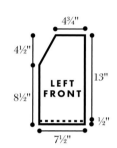

DANYA'S SOUTHWEST MOTIF JUMPER-VEST

BUTTERFLY: Transformation.
TEPEE OR SACRED MOUNTAIN: Mother Earth, home, sacred ground, peace, safety, and love.
COYOTE TRACKS: Coyote, the sacred teacher, reminds us not to take life or ourselves too seriously.
MORNING STAR WITH CIRCLE IN CENTER: To the Pueblo Indians, Morning Star is the messenger of the Four Old Men, the Sacred Four great primary forces who watch over the four quarters of the universe—North, South, East, and West. The circle in the center represents the sun, the earth, the universe, wholeness, perfection, and balance.
CORN: Sacred to all Indian Nations. To the Hopi, it represents creation and the unity of male and female elements.
CLOUDS: The Pueblo people believe that at death, the guardian spirits and souls of the most virtuous enter the rainmaker's world and come back to visit the Pueblo in the form of clouds. Including these in a design adds the protective energy of our elders.
TRACKS: Bright prospects.
SPIDER: The infinite possibilities of creation.
LIZARD: The medicine of dreamers— what you can dream or visualize you can create. This symbol is from the Arapaho; however, the Sioux women also wore it to protect against female disorders.
FEATHERS: Gifts from the gods; a reminder of a higher order.

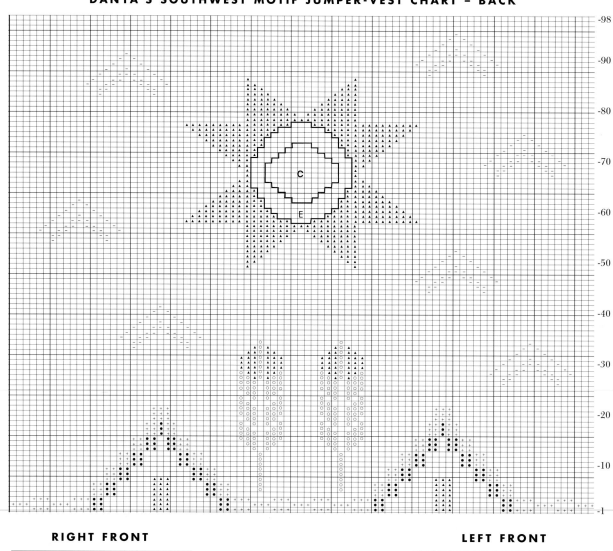

St st with MC

Rev St st MC

St st A

St st B

St st C

St st D

St st E

RIGHT FRONT

LEFT FRONT

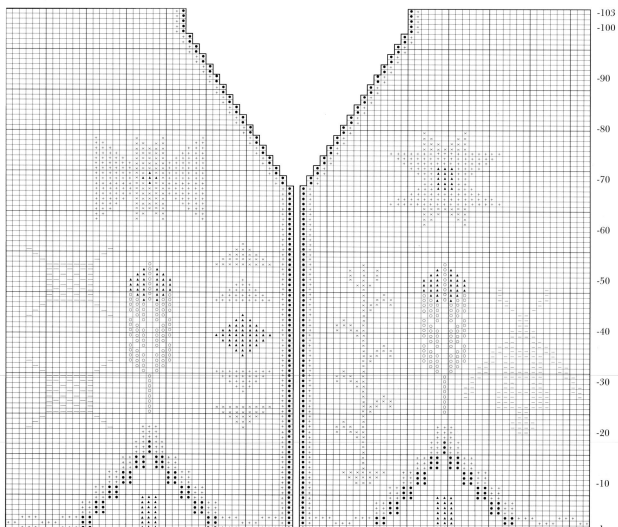

TREE OF LIFE MOSAIC JACKET

EXPERIENCED

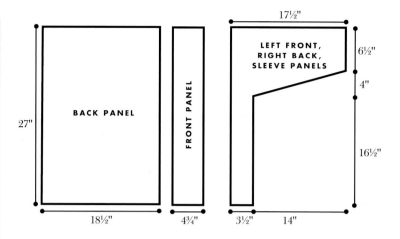

SIZES
One size. Shown on page 132.

FINISHED MEASUREMENTS
Bust at underarm (with front bands overlapping): 50½"
Length from shoulder: 30½"
Sleeve width at upper arm: 22"

MATERIALS
10 1¾oz/50g skeins (each approx 104yd/95m) of Tahki's Tweedy
    Lamb in #1911Black (A)
2 skeins #1915 Soft Red (C)
1 skein #1922 Violet (D)
10 1¾oz/50g skeins (each approx 106yd/96m) of Tahki's Chelsea
    Silk in #111 Natural (B)
One pair size 9 knitting needles *or size needed to obtain gauge*
Size 9 circular needle 29" long
Size F crochet hook
One double-pointed needle (dpn), size 7
Tapestry needle
Waste yarn to use in casting on and holding sts

GAUGE
18 sts and 36 rows to 4" over chart pat using size 9 needles. *To save time and to ensure accurate sizing, check gauge.*

Note 1: On RS rows, sl sts purlwise wyib; on WS rows, sl sts purlwise wyif. **Note 2:** Selvage sts are worked as foll: Sl first st of every row; k last st of every RS row and p last st of every WS row. Selvage sts do not appear on Left Front Panel and Back Panel charts. **Note 3:** Each line of chart represents 2 rows, 1 RS row and 1 WS row. **Note 4:** Black (A) sts of front and back panels are worked in St st; Natural (B) and Red (C) sts are worked in garter st. On sleeve panels, all sts are worked in garter st.

SEED ST PAT
Row 1: *K1, p1; rep from *. **Row 2:** K the purl sts, p the knit sts. Rep row 2 for Seed St Pat.

SLEEVE PAT (multiple of 4 sts plus 3)
Row 1 (RS): Sl 1 B wyib, *k1 A, sl 1 B, k2 A; rep from * to last 2 sts, k2A. **Row 2:** Sl 1 A wyif, k the A sts and sl the B sts wyif to last st, P1 A. **Row 3:** Sl 1 A, *sl 1 A, k3 B; rep from * to last 2 sts, sl 1 A, k1 B. **Row 4:** Sl 1 B, sl the A sts wyif and k the B sts to last st, p1 B. **Row 5:** Sl 1 B, *k3 A, sl 1 B; rep from * to last 2 sts, k2 A. **Row 6:** Rep row 2. **Row 7:** Sl 1 A, *k2 B, sl 1 A, k1 B; rep from * to last 2 sts, k2 B. **Row 8:** Rep row 4. Rep rows 1 – 8 for sleeve pat.

LEFT FRONT PANEL
With size 9 needles and A, cast on 21 sts using open cast-on as foll: Cut a length of waste yarn (about 4 times the width of the panel). With A, make a sl knot on needle. Holding waste yarn parallel to needle, take working yarn under waste yarn from front to back and over needle from front to back. Bring working yarn in front of and under waste yarn and over needle again. Cont in this way until all sts are cast on. Keep waste yarn in place until sts are ready to be picked up and worked. Purl 1 row on WS with A. MOSAIC PAT CHART *Pick up B and work as foll: **Row 1 (RS):** Sl 1 A wyib, work 19 sts of Chart for Left Front Panel (k all B sts, sl all A sts wyib), k1B. **Row 2 (WS):** Sl 1 B wyif, work 19 sts of chart (k all B sts, sl all A sts wyif), p1B. Pick up A and work as foll: **Row 3:** Sl 1 B wyib, work 19 sts of chart (k all A sts, sl all B sts wyib), k1A. **Row 4:** Sl 1 A wyif, work 19 sts of chart (p all A sts, sl all B sts wyif), p1A.* Cont to rep between *'s for basic mosaic pat, foll chart for color, for 238 rows. Work 2 rows St st with A. Do not bind off. Place sts on waste yarn. Mark lower edge of panel with a piece of CC yarn for ease in identifying later when picking up sts for lower edge.

RIGHT FRONT PANEL
Work to correspond to left front panel, reversing chart pat.

BACK PANEL
With size 9 needles and A, cast on 83 sts, using open cast-on. Purl 1 row on WS with A. Working selvage sts as for left front panel, work rem 81 sts in chart for back panel as foll: Work rows 1-62 once, then cont to rep rows 15-62 until 238 rows from beg. (**Note:** Use a separate bobbin of C for each motif.)

LEFT FRONT SLEEVE AND RIGHT BACK SLEEVE PANELS
With WS of left front panel facing, and lower edge of panel (marked with CC yarn) at LH side, and size 9 needles and B, pick up and k 121 sts evenly along side of left front panel. (Pick up sts inside of selvage edge, so that black and white selvage sts show on RS.) K 2 rows with B. Work sleeve pat for 32 rows. **Next row (RS):** With crochet hook and A, bind off 74 sts using ch bind-off as foll: insert hook knitwise into first st on needle, draw up a lp, letting st drop off needle. *Work in same way into next st, but pull lp through both st and lp on hook, 1 lp rem on hook; rep from * until all 74 sts are bound off, cont in pat to end. Work on rem 47 sts until a total of 54 rows have been worked. Dec 1 st (by SSK) at beg of next (RS) row, then cont to dec 1 st at same edge [every other RS row once, every 4th RS row once] 8 times, then every other RS row once more—29 sts. Work until 158 rows from beg. With B, k 2 rows. Do not bind off. Place sts on waste yarn. Work right back sleeve panel, picking up sts as for left front sleeve panel, working shaping as for left front panel.

RIGHT FRONT AND LEFT BACK SLEEVE PANELS
Work to correspond to left front and right back sleeve panels, reversing shaping and pat.

SLEEVE AND SHOULDER BORDERS
RIGHT FRONT SLEEVE AND SHOULDER BORDER With WS facing, circular needle and A, beg at sleeve cuff, pick up and k 1 st in each st along selvage edge at top of sleeve (pick up sts inside selvage, so that black and white sts show on RS). Slide sts of front panel on to same needle. **Next row (RS):** With B, k21. Change to A, k to end. K next row on WS, matching colors. Change to C and work 2 rows St st. With crochet hook and A, bind off all sts using ch st bind-off. LEFT FRONT SLEEVE AND SHOULDER BORDER With WS facing, slide sts of left front panel to circular needle, then with A pick up and k 1 st in each st along top of sleeve as for right sleeve. **Next row (RS):** With A, k to end of sleeve panel. Change to B, k to end. Complete as for right shoulder border. BACK SLEEVE AND SHOULDER BORDER With WS facing, circular needle and A, pick up and k 1 st in each st along selvage edge at top of left back sleeve. (Pick up sts inside selvage, so that black and white sts show on RS.) Slide all sts of back panel to needle, then with A, pick up and k sts along right back sleeve panel to end. **Next row (RS):** With A, k to end of sleeve panel. Change to B, k to end of back panel. With A, k to end. K next row on WS, matching colors. Change to D and work 2 rows St st.

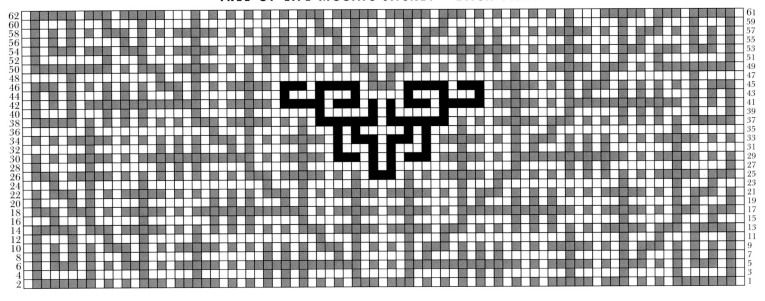

KEY

■ =Natural (B)
□ =Black (A)
■ =Red (C)

CUFF CHART

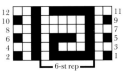

└─ 6-st rep ─┘

LEFT FRONT PANEL

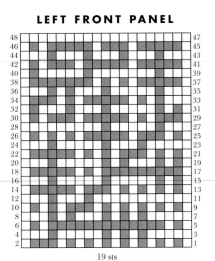

19 sts

RIGHT FRONT BAND & LOWER EDGE

└─ 6-st rep ─┘

With crochet hook and A, bind off all sts using ch st bind-off. JOIN SHOULDER SEAMS With WS of right front and right back tog, with crochet hook and A, work ch st loosely through bind-off ch to form seam on RS of fabric. Join left front to left back in same way.

SLEEVE CUFFS

With WS facing, slide open sts of left sleeve cuff of front and back sleeve panels to straight needles (there will be a gap in center where sleeve borders were joined). **Next row (RS):** With A, k to gap in sts. With A, pick up and k 7 sts along gap, k to end—65 sts. P 1 row with A. Change to B and k 2 rows. Pick up A and work row 1 of cuff chart across row. Cont in chart pat through row 8 (working B sts in garter st and A sts in St st as for body panels). Work 3 rows St st with A, then work 3 rows seed st. Bind off loosely. Work cuff for right sleeve in same way, reversing pat. JOIN SIDE AND SLEEVE SEAMS With RS facing, crochet hook and A, and beg at lower right edge, ch st loosely through bind-off ch of sleeve panels (side seam) to underarm. Fasten off, leaving 1 yd for finishing. Bring yarn to WS of work, sew sleeve seam to cuff. Pull yarn to RS of work. With crochet hook, work sl st crochet around edge of cuff to keep it from rolling as foll: insert hook from front to back into st, yo hook and draw yarn through to front, yo and draw through lp on hook, *insert hook into next st, draw yarn through to front and through lp on hook; rep from * in each st.

FRONT EDGE BAND

With WS facing, circular needle and B, pick up 125 sts along right front panel edge (inside selvage sts). K 2 rows B. **Next row (RS):** K1A, *sl 1 B, k1 A; rep from * to end. Rep last row once more. K 2 rows with B. Work 2 rows St st with A. Work 12 rows of chart for right front band. Work 2 rows St st with A. Do not bind off. Slide sts to waste yarn. Sew edge of front band to shoulder. Work left front edge band to correspond, reversing chart pat.

LOWER EDGE BAND

With RS facing, circular needle and A, beg at lower edge of left front band, pick up and k 7 sts along edge of left front band, sl 21 open sts of left front panel to needle. With A, pick up and k 37 sts along edge of sleeve panels. Sl 83 open sts of back panel to needle. With A, pick up and k 37 sts along edge of sleeve panels, sl 21 sts of right front panel to needle. With A, pick up 7 sts along right front band—213 sts. P 1 row on WS with A. **Next row (RS):** Knit in foll color sequence: 7 sts with A, 199 sts with B, 7 sts with A. **Next row:** P7 sts with A, k199 sts with B, p7 sts with A. Work 2 rows St st with A. ESTABLISH CHART PAT: **Next row (RS):** Work first 2 sts of chart for right front band, work 6-st rep 35 times, end with last (selvage) st of chart. Cont in chart pat as established

through chart row 12. Work 2 rows St st with A. K 2 rows with B. **Next row (RS):** K1A, *sl1B, k1A; rep from * to end. Rep last row once more. K 2 rows with B. With A, k 3 rows, then work 3 rows in seed st. With crochet hook and A, bind off sts using ch st bind-off. Work sl st crochet around edge to keep it from rolling.

NECKBAND

With RS facing, circular needle and A, beg at lower edge of right front, pick up and k 14 sts along edge of lower band. Sl 125 open sts of right front band to needle. Pick up sts along back neck as foll: With WS facing, dpn and A, pick up and k 17 sts along back neck edge, pulling yarn through bind-off lp from back to front so that chained edge of shoulder seams rem uninterrupted along neck edge. Sl these sts from dpn on to circular needle. Sl 125 open sts of left front band to needle. With A, pick up and k 14 sts along edge of lower band—295 sts. Return to lower edge of right front (so that first row is a RS row). K 2 rows with B. **Next row (RS):** K1A, *sl 1B, k1A; rep from * to end. Rep last row once more. K 2 rows with B. Work 2 rows St st with A, 2 rows St st with C, 9 rows St st with A. K next row on WS with A for turning ridge. K 1 row with A. Work 9 rows St st with D, 6 rows St st with B. With crochet hook and B, bind off loosely using ch st bind-off. Fasten off. Fold band to WS at turning ridge and sl st in place with B.

SIZES

To fit woman's or man's Small (Medium, Large, X-Large). Directions are for smallest size with larger sizes in parentheses. If there is only one figure it applies to all sizes. Shown on page 138 in size Medium.

FINISHED MEASUREMENTS

Bust/chest at underarm: 38 (42, 46, 50)"
Length from shoulder: 25 (26, 27, 27)"
Sleeve width at upper arm: 15 (17, 19, 20)"

MATERIALS

8 (8, 9, 10) oz each Shetland fingering-weight wool in Loch
    Maree (Dark - D) and Slate Blue (Light -L)
One each size 4 circular needle 24", 16", and 11" long (or one set
    dpn instead of 11") *or size needed to obtain gauge*
Sewing machine (optional)
Stitch holder

GAUGE

28 sts and 28 rnds to 4" over St st and colorwork pat using size 4 needles. *To save time and to ensure accurate sizing, check gauge.*

BODY

With 24" needle and D, cast on 240 (268, 296, 324) sts. Join, taking care not to twist sts on needle. **Next rnd:** P 111 (125, 139, 153) sts (front), pm, 9 sts (side panel), pm, 111 (125, 139, 153) sts (back), pm, 9 sts (side panel), pm. ESTABLISH CHART PATS **Next rnd:** *Work rnd 1 of chart #1 as foll: work 14-st rep 7 (8, 9, 10) times, work first 13 sts once more (front), work rnd 1 of side panel chart over 9 sts; rep from * once. Cont as established until 14 rnds of chart have been worked. Work rnd 15 of chart as foll: *Inc 14 sts evenly across front sts, cont side panel; rep from * once — 268 (296, 324, 352) sts. Work front and back sts in chart #2 (working one extra 14-st rep for each) and keep 9 sts in side panel, until 14 rnds of chart #2 have been worked 7 times. K 1 rnd D, 1 rnd L. Work chart #3 on front and back as foll: *Work first 5-st rep of chart over 61 (68, 75, 82) sts as foll: beg with st 5 (3, 1, 4), work 5-st rep; work center 3 sts of chart, beg with st 1, work last 5-st rep of chart to side panel, cont side panel; rep from * once. Cont as established through rnd 8 of chart #3. K 1 rnd L, 1 rnd D. UNDERARMS Put the 9 side panel sts on a thread. Cast on 5 steek sts in alternating colors. **Note:** All steek sts are worked in St st alternating 1 st D and 1 st L, forming a speckled pat. YOKE Work chart #4 as foll: *Work 5 steek sts, beg with st 3 (22, 15, 8) of chart, work 26-st rep to next steek sts; rep from * once. Cont as established until piece measures 22½ (23½, 24½, 24½)" from beg. NECK SHAPING **Next rnd:** Work 5 steek sts, work 33 (40, 45, 52) sts of front, place center 59 (59, 63, 63) sts on a holder for neck, cast on 5 steek sts in their place, work to end of rnd. Cont as established until 26 rnds of chart #4 have been worked twice, then work first 1 (7, 13, 18) rnds once more. K 1

rnd L, binding off 3 sets of steek sts as you go. Place rem sts on a thread or holder. Baste down center of each steek. With a small st and loose tension, machine stitch down one side of the basting, across the bottom, and up the other side - staying as close to the center st as possible while still leaving enough space for the blade of the scissors. Cut on basting. JOIN SHOULDERS With L, bind off shoulder sts while working I-cord as foll: Sl 33 (40, 45, 52) sts of front shoulder to one needle and 33 (40, 45, 52) sts of back shoulder to a 2nd needle. With a 3rd needle, beg at armhole edge, cast on 2 sts, *k1, sl 1, k 1 st from front needle tog with 1 st from back needle, psso; rep from * across shoulder, and put the 2 I-cord sts on a thread. Join other shoulder in same way, but work from neck edge to armhole.

SLEEVES

Note: If desired, continue the shoulder line of I-cord down the finished sleeve (as in the model), knit up a st of L somewhere underneath the existing I-cord. If you want the I-cord to end at the shoulder, k the 2 cord sts tog at shoulder top. Whichever method you use, that single shoulder-top will be the center of the double decs that are to come. Beg at one side panel, slip 9 sts from holder to 16" circular needle. Turn the body sideways in your lap, and find the two final vertical rows of color pat just before the steek sts beg. Insert the needles between the two rows and pick up the yarn in the color that matches the final row (above the needle). Using the final row as a guide, copy the color of each side as you go. Pick up and k 1 st in each row to the shoulder seam, (pick up and k1 L at seam and work 2 I-cord sts with L), or (knit the 2 cord sts tog with L), pick up and k sts on 2nd side of armhole the same as first side. Join. Work 9 sts side panel, cont chart #4 on sts either side of center and cont center 3 sts in I-cord with L. SLEEVE DEC For a bloused sleeve, work a double dec at sleeve top every 6th or 7th rnd. For a more tapered sleeve, work the dec every 5th rnd. The further apart the decs, the more sts you will have left at the lower edge. Meg's sweater is slightly bloused at a dec rate of 2 sts every 6th rnd. (**Note:** change to 11" circular or dpn when necessary). Work even in pats until sleeve measures 18" for woman or 20" for man. With L, k next rnd, dec enough sts each side of center (do not dec in side panel) so that there are 21 sts each side. Work these 21 sts in chart #1 (beg with rnd 2), cont side panel as established, to end of chart. Bind off with D.

NECK FINISHING

With RS facing and L, pick up all neck sts. Beg at one shoulder, k 1 rnd L. Work 2-st I-cord bind off as foll: on a spare dpn, cast on 2 sts, transfer them to LH needle and *k1, k2tog tbl. Replace 2 sts to LH needle and rep from * around. Weave end to beg. Rep the above with D, but work from the WS.

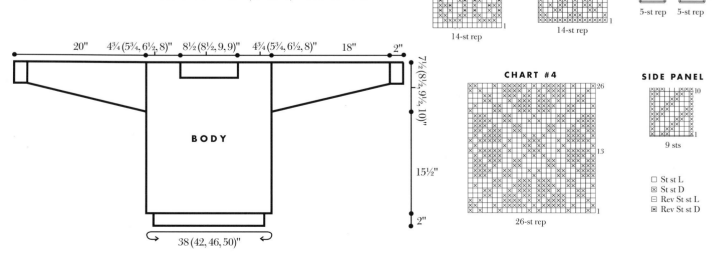

SAND CASTLE & STARFISH BEACH TUNIC

INTERMEDIATE

SIZES
BEACH TUNIC: To fit sizes 2 (4, 6, 8) or chest sizes 21 (23, 24½, 26½)". Directions are for smallest size with larger sizes in parentheses. If there is only one number, it applies to all sizes. Shown on page 144 in size 4.
STARFISH TAM: To fit sizes 2 - 4 (6 - 8).

FINISHED MEASUREMENTS
Chest at underarm: 27 (29½, 31½, 33½)"
Length from shoulder: 14½ (16½, 17½, 18½)"
Sleeve width at upper arm: 11 (12, 14, 15)"

MATERIALS
BEACH TUNIC:
3 (3, 4, 4) 3½oz/100g skeins (each approx 185yd/166m) of
    Reynolds Saucy in #817 Natural (MC)
1 (1, 2, 2) skeins in #753 Taupe (A)
1 skein each in #071 Blue (B), #528 Sage (C) and #396 Ashes
    of Roses (D)
One pair size 7 needles *or size needed to obtain gauge*
STARFISH TAM:
1 skein #753 Taupe (A)
Small amount #817 Natural (MC)
Size 5 circular needle, 16"
Size 7 double-pointed needles (dpns)
STARFISH PURSE:
1 skein #396 Ashes of Roses (D)
Size 7 double-pointed needles (dpns)
Snap or small piece of Velcro
FOR ALL:
Size 7 circular needle 16" long
Tapestry needle
Stitch markers

GAUGE
19 sts and 28 rows to 4" over St st using size 7 needles. 18 sts and 18 rows to 4" over Fishnet Pat using size 7 needles. *To save time and to ensure accurate sizing, check gauges.*

STITCH GLOSSARY
Double Vertical Dec on a RS row (Dec2K): Wyib, sl 2 sts tog knitwise, k1, p2sso.
Double Vertical Dec on a WS row (Dec2P): Wyif, sl 2 sts knitwise, one at a time, to RH needle; sl same 2 sts back to LH needle; sl same 2 sts tog as if to p tbl, p1, p2sso.

FISHNET PAT (over an even # of sts):
Rows 1 and 3 (RS): Knit. **Row 2 (WS):** K1 (selvage st), *yo, k2tog; rep from *, end k1 (selvage st). **Row 4:** K1 (selvage st), *k2tog, yo; rep from *, end k1 (selvage st). Rep rows 1 – 4 for Fishnet Pat.

BEACH TUNIC

BACK
With size 7 circular needle and B, cast on 157 (170, 183, 196) sts. Work back and forth on circular needle as foll: **Row 1 (RS):** K5, [dec2K, k10] 12 (13, 14, 15) times, end last rep k6, instead of k10. **Row 2 (WS):** P5, [dec2P, p8] 12 (13, 14, 15) times, end last rep p4, instead of p8. **Row 3:** K3, [dec2K, k6] 12 (13, 14, 15) times, end last rep k4, instead of k6. **Row 4:** P3, [dec2P, p4] 12 (13, 14, 15) times, end last rep p2, instead of p4—61 (66, 71, 76) sts. Change to straight needles, if desired. With B, work in St st (k on RS rows, p on WS rows) for 2 rows. ESTABLISH WAVE PAT CHART **Next row (RS):** Beg with st 3 (5, 7, 2) of chart, work to st 7, then

work 7-st rep to end of row. Cont in pat as est through row 6 of chart. With A, work in st st for 3 rows, then k next row on WS row to form purl ridge on RS. ESTABLISH SANDCASTLE CHART **Next row (RS):** Beg where indicated, work row 1 of chart pat to end of row. Cont in chart pat through row 50. **Note:** For sizes 2 (4, 6) only: When working Fishnet Pat on chart, work last 2 (1, 2) sts of WS rows as foll: P1 (0, 1), k1. Cont in Fishnet Pat until piece measures 13½ (15½, 16½, 17½)" from beg, end with a WS row. NECK SHAPING **Next row (RS):** Work 21 (23, 25, 27) sts, join 2nd ball of yarn and bind off 19 (20, 21, 22) sts, work to end. Working both sides at once, bind off 3 sts each neck edge once, work 1 row even. Bind off rem 18 (20, 22, 24) sts each side for shoulders.

FRONT
Work as for back until piece measures 13 (15, 16, 17)" from beg, end with a WS row. NECK SHAPING **Next row (RS):** Work 25 (27, 29, 31) sts, bind off 11 (12, 13, 14) sts, work to end. Working both sides at once, bind off from each neck edge 4 sts once, 3 sts once. Work 1 row even. Bind off rem 18 (20, 22, 24) sts each side.

SLEEVES
With size 7 straight needles and B, cast on 66 (66, 79, 79) sts. Work as foll: **Row 1 (RS):** K5, [dec2K, k10] 5 (5, 6, 6) times, end last rep k6, instead of k10. **Row 2 (WS):** P5, [dec2P, p8] 5 (5, 6, 6) times, end last rep p4, instead of p8. **Row 3:** K3, [dec2K, k6] 5 (5, 6, 6) times, end last rep k4, instead of k6. **Row 4:** P3, [dec2P, p4] 5 (5, 6, 6) times, end last rep p2, instead of p4—26 (26, 31, 31) sts. With B, work in st st for 2 rows. ESTABLISH WAVE PAT CHART **Next row (RS):** Beg with st 3 (3, 5, 5) of chart, work to st 7, then work 7-st rep to end of row. Cont in pat as est through row 6 of chart. With A, work in st st for 3 rows, then k next row on WS row to form purl ridge on RS. K 1 row on RS. Change to MC. ESTABLISH FISHNET PAT **Next row (WS):** K1, [yo, k1, yo, k2tog] 8 (8, 9, 9) times, [yo, k2tog] 0 (0, 1, 1) time, k1—34 (34, 40, 40) sts. Cont in Fishnet Pat (beg with row 3, then rep rows 1 - 4) to end of piece, AT SAME TIME, inc 1 st each side (working inc sts into pat) every other row 5 (7, 10, 13) times, then every 4th row 3 (3, 2, 1) times—50 (54, 64, 68) sts. Work even until piece measures 9 (10, 10½, 11)" from beg. Bind off.

FINISHING
Block pieces to measurements. Sew shoulder seams. Embroider chain st with C to outline handle of pail. NECKBAND With RS facing, circular needle and MC, pick up and k64 (66, 68, 70) sts evenly around neck edge. Join, and work in rnds of garter st (k 1 rnd, p 1 rnd) for 6 rnds. Bind off. STARFISH (make 2 with B, 2 with C, 2 with D): With size 7 needles and desired color, cast on 55 sts. **Row 1 (RS):** K4, [dec2K, k8] 5 times, end last rep k4, instead of k8. **Row 2 (WS):** P3, [dec2P, p6] 5 times, end last rep p3, instead of p6. **Row 3:** K2, [dec2K, k4] 5 times, end last rep k2, instead of k4. **Row 4:** P1, [dec2P, p2] 5 times, end last rep p1, instead of p2, **Row 5:** [Dec2K] 5 times. Thread yarn through rem 5 sts and pull tightly. Sew starfish seam. Sew 3 starfish (1 of each color) along back neck edge, and 3 along front neck edge, as shown in photo. Place markers 5 ½ (6, 7, 7½)" down from shoulders on front and back for armholes. Sew sleeves between markers. Sew side and sleeve seams.

STARFISH TAM

With size 5 circular needle and A, cast on 90 (100) sts. Join, place marker, and work in rnds of k1, p1 rib as foll: *K1A, p1 MC; rep from * around. Cont in k1, p1 rib as est for 6 rnds more. Change to size 7 circular needle and cont with A only, work as foll: **Rnd 1:** *K17 (19) sts, place marker (pm) in next st; rep from * around. **Rnd 2:** *P to marked st (do not work marked st, M1 (insert LH needle from front to back under strand between st just worked and next st, k this strand tbl), k marked st, M1; rep from * 4 times more—100 (110) sts. **Rnd 3:** *K to marked st, M1, k1, M1;

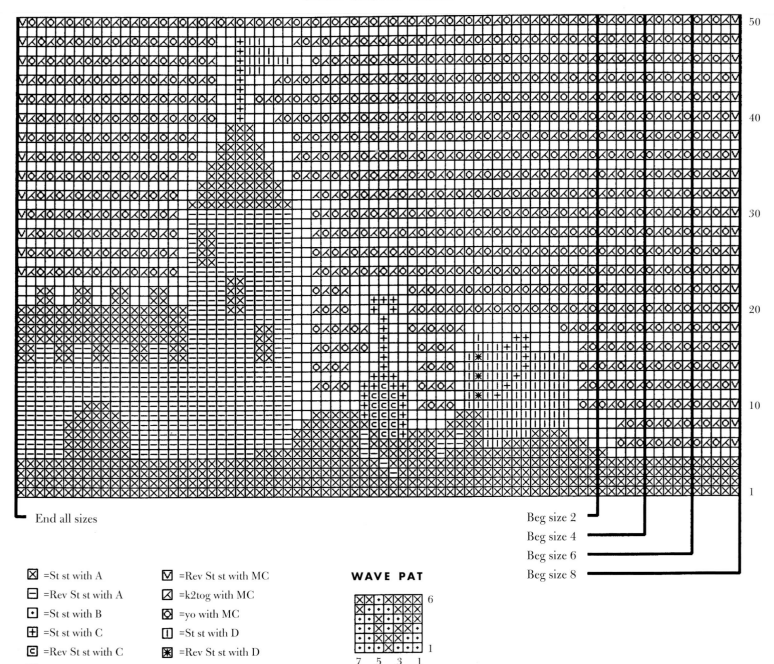

└ End all sizes

Beg size 2
Beg size 4
Beg size 6
Beg size 8

⊠ =St st with A   ☑ =Rev St st with MC

⊟ =Rev St st with A   ◿ =k2tog with MC

· =St st with B   ⊙ =yo with MC

⊞ =St st with C   ▯ =St st with D

c =Rev St st with C   ✳ =Rev St st with D

□ =St st with MC

WAVE PAT

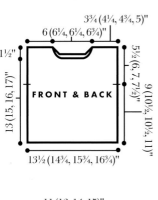

7 5 3 1

rep from * 4 times more, k to end of rnd. **Rnd 4:** *P to marked st, M1, p1, M1; rep from * 4 times more, p to end of rnd. Rep rnds 3 and 4 until there are 230 (240) sts. Work even in garter st for 4 rnds. **Next rnd:** *K to 1 st before marked st, dec2K; rep from *4 times more, k to end of rnd. Rep last rnd until 10 sts rem (change to dpns when there are too few sts for circular needle). Fasten off. Pull sts tog tightly. Weave in ends.

STARFISH PURSE

With size 7 circular needle and D, cast on 115 sts. Join and work in rnds as foll: **Rnd 1:** *K22, pm in next st; rep from * 4 times more. **Rnd 2:** *K to 1 st before marked st, dec2K; rep from * around. Rep last rnd until 5 sts rem (change to dpns when needed). Fasten off. Thread sts tog. Make another starfish in same way. With WS of each starfish tog, sew side seams, leaving 1 side unsewn for opening at top of purse.
I-CORD STRAP With dpn and D, cast on 3 sts. *K3, slide sts to opposite end of dpn, k3; rep from * until cord measures approx 30". Bind off. Attach cord at 2 points of starfish at each side of purse opening. Sew snap or Velcro in purse opening.

3¾ (4¼, 4¾, 5)"
6 (6¼, 6¼, 6¾)"
1½"
5½ (6, 7, 7½)"
FRONT & BACK
13 (15, 16, 17)"
9 (10½, 10½, 11)"
13½ (14¾, 15¾, 16¾)"

11 (12, 14, 15)"
SLEEVE
9 (10, 10½, 11)"
5½ (5½, 6½, 6½)"

CHILD'S MITTENS

For large child or petite woman. All mittens shown together on page 152.

MATERIALS

1 1¾oz/50g skein (each approx 95yd/86m) of Peer Gynt 4-ply in #270 Teal (A), #257 Bright Pink (B), #215 Gold (C), #658 Purple (D), #17 White (E).
One set (5) size 2 dpn *or size needed to obtain gauge*

GAUGE

28 sts and 30 rnds to 4" over St st and colorwork pat using size 2 needles. *To save time and to ensure accurate sizing, check gauge.*

RIGHT MITTEN

CUFF With B as border and A as St st color, using 2-strand cast on (basically the same as a long-tail cast-on except the two strands of yarn are each a different color), cast on 48 sts as foll: Hold 2 needles tog in the right hand and make a slip knot on needles with both yarns. *Still holding needles in right hand, wrap B back to front around left thumb, wrap A front to back around left index finger, and secure ends of yarn coming from your balls of yarn (not the slip knot) with your remaining fingers in your left palm. Insert needles under B, over, behind and under A, then through the opening made in B. Release A. Tighten the sts on needles while re-inserting thumb into B.* Rep the steps between the asterisks until there are 48 sts, not including the slip knot. Remove one needle, release slip knot, and divide sts evenly over 4 dpn (12 sts on each dpn). Join, being careful not to twist sts, place marker for beg of rnd. K 5 rnds A. **Picot edge: Next rnd:** With A, *k2tog, yo; rep from * around. K 5 rnds A. Cont in St st (k every rnd) as foll: Work 17 rnds chart #1, inc 8 sts evenly spaced on last rnd; 14 sts on each dpn — 56 sts. PALM Beg with rnd 1 of chart #2, work center 28 sts of chart (as marked) twice. Cont as est for 10 rnds above cuff. DIVIDE FOR THUMB **Next rnd:** First & 2nd dpn: Pat across; 3rd dpn: k 1 st, then using backward cast-on, cast on 12 sts in color pat as designated, as foll: Holding your knitting in your right hand, wrap the yarn around your left thumb so that the yarn travels around the outside of your thumb and finishes between your thumb and index finger (hold yarn from ball in your palm with your other fingers). Insert the needle upwards through center of strand around thumb. Slip loop from thumb onto needle, pulling yarn from ball to tighten. When finished, you will have 13 sts on RH needle. Sl 12 sts from LH needle to a holder for thumb, k rem st on LH needle (14 sts on 3rd dpn); 4th dpn: pat to end of dpn. Cont chart #2 until Rnd 33 has been completed. HAND SHAPING **Note:** The first st on both sides is a contrasting center st running between the dec sts at the edges. **Rnd 34:** First dpn: k 1 E, k 2 D, pat to end of dpn; 2nd dpn: pat to last 2 sts on dpn, k 2 D; 3rd & 4th dpn: work same as for first and 2nd dpn. **Dec rnd:** First dpn: K 1 E, with D ssk, k 1, pat to end of dpn; 2nd dpn: pat to last 3 sts on dpn, with D, k 1, k2tog; 3rd & 4th dpn: work same as for first and 2nd dpn. Cont foll chart #2, rep dec rnd every rnd until 8 sts rem. **Note:** As sts dec and needles beg to slide, you may want to work with 1 needle holding all sts for mitten front and a 2nd needle holding all sts for mitten back working with a 3rd needle. **Next rnd:** [K 1 E, with D, sl 1, k2tog, psso] twice — 4 sts. Cut both yarns leaving approx 6", thread blunt needle with D and pass through 2 rem D sts; pass to inside of mitten. Thread needle with E, pass through 2 E sts and into center of mitten. Turn mitten to wrong side and tug both yarns firmly to seal the point, then sew through back of work to secure. RIGHT THUMB Sl 12 sts from holder to 2 dpns, pick up 12 sts from cast-on edge at top of thumb opening and place on 2 dpns, then pickup the outer loop of the st adjacent to thumb opening, twist, and put on needle which will produce 4 extra sts on rnd — 28 sts; divide sts over 4 needles (7 sts on each dpn). **Note:** Front thumb (first & 2nd dpn) will have a different pat than back (3rd & 4th dpn) because each side cont in pat from original thumb rnd. Pats build on different rows but cont unbroken up thumb for front or back. **Rnds 1-2:** Work in pat. **Rnd 3:** First dpn: K2tog, pat to end of dpn; 2nd dpn: Pat to end of dpn; 3rd & 4th dpn: Work same as for first & 2nd dpn. **Rnd 4:** First dpn: Work pat to end of dpn; 2nd dpn: pat to last 2 sts on dpn, ssk; 3rd & 4th dpn:

work same as for first & 2nd dpn — 24 sts; divide over 4 needles (6 sts on each dpn). Cont in pat until 11 rnds from beg. THUMB SHAPING Dec as for hand shaping. Keep contrasting color up the center of dec sts. Finish and sew to inside as on mitten top.

LEFT MITTEN

Using Right Mitten as pat for Left Mitten, make palms and backs to match. Foll chart #2 from left to right instead of right to left, always keep the pats flowing around the mittens and joining the rnd at the opposite side. Work Left Mitten same as Right until thumb opening (10 rnds above cuff). DIVIDE FOR THUMB **Next rnd:** First dpn: Work pat across; 2nd dpn: k 1 st, using backward loop cast on, cast on 12 sts (13 stson RH needle), sl 12 sts from LH needle to a holder for thumb, k rem st on LH needle (14 sts on 2nd dpn); 3rd & 4th dpn: pat across. Foll chart #2 until Rnd 34 has been completed. HAND SHAPING Work same as Right Mitten hand shaping. LEFT THUMB Work same as for Right Mitten thumb. Fold cuff to inside along picot edges; sew in place.

WOMAN'S MITTENS

MATERIALS

1 3½oz/100g skein (each approx 363yd/330m) of Satakieli 2-ply yarn from Helmi Vuorelma Oy, Finland #97 Black (A), #890 Forest Green (B), #9 Lt Violet Gray (C), #491 Burnt Red (D), #184 Gold (E), and #894 Dk Green (F)
One set (5) size 0 dpn *or size needed to obtain gauge*

GAUGE

40 sts and 44 rnds to 4" over St st and colorwork pat using size 0 needles. *To save time and to ensure accurate sizing, check gauge.*

RIGHT MITTEN

CUFF With A as border and B as st color, using 2-strand cast on (see cuff instructions for Child's Mitten), cast on 92 sts; divide sts evenly over 4 needles (23 sts on each dpn). Join, being careful not to twist sts, place marker for beg of rnd. **Hem: Rnds 1-9:** With B, work in St st knitting in initials, name, or date in A on this hem, if desired. **Rnds 10-11:** With A, knit. **Picot edge:** With A, *k2tog, yo, rep from * around. **Next rnd:** With A, inc 4 sts evenly spaced on rnd — 96 sts; divide over 4 needles (24 sts on each dpn). **Next 2 rnds:** *K2 B, k2 C; rep from * around. K 1 rnd each D, E, B, C, and D. **Next rnd:** *K1 A, k1 C; rep from * around. K 1 rnd A. Work 17 rnds chart #3. K 1 rnd A. **Next rnd:** *K 1 A, k 1 C; rep from * around, AT THE SAME TIME, dec 6 sts evenly around (k2tog on A sts) — 90 sts. K 1 rnd each D, C, and B. **Next rnd:** *K 2 A, k 1 D, k 1 C, k 1 D; rep from * around. **Next rnd:** *K 1 D, k 2 A, k 1 D, k 1 C; rep from * around. K 1 rnd each B, C, and D. **Next rnd:** *K 1 A, 1 C; rep from * around, dec 6 sts as before — 84 sts divided evenly over 4 needles (21 sts on each dpn). K 1 rnd A. Work 4 rnds chart #4. K 1 rnd A. **Next rnd:** *K 1 A, 1 C; rep from * around. K 1 rnd each D, C, and F. PALM Beg on Rnd 8, work center 42 sts of chart #2 twice (1 complete pat on front and back, so beg at the right edge of 1 pat) for 17 rnds. DIVIDE FOR THUMB **Next rnd:** First & 2nd dpn: Pat across; 3rd dpn: k 1 st, using backward loop cast on, cast on 19 sts (20 sts on RH needle), sl 19 sts from LH needle to holder for thumb, k rem st on LH needle (21 sts on 3rd dpn); 4th dpn: pat to end of dpn. Work even until 68 rnds of chart #2 has been completed. (Note: After working rnd 42, cont to rep rnds 1-42.) HAND SHAPING **Note:** The first st on both sides is a contrasting center st running between the dec sts at the edges. **Next rnd:** First dpn: K 1 F, k 2 C, pat to end of dpn; 2nd dpn: pat to last 2 sts on dpn, k 2 C; 3rd & 4th dpn: work same as for first & 2nd dpn. **Dec rnd:** First dpn: K 1 F, with C, SSK, k 1, pat to end of dpn; 2nd dpn: pat to last 3 sts on dpn, with C, k 1, k2tog; 3rd & 4th dpn: work same as first & 2nd dpn. Cont foll chart rep dec rnd every rnd until 8 sts rem. **Note:** As sts dec and needles beg to slide, you may want to work 1 needle holding all sts for mitten front and 2nd needle

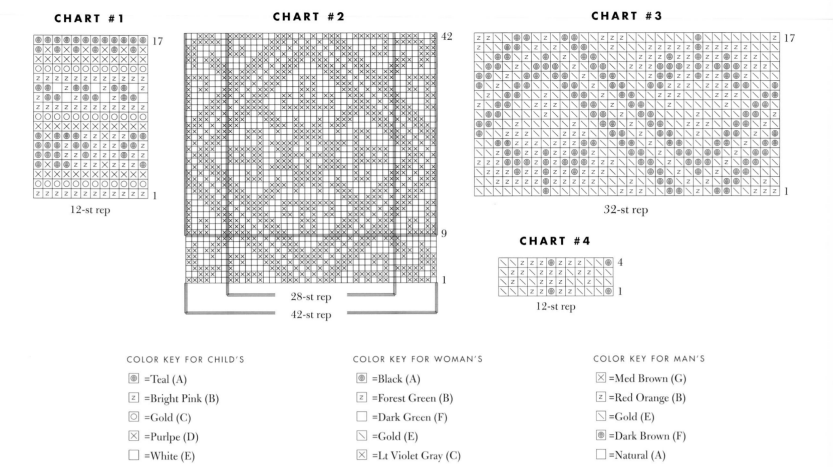

CHART #1

17

1

12-st rep

CHART #2

42

9

1

28-st rep

42-st rep

CHART #3

17

1

32-st rep

CHART #4

4

1

12-st rep

COLOR KEY FOR CHILD'S

⊙ =Teal (A)

z =Bright Pink (B)

○ =Gold (C)

✕ =Purlpe (D)

☐ =White (E)

COLOR KEY FOR WOMAN'S

⊙ =Black (A)

z =Forest Green (B)

☐ =Dark Green (F)

◣ =Gold (E)

✕ =Lt Violet Gray (C)

COLOR KEY FOR MAN'S

✕ =Med Brown (G)

z =Red Orange (B)

◣ =Gold (E)

⊙ =Dark Brown (F)

☐ =Natural (A)

holding all sts for mitten back working with a 3rd needle. **Next rnd:** [K 1 F, with C, sl 1, k2tog, psso] twice — 4 sts. Cut both yarns leaving approx 6", thread blunt needle with C, and pass through the 2 sts rem of that color to the inside of mitten. Thread needle with the contrasting yarn, pass through those 2 sts and into center of mitten. Turn mitten to wrong side and tug both yarns firmly to seal the point. Sew through the back of work to secure. RIGHT THUMB Sl 19 sts from holder to 2 dpns, pick up 19 sts from cast-on edge at top of thumb opening and place on 2 dpns, pick up the outer loop of the st adjacent to thumb opening, twist and put on needle which will produce 4 extra sts on the rnd — 42 sts; divide on 4 dpns. **Note:** Front thumb (first & 2nd dpn) will have a different pat than back (3rd & 4th dpn) because each side cont in pat from original thumb rnd. Pats build on different rows but cont unbroken up thumb for front or back. **Rnds 1-2:** Work in pat. **Rnd 3:** First dpn: K2tog, pat to end of dpn; 2nd dpn: pat to end of dpn; 3rd & 4th dpn: work same as first & 2nd dpn. **Rnd 4:** First dpn: Work pat to end of dpn; 2nd dpn: pat to last 2 sts on dpn, ssk; 3rd & 4th dpn: work same as first & 2nd dpn — 38 sts; divide on 4 dpns. Cont in pat until 19 rnds from beg. THUMB SHAPING Dec as for hand shaping. Keeping contrasting color up the center of dec sts. Finish and sew to inside as on mitten top.

LEFT MITTEN

When there is an odd number of reps around mitten (chart # 3 has 3 reps) there is a different beg point for the Right and Left Mitten. Use Right Mitten as pat for Left Mitten, make palm and backs to match. Mark the beg line on chart and foll pat left to right instead of right to left from beg line, always keeping the pats flowing around mitten and joining the rnd at the opposite side. Work Left Mitten as Right Mitten until thumb opening (17 rnds above cuff). DIVIDE FOR THUMB **Next rnd:** First dpn: Work pat across; 2nd dpn: k 1 st, using backward loop cast on, cast on 19 sts (20 sts on RH needle), sl 19 sts from LH needle to a holder for thumb, k rem st on LH needle (21 sts on 2nd dpn); 3rd & 4th dpn: pat across. Foll chart until Rnd 68 has been completed. HAND SHAPING Work same as Right Mitten hand shaping. LEFT THUMB Work same as Right Mitten thumb. Fold cuff to inside along picot edge; sew in place.

MAN'S LINED MITTENS

MATERIALS

1 3½oz/100g skein (each approx 363yd/330m) of Satakieli 2-ply yarn from Helmi Vuorelma Oy, Finland #3 Natural (A), ½ skein each #491 Red Orange (B), #890 Dk. Green (C), #184 Gold (E), #385 Dk. Brown (F), #388 Med. Brown (G)

One set (5) sizes 000 and 0000 dpn *or size needed to obtain gauge*

GAUGE

26 sts and 28 rnds to 2" over St st and colorwork pat using smaller needles; 24 sts and 26 rnds to 2" over St st and colorwork pat using larger needles. *To save time and to ensure accurate sizing, check gauges.*

RIGHT MITTEN LINER

With A and larger needles, loosely cast on 112 sts using the 2-strand technique (see cuff instructions for Child's Mitten). Divide sts evenly over 4 needles (28 sts on each dpn). Join, being careful not to twist sts, place marker for beg of rnd. Work in k 2, p 2 rib for 8 rnds. Change to St st (k every rnd) and work until 4" from cast-on edge. DIVIDE FOR THUMB **Next rnd:** First dpn: K 28 sts; 2nd dpn: k 1 st, using backward cast on (see Child's Mittens) cast on 26 sts (27 sts on RH needle), sl 26 sts from LH needle to holder for thumb, k rem st on LH needle (28 sts on 2nd dpn); 3rd & 4th dpn: pat to end of dpn. Work even until 4½" above thumb opening. HAND SHAPING **Next rnd:** First dpn: k 1, SSK, k to end of dpn; 2nd dpn: k to last 2 sts on dpn, k2tog; 3rd & 4th dpn: work same as first & 2nd dpn. Cont in this way dec 4 sts on every rnd until 8 sts rem. **Note:** As sts dec and needles beg to slide, you may want to work with 1 needle holding all sts for mitten front and 2nd needle holding all sts for mitten back working with a 3rd needle. **Next rnd:** [K1, sl 1, k2tog, psso] twice — 4 sts. Cut yarn leaving approx 6", thread through the rem 4 sts, pass yarn to wrong side and finish by sewing through back of work for about 1". RIGHT LINER THUMB Sl 26 sts from holder to 2 dpns, pick up 26 sts from cast-on edge at top of thumb opening, then pick up the outer loop of the st adjustment

to thumb opening, twist and put on needle which will produce 4 extra sts on the rnd — 56 sts; divide on 4 dpns. **Rnds 1-2:** Beg on thumb front, k. **Rnd 3:** First dpn: K2tog, k to end of dpn; 2nd dpn: k to end of dpn: 3rd & 4th dpn: work same as first & 2nd dpn. **Rnd 4:** First dpn: K to end of dpn; 2nd dpn: pat to last 2 sts on dpn, ssk; 3rd & 4th dpn: work same as first & 2nd dpn — 52 sts; divide sts over 4 needles (13 sts on each dpn). K until thumb measures 2½" from beg. THUMB LINER SHAPING Dec as for Right Mitten Liner hand shaping.

LEFT MITTEN LINER

Use Right Mitten Liner as pat for Left Mitten Liner, make palms and back to match. Work Left Liner same as Right Liner for 4" until thumb opening. DIVIDE FOR THUMB **Next rnd:** First & 2nd dpn: Pat across; 3rd dpn: k 1, using backward cast on, cast on 26 sts (27 sts on RH needle), sl 26 sts from LH needle to holder for thumb, k rem st on LH needle (28 sts on 2nd dpn); 4th dpn: pat to end of dpn. Work even until 4½" above thumb opening. HAND SHAPING Work same as Right Mitten Liner hand shaping. LEFT LINER THUMB Work same as Right Mitten Liner thumb. THUMB SHAPING Dec as for hand shaping.

OUTER RIGHT MITTEN

CUFF Pick up 112 sts from cast-on edge of Right Mitten Liner; divide on 4 dpns. With smaller needles and B, k 1 rnd inc 8 sts evenly spaced — 120 sts; divide sts evenly over 4 needles (30 sts on each dpn). Join, being careful not to twist sts, place marker for beg of rnd. HEM **Rnds 1-9:** With B, work in St st knitting in initials, name, or date in E on this hem, if desired. **Rnds 10-11:** With B, knit. PICOT EDGE With B, *k2tog, yo, rep from * around. **Next rnd:** With B, inc 8 sts evenly spaced on rnd — 128 sts; divide: 32 sts on each dpn. Cont in St st as foll: **Next 2 rnds:** *2A, 2B; rep from * around. K 1 rnd each C, A, C, E, B. **Next rnd:** *1A, 1F; rep from * around. K 1 rnd F. Beg with 26th st of chart #3, work 17 rnds of chart. K 1 rnd F. **Next rnd:** *1F, 1A; rep from * around. K 1 rnd each B, E, and C, inc 2 sts on last rnd — 130 sts. **Next rnd:** *2 F, 1 B, 1 A, 1 B; rep from * around. **Next rnd:** *1 B, 2 F, 1 B, 1 A; rep from * around. **Next rnd:** *1 A, 1 B, 2 F, 1 B; rep from * around. K 1 rnd each C, E, and B. **Next rnd:** *1 A, 1F; rep from * around. K 1 rnd F, inc 2 sts — 132 sts. Work rnds 1-4 of chart #4. K 1 rnd F, dec 2 sts — 130 sts. **Next rnd:** *1 A, 1 F; rep from * around. K 1 rnd each B, E, and C. PALM Change to larger needles. Work chart #2 as foll: Beg on Rnd 1, work 42-st rep of chart 3 times (you have 3 pat reps encircling the band so mitten palm and back are not identical), dec 4 sts evenly spaced on first rnd — 126 sts; divide: 32 sts on first & 3rd dpn and 31 sts on 2nd & 4th dpn. Cont until 18 rnds above cuff have been completed. DIVIDE FOR THUMB **Next rnd:** First & 2nd dpn: Pat across; 3rd dpn: k 1 st, using backward loop cast on, cast on 30 sts in color as designated on chart (31 sts on RH needle), sl 30 sts from LH needle to holder for thumb, k rem st on LH needle (32

sts on 3rd dpn); 4th dpn: pat to end of dpn. Work even until 77 rnds have been worked. HAND SHAPING **Note:** The first st on both sides is a contrasting center st running between the dec sts at the edges. **Rnd 78:** First dpn: K1 A, k2 F, pat to end of dpn; 2nd dpn: pat to last 2 sts on dpn, k 2 F; 3rd & 4th dpn: work same as first & 2nd dpn. **Dec rnd:** First dpn: k1 A, with F ssk, k 1, pat to end of dpn; 2nd dpn: pat to last 3 sts on dpn, with F k 1, k2tog; 3rd & 4th dpn: work same as first & 2nd dpn. Foll chart, rep dec rnd until 10 sts rem. **Note:** As sts dec and needles beg to slide, you may want to work 1 needle holding all sts for mitten front and 2nd needle holding all sts for mitten back working with a third needle. **Next rnd:** [With A k 1, with F ssk, k2tog, then pass first st over 2nd st] twice — 4 sts. Cut both yarns leaving approx 6" end, thread blunt needle with the dec yarn and pass through 2 rem sts of that color; pass to inside of mitten. Thread needle with the contrasting yarn, pass through these 2 sts and into center of mitten. Lined mittens need to be secured and sewn through from outside as the center is inaccessible. RIGHT THUMB Sl 30 sts from holder to 2 dpns, pick up 30 sts from cast-on edge at top of thumb opening and place on 2 dpns, then pick up the outer loop of the st adjacent to the thumb opening and put on needle which will produce 4 extra sts on the rnd — 64 sts; divide: 16 sts on each dpn. **Note:** Front thumb (first & 2nd dpn) will have a different pat than back (3rd & 4th dpn) because each side cont in pat from original thumb rnd. Pats build on different rows but cont unbroken up thumb for front or back. **Rnds 1-2:** Work in pat. **Rnd 3:** First dpn: K2tog, pat to end of dpn; 2nd dpn: pat to end of dpn; 3rd & 4th dpn: work same as first & 2nd dpn — 60 sts; divide: 15 sts on each dpn. Cont in pat until 26 rnds from beg. THUMB SHAPING Dec as for hand shaping, keeping contrast color up center of dec sts. Finish as for mitten.

LEFT MITTEN

Note: Whenever an odd number of pats rep around the mitten (Chart 3 has 3 reps) there is a different beg point for the Right and Left Mitten. Use Right Mitten as the pat for the Left Mitten and make palms and backs match. Mark the beg line on chart and foll pat left to right instead of right to left from beg line always keeping the pats flowing around the mitten and joining rnd at the opposite side. Work Left Mitten same as Right Mitten until 18 rnds above cuff. DIVIDE FOR THUMB **Next rnd:** First dpn: Work pat across; 2nd dpn: sl last st from first dpn to beg of 2nd dpn (32 sts on 2nd dpn), then k 1, using backward cast on, cast on 30 sts (31 sts on RH needle), sl 30 sts from LH needle to holder for thumb, k rem st on LH needle (32 sts on 2nd dpn); 3rd & 4th dpn: pat across. Foll chart until 77 rnds have been worked. Hand shaping Work same as Right Mitten hand shaping. LEFT THUMB Work same as Right thumb. THUMB SHAPING Dec as for hand shaping. **Block:** Soak a handkerchief or light cotton cloth in water and wring out. Lay mitten flat, align sides and top then press with hot iron. Rep on both sides of mitten and thumb. Let dry flat.

LIU HAD A DREAM CARDIGAN & SHORT VEST

INTERMEDIATE

SIZES
To fit Small (Medium/Large). Directions are for smallest size with larger size in parentheses. If there is only one figure it applies to both sizes. Shown on page 158 in size Medium/Large.

KNITTED MEASUREMENTS
Bust at underarm (buttoned): 46½ (50½)"
Length from shoulder: 23½" - cardigan; 17" - vest
Sleeve width at upper arm: 18"

MATERIALS
CARDIGAN:
16 (17) 1¾ oz/50g skeins (each approx 165yd/148m) of Muench Wuhan in #531 (A)
1 (1) 1¾ oz/50g skeins (each approx 220yd/198m) of Muench GGH Sprint #103 (B)
Small amount of a color darker than Wuhan for crochet trim
VEST:
4 (4) skeins Wuhan in #531
3 (3) skeins GGH Sprint in #103
BOTH STYLES:
One pair each sizes 7 and 9 needles *or size needed to obtain gauge*
Size I crochet hook
Cable needle (cn)
6 buttons for cardigan; 3 buttons for vest

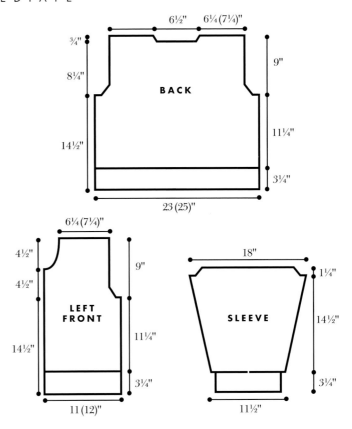

GAUGE
16 sts and 32 rows to 4" over pat st #1 using 2 strands of yarn and larger needles. *To save time and to ensure accurate sizing, check gauge.*

STITCH GLOSSARY
RPT: Sl next st to cn and hold to *back* of work, k1, p1 from cn.
LPT: Sl next st to cn and hold to *front* of work, p1, k1 from cn.
Cr2P: Sl next st to cn and hold to *back* of work, p1, then p1 from cn.

PATTERN STITCH #1 (multiple of 8 sts plus 4)
Row 1: K4, *p4, k4, rep from * to end.
Row 2 K the purl sts and p the knit sts.
Rep row 2 for pat st #1.

PATTERN STITCH #2 (worked over 18 sts)
Row 1 (RS): P1, [RPT, LPT, p2] twice, RPT, LPT, p1.
Row 2: K1, [p1, k2] 5 times, p1, k1.
Row 3: [RPT, p2, LPT] 3 times.
Row 4: P1, [k4, Cr2P] twice, k4, p1.
Row 5: [LPT, p2, RPT] 3 times.
Row 6: Rep Row 2.
Row 7: P1, [LPT, RPT, p2] twice, LPT, RPT, p1.
Row 8: K2, [Cr2P, k4] twice, Cr2P, k2.
Rep Rows 1 – 8 for pat st #2.

CARDIGAN

BACK
With smaller needles and 1 strand each A and B, cast on 96 (102) sts.
Border: Row 1: Work 3 (6) sts rev St st, [18 sts pat #2, 6 sts rev St st] 3 times, 18 sts pat #2, 3 (6) sts rev St st. Cont in pat as established until border measures 3¼" from beg. Change to larger needles. Cut B, join 2nd strand A. Work in pat st #1 dec 4 (2) sts evenly spaced on first row — 92 (100)sts. Cont until piece measures 14½" from beg. ARMHOLE SHAPING Keeping to pat, bind off 4 sts at beg of next 2 rows. Dec 1 st each side every other row 4 times — 76 (84) sts. Work even until armholes measure 8¼". NECK AND SHOULDER SHAPING Keeping to pat,

work 27 (31) sts, join 2nd balls of yarn, bind off center 22 sts, work to end. Working both sides at once, dec 1 st at each neck edge every other row twice. Bind off rem 25 (29) sts each side.

LEFT FRONT
With smaller needles and 1 strand each A and B, cast on 48 (51) sts.
Border: Row 1: Work 3 (6) sts rev St st, 18 sts pat #2, 6 sts rev St st, 18 sts pat #2, 3 sts rev St st. Cont pat as established until border measures 3¼" from beg. Change to larger needles. Cut B, join 2nd strand A. Work pat st#1 dec 4 (3) sts on first row — 44 (48) sts. Work until piece measures 14½" from beg, end with a WS row. ARMHOLE SHAPING Work at side edge as for back — 36 (40) sts. Cont in pat st #1 until armhole measures 4 ½", end with a RS row. NECK AND SHOULDER SHAPING **Next row (WS):** Bind off 5 sts (neck edge), work to end. Cont to dec 1 st at neck edge every other row 6 times. Cont pat st #1 until armhole measures same as back. Bind off rem 25 (29) sts.

RIGHT FRONT
Work as for left front, reversing pat and shaping.

SLEEVES
With smaller needles and one strand each A and B, cast on 48 sts. CUFF **Row 1:** Work 3 sts rev St st, 18 sts pat st #2, 6 sts rev St st, 18 sts pat st #2, 3 sts rev St st. Cont in pat as established until cuff measures 3¼" from beg. Change to larger needles. Cut B, join 2nd strand A. Cont in pat as established, inc 1 st each side (working inc sts into pat and beg additional pat #2 after there are 6 sts rev St st and enough sts to beg pat, or work inc sts into rev St st) every 8th row 13 times - 74 sts. Work even until sleeve measures 17¾" from beg, or desired length. CAP SHAPING Work as for back armhole shaping. Bind off rem sts.

FINISHING
Block pieces to measurements. Sew shoulder seams. LEFT FRONT BAND With RS facing, smaller needles and 2 strands A, pick up and k 91 sts along left front opening edge. Work k 1, p 1 rib for 1½". Bind off in rib. Sew 6 buttons inside left front band, the first 1" from lower edge, the last ½" from neck edge with 4 others evenly between. RIGHT FRONT BAND Work as for left front band. With RS facing and a darker color yarn, cro-

chet 1 row sc along right front edge working 3 or 4 chains for each buttonloop opposite buttons. COLLAR With RS of cardigan facing, smaller needles and 2 strands A, pick up and k 95 sts around neck edge, including top of front bands. Work k 1, p 1 rib for 4". Bind off in rib. Sew in sleeves. Sew side and sleeve seams.

SHORT VEST

BACK

With smaller needles and one strand each A and B, cast on 96 (102) sts. Work border as for cardigan back for 3¼". Change to larger needles. Cont pat st #1, dec 4 (2) sts across first row - 92 (100) sts. Work until piece measures 8" from beg. ARMHOLE, NECK AND SHOULDER SHAPING Work as for cardigan back.

LEFT FRONT

With smaller needles and one strand each A and B, cast on 48 (51) sts. Work as for left front cardigan border for 3¼". Change to larger needles. Cont pat st #1, dec 4 (3) sts on first row - 44 (48) sts. Work until piece measures 8" from beg. ARMHOLE, NECK AND SHOULDER SHAPING Work as for cardigan left front.

RIGHT FRONT

Work as for left front, reversing pat and shaping.

FINISHING

Block pieces to measurements. Sew shoulder seams. LEFT FRONT BAND With RS facing, smaller needles and one strand each A and B, pick up and k 51 sts along left front opening edge. Work k 1, p 1 rib for 1½". Bind off in rib. Sew 3 buttons inside left front band, the first just below neckband, the second 2" and third ½" from lower edge. RIGHT FRONT BAND Work as for left front band. With RS facing and darker color yarn, crochet 1 row sl st along right front band edge working 3 or 4 chains for each buttonloop opposite buttons. NECKBAND With RS facing, smaller needles, and one strand each A and B, pick up and k 105 sts around neck edge, including top of front bands. Work k 1, p 1 rib for 1". Bind off in rib. ARMBAND With RS facing, smaller needles, and one strand each A and B, pick up and k 79 sts around armhole edge. Work k 1, p 1 rib for 1". Bind off in rib. Sew side seams.

YARN SOURCES

Kathryn Alexander
(Entrelac Christmas Sock)
1250 Addison #211A
Berkeley, CA 94702

Brown Sheep Yarn Company
(Danya's Southwest Motif
Jumper-Vest, Lee's Crow
Bear Cardigan, Faux Cable
Sage Pullover)
100662 County Road 16
Mitchell, NE 69357
308-635-2198

Cashmere America
(Colorado Cashmere Wimples)
210 SW College Street
POB 1126
Sonora, TX 76950
915-387-6052

Castle Crags Ranch
894 Pheasant Run
Hamilton, MT 59840
406-961-3058

Classic Elite Yarns
(Girl's Jacket with Mitten Motif,
plus Hat and Mittens, Moss
Stitch and Cable Pullover and
Cardigan, Kestrals Alight
Cropped Kimono)
12 Perkins Street
Lowell, MA 01854
508-453-2837

Creative Yarns International
(Snoqualmie Stripes Jacket)
911 Western Avenue, Suite 311
Seattle, WA 98104
206-343-5142

Dale of Norway
(Patchwork-Sunflower Jacket)
206 Travis Lane #5
Waukesha, WI 53186
414-544-1996

Valentina Devine
1222 Big Rock Loop
Los Alamos, NM 87544
505-662-1440

Fiesta Yarns
(mohair and rayon bouclé for
Pre-Columbian Shawl)
PO Box 2548
Corrales, NM 87048
505-897-4485

Folknits
(Kousa Dogwood Shawl)
2151 Second Avenue
Whitehorse, Yukon, Canada
YIA 1C6
403-633-2530

Happy Trails Yarn
(La Plata Socks)
The Wooly West
208 South 1300 East
Salt Lake City, UT 84102
801-583-9373

Henry's Attic
(undyed silk for
Pre-Columbian Shawl)
5 Mercury Avenue
Monroe, NY 10950
914-783-3930

Knitting Traditions
(At Sea Gansey)
604 Main St
PO Box 421
Delta, PA 17314
717-456-7950

La Lana Wools
(Navajo Pullover)
136 Paseo Norte
Taos, NM 87571
505-758-9631

Manos del Uruguay
(Spice Market Wrap and Hat)
Simpson Southwick
350 Route 513
Califon, NJ 07830
908-832-9370

Morehouse Farm
(Morehouse Family Cardigan
and Pullover)
RD2 Box 408
Red Hook, NY 12571
914-758-6493

Mt. Bruce Station
6440 Bordman Road
Romeo, Michigan 48065
313-798-2660

Mountain Colors
PO Box 156
Corvallis, MT 59828
406-777-3377

Muench Yarns
(Liu Had a Dream Cardigan
and Short Vest)
118 Ricardo Road
Mill Valley, CA 94941-2461
415-383-1005

The Muskox Company
633 Fish Hatchery Road
Hamilton, MT 59840
406-363-6818

**Northwest Alpacas Ranch &
Country Store**
11785 S.W. River Road
Scholls, OR 97123
503-257-2227

Reynolds
(Alice's Sand Castle and
Starfish Beach Tunic, Cable
Raglan Pullover) and

Adrienne Vittadini
(Centered Cable and
Rib Pullover)
JCA Fashion Yarns
50 North Broadway
Rumford, RI 02916
401-434-4018

Rowan Yarns
(Southwestern Geometric
Jacket, Counterpane Pullover,
Harvest Fruit Pullover)
Westminster Fibres
5 Northern Boulevard
Amherst, NH 03031
603-886-5041

Schoolhouse Press
(Schoolhouse Shetland Pullover)
6899 Cary Bluff
Pittsville, WI 54466
715-884-2799

Swedish Yarn Imports
(Child-Sized Latvian Mittens)
126-A Wade Street
PO Box 2069
Jamestown, NC 27282
910-883-9939

Tahki Yarns
(Tree of Life Mosaic Jacket)
11 Graphic Place
Moonachie, NJ 07074
201-807-0070

Lizbeth Upitis
(Adult-Sized Latvian Mittens)
620 Morgan Ave S.
Minneapolis, MN 55405

**Vreseis Limited/Natural
Cotton Colours**
PO Box 87
Wickenburg, AZ 85358-0087
602-684-5022

ACKNOWLEDGMENTS

THIS BOOK COULD NEVER HAVE BEEN completed without the hard work, dedication, creativity, and support of many wonderful people. Barbara Albright pushed me to write the proposal for several years after hearing the initial idea. Without her nudging I might not have written it at all. Publisher Leslie Stoker's enthusiasm and confidence were unwavering from start to finish. I feel very fortunate that Sallie Gouverneur, my agent, lent her publishing expertise to this project. I also feel fortunate that Chris Hartlove agreed to do the photography and that Susi Oberhelman designed the book despite her already busy schedule. Thank you to copyeditor Babara Clark, to proofreaders Christina Sheldon, Dee Neer, and Kerry Acker, and to everyone at Artisan and Workman who worked so hard to make this book as fine as it could possibly be.

The endorsement that Nancy Thomas gave *Knitting in America* in the proposal stage was invaluable. The staff at Interweave Press, especially Veronica Patterson, Jane Fournier, Deb Robson, and Dale Petigrew, offered me guidance and encouragement when I visited them in Colorado. Throughout the project Margery Winter generously answered my questions about design. Carla Scott meticulously edited the patterns and created the charts with the assistance of Joni Coniglio, Rita Greenfeder, and Jennifer Madara. Anne Hanson, Heather Slaughter, and Charle Kappel tested patterns and knit samples with speed and expertise. Joan Davis gave me the opportunity to participate in her knitting cruise and tested the Kousa Dogwood Shawl pattern. I also owe a special thank you to all of the companies that donated the yarn with which the designers worked.

Traveling around the country, Chris Hartlove and I were welcomed into the homes of more people than I have space to mention here. In particular, I would like to thank Sandy and Bob Morris, Karen Kendrick-Hand and family, Denise Kavanagh and her partners at The Fine Line in St. Charles, Illinois, Sue Drummond, Meryl Perlson and Jim Ospenson, Jaclyn Hausman, Eugene Beugler, and Michelle Andonian. I am also grateful to the Lacy Knitters who came to the meeting I attended in Sunnydale, California, and the Latvian knitting group in Minneapolis, Minnesota.

Our models for this project were patient and spirited. Thank you David Ashton, Lee Axelrad and Danya Axelrad-Hausman, Noah Barnes, Jim Brown, Betsy Campbell, Jenny and Tita Cocq, Dede Coyne, Andrea Danese, Alan Dobbs, Mark Duprey, Elena Erber, Caitlin FitzGerald, Alice Flanders, Andy Glantz, Heather Harrington, Jennifer Jewell, Janine Keller, Mara Jonas, Carrie Kappel, Annie Kordesh, Sasha Pearl, Kate Riley, and Nick Stoker.

Chris Hartlove would like to thank everyone at KC Color Lab, Service Photo, Peter Whedbee Camera Repairs, and, most of all, Shelley Sirmans. Both of us are grateful to Jackie Billier of Gulf Stream Travel.

I have been fortunate to be guided over the years by several wise women. Gisela Weinland, Sandra Kolber, Kitty Boles, Irene Preston Miller, and Trudy Taylor came into my life, like guardian angels, at different points and gave me the courage to hold on to my dreams. I must also thank my family, especially my mother, Diana Waill. Their love and support form the safety net that allows me to take on new and uncertain challenges.

Most of all, I would like to thank all of the people who are profiled in this book. Working with them was a great privilege.

THE HAT PROJECT

IN ORDER TO GIVE AS MANY PEOPLE AS possible the opportunity to contribute something meaningful to this book, I originated the *Knitting in America* Hat Project. Over the course of one year, I collected handknit head coverings from all over the country, then had them photographed together to create what I perceive as a mosaic of knitting in America.

Soon after an announcement of my efforts appeared in print, mostly in magazines, the hats started arriving in every imaginable size, shape, and color. Opening my mailbox was, for the course of the collection period, continually exciting. Participants—one hundred seventy-six women and two men from all age groups and walks of life and nearly every state—sent me a total of two hundred twenty-six hats, and often also included in their packages long, thoughtful letters in which they explained how they made their hats and the important role knitting plays in their lives. I gave the knitters the option of having me return their hats after photography or allowing me to donate them to a charity, and in the fall of 1996, I donated one hundred handknit hats to Women in Need, a nonprofit organization that offers housing and social services to homeless women and their children in New York City. The following is a list of all of the knitters who made this project possible.

ALABAMA Barbara Clapp, Pleasant Grove **ALASKA** Therese Elkins, Homer; Jana Peirce, Fairbanks; Martie Rozkydal, Palmer **ARIZONA** Terry Neal, Phoenix **ARKANSAS** Mrs. R.A. Patton, Monticello **CALIFORNIA** Ethel Mae Boswell Colacomazzi, Monterey County; Margaret Eilrich, Columbia; Martha Jansz, Ventura; Dee Jones, Nevada City; Jasie Loving, Oak View; Diane Sack, Novato; Judith Tarrant, Sacramento; Helen Von Ammon, San Francisco; Margaret L. Whyte, Ojai; Julia Wright, Los Osos **CONNECTICUT** Barbara Albright, Wilton; Virginia S. Dugan, Pawcatuck; Ellen Harvey, New Canaan; Mae Karbonik, New Britain; Selma Miriam, Westport; Sherilyn Pearce, New Haven; Cristine Piane, East Granby **FLORIDA** Rose Epstein, Plantation; Melissa Gleeson, Jacksonville; Raymonda Schwartz, Crestview; Lorraine Van Lathem, Jacksonville; Jean P. Williams, Pinellas Park **GEORGIA** Suzane Chancey, Monroe **IDAHO** Anne Adams, Moscow; Nancy Draznin, Challis **IOWA** Vera R. Giertz, Bettendorf **ILLINOIS** Ann Cibulskis, Chicago; Lynn Gray Lightfoot, Crystal Lake; Mary Stowe, Lombard **INDIANA** Barbara Bealor, New Carlisle; Julia Galbus, Evansville **KANSAS** Nora Clements, Shawnee; Ardith Drummond, Overland Park; Julie Simons, Topeka **KENTUCKY** Adele R. Marano, Stanford **MAINE** Janet Clark and Dr. Michael Clark, Moody; Liz Clouthier, Phippsburg; Elaine Davey/Pine Tree Yarns, Damariscotta; Joan Davis, Northport; Laurie Doran, Brunswick; Jo Eaton, Rockland; Darcy J. Engholm, Brunswick; Norma Lou Shearer, Berwick; Janice Davis and Michele Smith/Stitchery Square, Camden; Ingrid C. Waite, Durham **MARYLAND** Joanne Backhaus, Baltimore; Mary Julius, Lanham; Margaret B. Todd, Adelphi; Joanne Whitacre

Bittner, Gaithersburg **MASSACHUSETTS** Jacqueline Fee, Hingham; A. Tearle Harding, Bernardston; Cheryl Marsolais, West Boylston; Bonnie Norkin, Springfield; Evelyn Portrait, Lynn; Phyllis Rodgers, Hingham; Carol B. Seitz, Woburn; Mary Vogt, Arlington; Rebecca Williams, Rochester **MICHIGAN** Jane Hill, Royal Oak; Diana Matusik, Allenton; Ruthanne M. Morningstar, Dryden; Rise' St. Arno, Ann Arbor; Leanna Smith, Ann Arbor; Melinda Stees, East Lansing; Janice Y. Van Arsdol, Center Line **MINNESOTA** Norma Buscher, St. Paul; Jvonne Granlund Gray, Bemidji; Cheryl Gray Christlieb, Moorhead; Marleen Gray Webb, Bemidji; Nancy Lindberg, Circle Pines; Sandra Morris, Minneapolis; Colleen O'Leary Nelson, Winona **MISSISSIPPI** Deborah Levine, Jackson **MISSOURI** Marsha Gray Young, Columbia **MONTANA** Diana Hachenberger, Hamilton; Chris Moisey, Missoula; Peggy Shunick, Missoula **NEBRASKA** Margaret Eilrich, Columbia; Ruth Lund, Fremont; Jean Schafer-Albers, Lincoln **NEW HAMPSHIRE** Dorothy S. Grubbs, Lebanon; Dee Neer, Dumbarton; Bettie Stark, Charlestown **NEW JERSEY** Mrs. Ann S. Cooper, Chester; Therese M. Inverso, Camden; Sandra Sgarro, Highland Park; Diana Waill, Englewood; Anne Zaller, Jersey City **NEW MEXICO** Cynthia Atkinson, Albuquerque; Molly Geissman, Albuquerque; Patricia Werner, Placitas; Jaque Wright, Albuquerque **NEW YORK** Lauri Aibel, New York; Sharon Berger, Rochester; Dorothy M. Bosket, Binghamton; Martha Fisher, Little Falls; Gretchen Flint, White Plains; Charlotte Nee, Palisades; Nancy Rivera, Sunnyside; Nadine Stewart, New York; Vivian Wachsberger, New York; Doris Walton, Brooklyn Heights; Matthew Wise, New York; Elaine K. Yale, Bronxville **NORTH CAROLINA** Nicole Bolduc, Boone; Marielena Bresnen, Hendersonville; Roberta D. Kelsh, Tarboro; Rose Wignall, Chapel Hill; Betsey Young Hoyt, Arden **NORTH DAKOTA** Dorothea Nelson, Mayville; Judy Sopher, Grand Forks **OHIO** Vickie Starbuck, Columbus **OKLAHOMA** Joan Almeida, Sapulpa; Jodi Champlin, Enid **OREGON** Francisco J. Camacho, Corvallis; Sharon Heisel, Central Pt; Frances Keeney, Tigard; Celeste Pinheiro, Beaverton; Betty Jo Reynolds, Ashland **PENNSYLVANIA** Jane A. Armstrong, Pittsburgh; Betty Clarkson, Lancaster; Joan H. Debolt, Bradford; Cheryl Fischer Breckinridge, Loretto; Debbie Goldberg, Pittsburgh; Rita Levine, Pittsburgh; Marion Markovitz, Pittsburgh; Joan H. McAnulty, Pittsburgh; Emily B. Sippel, Doylestown; Polly Van Hyning, East Berlin; Susan Van Hyning, East Berlin; Kathy Zimmerman, Ligonier **RHODE ISLAND** Norma Smayda, Saunderstown **SOUTH CAROLINA** Betty Hass, Aiken **TENNESSEE** Shannon Stoney, Cookeville **TEXAS** Betty Benson, Keller; Mary Lynn Brown, Missouri City; Rena Brown, Ft Worth; Pat Cale, Dallas; Maria Larson, San Antonio **UTAH** Betsy Campbell, Salt Lake City; Betty Jacobsen, Bountiful; Kathie Zabell, Orem **VERMONT** Lee Ann Bonson, Burlington; Beverly Creller, Alburgh; Kathy Dowd Hill, Hinesburg; Matilda B.R. White, Norwich **VIRGINIA** Susan B. Alkhadra, Roanoke; Michèle Gerards, Afton; Michele Jensen, Ashland; Jinann Larson, Herndon; Wendy Levy, Richmond **WASHINGTON STATE** Marianne Burr, Coupeville; Evelyn A. Clark, Seattle; Mary E. Cooke, Kent; Jody Grage Haug, Seattle; MayLynn Howell, Seattle; Ann Jones, Olga; Betsy Leggat, Seattle; Kathleen McCrabb, Redmond **WASHINGTON, DC** Gayle Roehm **WEST VIRGINIA** Stitch & Bitch, Wheeling **WISCONSIN** Amy E. Anderson, Shorewood; Nancy Byers, Kenosha; Mary Dominski, Madison; Beverly M. Keller, Richfield; Joyce Lesar, Mt. Horeb; Lorna Schnell, Sparta **WYOMING** Martha Hanscom, Laramie; Audrey A. B. Philips, Thermopolis; Ruth Lee Reissig, Powell **CANADA** Lee Dyke, Abbotsford, BC; Vermell Stevens, Ingersoll, Ontario.

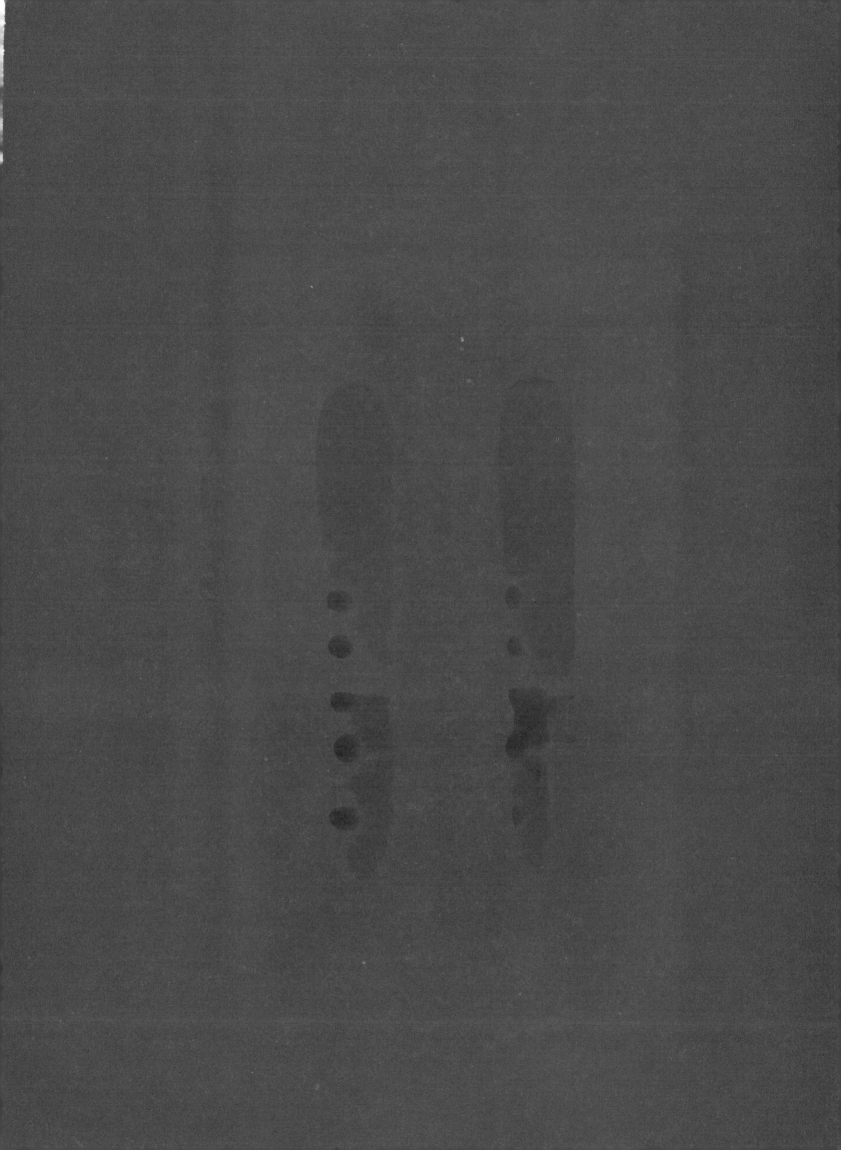